Soul Searching

The Unofficial Guide to the Life and Trials of Ally McBeal

Soul Searching

The Unofficial Guide to the Life and Trials of Ally McBeal

Mark Clapham and Jim Smith

Virgin

This edition first published in 2000 by
Virgin Publishing Ltd
Thames Wharf Studios
Rainville Road
London W6 9HA

ISBN 0 7535 0474 X

Typeset by Galleon Typesetting, Ipswich
Printed and bound in Great Britain by Mackays of Chatham PLC

Contents

Acknowledgements

My half of this book, such as it is, is for:

Alex Comer, James Mellor and Brian Bussey – oldest and
most valued friends.
Jane Dunton – who doesn't even *like* the series.
My sister Louisa – who does.
Jim Sangster – for endless help and always believing in me.
David Bailey – who gave me a break.
Maria Wasilewski – who proofread when she didn't have to.
David Hampton, Steve Lavington, Matt Symonds and Clive –
has it really been three years?
Johnny Minkley, Jonny (de Burgh) Miller, Eddie Robson –
fraternity.

But mostly: for Mum and Dad – for everything.

JES

To my sister, who loved this show before I did.

MCC

Contents

Acknowledgements

My half of this book, such as it is, is for:

Alex Comer, James Mellor and Brian Bussey – oldest and most valued friends.
Jane Dunton – who doesn't even *like* the series.
My sister Louisa – who does.
Jim Sangster – for endless help and always believing in me.
David Bailey – who gave me a break.
Maria Wasilewski – who proofread when she didn't have to.
David Hampton, Steve Lavington, Matt Symonds and Clive – has it really been three years?
Johnny Minkley, Jonny (de Burgh) Miller, Eddie Robson – fraternity.

But mostly: for Mum and Dad – for everything.

JES

To my sister, who loved this show before I did.

MCC

Introduction

There are already many books available about the award-winningly wonderful *Ally McBeal*. Some are tell-alls from the set of one of the world's most popular TV series, others are biographies of its stars. That's fine as far as it goes, but that isn't what we've set out to do here.

In its most basic form this is a 'fan's guide' to the programme, an aide-mémoire and guide compiled by watching and enjoying three seasons of superb television.

What we do is go through every episode, in order, noting down the best and worst moments in Ally's life and trials. How she deals with the men she encounters and how she fares in court. How she copes day to day with people that populate the offices of the world's least sensible law firm, Cage & Fish.

Each episode is divided into categories, which allow us to break down each hour episode into a few pages of witty, pithy informative chunks.

Well, that's the idea.

Each episode looks something like this.

Episode Number: We've given every episode a three-digit number. The first is the season it's in, the second and third digits indicate where it comes. For example, 316 is episode 16 of Season Three.

Title: As a series made by FOX, *Ally McBeal* doesn't have onscreen episode titles, but internal documentation gives every episode a name. So we tell you it.

Production Number: A code used by the production team to identify the episode, usually found at the end of the credits.

First US Transmission Date: The episode's original showing in its primary market.

Written by: It's usually series creator David E. Kelley, but sometimes it isn't. We note who wrote the words our cast are speaking.

Directed by: Who's calling the shots this week.

Cast: Featured actors who aren't part of the permanent cast.

Following a brief taste of the episode's plotline we go into the main categories:

Everything Stops For Ally: Our heroine's self-obsession as revealed through the series about her life.

The Boy Next Door: Billy Alan Thomas, the love of Ally McBeal's life and her best friend since the age of eight. Developments on the rollercoaster ride that is the series' primary frustrated love affair will be recorded here. Every aspect of Billy and Ally's relationship, both past and present, will be noted as it is revealed.

We Got It Together, Didn't We?: In the second season the romance between John Cage and Nelle Porter often takes centre stage, sidelining Ally and Billy. This category will point out when these two supporting characters hijack the show from its star.

Fishisms: The Richard Fish guide to life, presented in easily digestible fragments.

Bygones: Those thoughts, words and actions Richard wants us all to forget.

Smile Therapy: The life, work and problems of John Cage, Richard Fish's partner in the firm that employs Ally and most of the regular cast.

Georgia On My Mind: Billy's long-suffering wife, ace lawyer and sometime colleague of both Ally and Billy. The tribulations of her life – and hair – will be recorded here.

Sub Zero: 'Eskimo' Nelle Porter, the ice-queen lawyer introduced in the second season.

Office Gossip: Elaine, her gossiping, bitching and back-stabbing. Her apposite summings-up of any given situation, her insane plans for world domination, and her occasional attempts to help.

Grrr!: The frightening world of Ling, the Wicked Witch of Ally's world.

DA Renee: Ally's roommate, District Attorney Renee Raddick; her attempts at giving Ally advice, her personal history and her own problems.

Girl Talk: What the girls say about the guys when they're not there.

Guy Talk: And vice versa.

Men: Ally's beaux, the most suitable to the obnoxious, the sane and the mad. The longer running ones will get their own categories where appropriate (for example, **Doctor's Orders** for Greg, Ally's man-in-the-emergency-room).

Quotes: Good lines (often from guest actors) that simply don't fit into the categories related to the above regulars.

Fantasy: From metaphorical dumper trucks to underwater nightmares to Ally turning to ice, those frequent moments when the series takes temporary leave of reality.

Oogachaka!: That most famous of Ally fantasies: the dancing baby.

Fetishes: We get a lot of them in this show. Not simply wattles and shoes. They'll be recorded here – all in good taste, of course.

Song: Music is a vital part of this series. Not simply in the form of Vonda Shepard's on-screen renditions of old classics, but also when music is heard as part of a character's thought process, or used to underscore a dramatic or thematic point. We'll note the songs and, when we feel it's appropriate, the performer, composer and where you might have heard it before.

. . . And Dance: Those moments when the characters indulge in lengthy, often well-choreographed dance routines, real or imaginary.

Shrink Wrapped: Ally's obnoxious therapist and her bizarre and usually utterly useless advice, with cameos from the variety of therapists and marriage guidance counsellors who make our heroes' lives . . . worse.

Fashion Victims: The clothes. The look of this show is so important that it is worth referencing those designer labels that turn up, as well as references, both sneering and complimentary, to the world of fashion.

The Case; The Defendant; The Defence; Guilty?: Four interlinked categories, which between them deal with most aspects of whatever case is presented during the course of the episode. Covers whether they win or lose, the validity of their argument, the nature of the accused and the accuser.

Withdrawn: Examples of unorthodox court technique from these inexplicably successful lawyers. Fish's continual withdrawing of testimony, Cage's performance oddities, Ally's rants; all those little things they do that'd get you thrown out of any court in the land yet usually manage to win their case for them.

Judge Not: The judges are often as confused or confusing as the lawyer or defendants. Whether it's Albert Hall as Seymore Walsh or another judge we only meet once, we will note their quirks every time they hold court. Regular judges, such as Dennis 'Happy' Boyle the dental fetishist or Fish's girlfriend Whipper Cone get their own categories (**Let Me See Your Teeth** and **Whip-Lash!**, respectively).

Also Starring: Guest stars of note, be it Bruce Willis's turn as a replacement psychiatrist, or the appearance of an actor you don't quite recognise from another US TV show. We'll tell you who they are, where you've seen them, and what we think of them.

Kisses: The series' various assorted moments of lip-play. We'll keep a tally of who's kissed whom, when and why.

Toilet Humour: A surprising amount of this series takes place in the firm's spacious unisex toilets, including dancing, fighting, isometric exercises . . .

Other categories will turn up as needed, but as some of them are specific to the events of particular episodes (some as yet unseen in the UK) we won't spoil them for you by mentioning them here.

The Verdict: A final (brief) opinion on the episode in question, subjectively summing up its relative merits. We love this show, but if we aren't impressed with it one week, or feel that David E. Kelley has let us down, we won't shrink from telling you.

Season One

Regular Cast

Calista Flockhart (Ally McBeal)
Courtney Thorne-Smith (Georgia Thomas)
Greg Germann (Richard Fish)
Lisa Nicole Carson (Renee Raddick)
Jane Krakowski (Elaine Vassal)
Vonda Shepard (Vonda Shepard)*
with
Peter MacNicol (John Cage)**
and
Gil Bellows (Billy Alan Thomas)

Created By David E. Kelley

* Vonda Shepard is not featured in the title sequence this season, but is often credited as part of the guest cast. Her credit is erratic but as she appears either in person or as a voice in every episode we choose to bracket her with the regular cast.

** Peter MacNicol officially joined the regular cast with episode 112 'Cro-Magnon'. Up until this point he is credited in each episode in which he features as making a 'Special Appearance'.

The Episodes

101
Pilot/*Ally McBeal*

#AM00
8 September 1997

Written by David E. Kelley
Directed by James Frawley

Cast: Richard Riehle (Jack Billings),
Larry Brandenburg (Judge Hopkins),
Pat McNamara (Ralph Lyne), David S. Dunard (Judge Hupp),
Paul Collins (Judge Williams),
Michael Mantell (Joseph Shapiro),
Michael Laskin (Henry Thorton),
Susan Knight (Joanne Wilder), Tom Virtue (Ally's Father),
Jeffrey Kramer (Pedestrian), Kim Delgado (Court clerk),
Ashley Marie (Ally aged 12–14),
Michael Galeota (Billy aged 12–14),
Mika Boorem (Ally aged 7), Nicholas Pappone (Billy aged 7),
Steve and Eric Cohen (The Twins)

Twenty-something lawyer Ally McBeal leaves her job due to the complications of a sexual harassment case, and quickly winds up working for an old college friend, Richard Fish, who has set up his own law firm. Introduced to the hectic life and 'interesting' staff of the firm, Ally loses her first case, sues her old firm for sexual harassment, and is appalled to discover her childhood sweetheart Billy Thomas is not only also working for Richard, but is happily married.

The Boy Next Door: As you'd expect from a first episode there's a huge amount of Billy/Ally angst. We learn that Ally and Billy were childhood sweethearts, that they dated through high school and that Ally followed Billy to Harvard where they both read law. Billy left Ally and Harvard to study elsewhere.

Billy acts as counsel in Ally's sexual harassment case. He realises that Ally wants to grind up Billings' head and beat it through his intestines.

The two of them discuss their past and resolve to work through it together, realising that this will take time.

Ally still keeps a picture of her and Billy in her apartment.

Fishisms: Richard reveals that he didn't become a lawyer because he likes the law. In fact 'The Law sucks! It's boring.' He relishes it as a weapon however. 'Bankrupt somebody, cost him all he's worked for. Make his wife leave him. Maybe even cause his kids to cry.' In flashback we see him laying out his approach to legal practice. 'Piles and piles of money. If I help someone along the way, that's great!'

'Look at this office,' he expounds as he shows Ally his firm. 'It stinks of money.'

Richard's solution to the sexual harassment case, to offer Billings a job at the firm, and tape him admitting he made the OCD defence up, is brilliant, and implies a chink of compassion in his veneer of cynicism.

The first real Fishism is invoked right at the end. 'Make enough money, everything else will follow.' Richard demands Ally quote him and explains that it's Fishism.

Bygones: Two small ones, both when rows break out in the office, and Richard tries to use the B-word to end it. He fails.

Smile Therapy: Oddly, in an episode that carefully introduces the entire season-one cast, John Cage is nowhere to be seen. His absence is explained by the fact that he's having his frown lines detoxed. Richard points out John 'makes rain in his sleep'.

Georgia On My Mind: Billy correctly deduces that Ally wanted his wife to be fat, or stupid or missing teeth. Unfortunately for Ally she's beautiful, a lawyer and seems to be a very nice person. Grilling Billy for flaws, he reveals that she snores, the blonde hair comes out of a bottle, and that she has a bunion on her left little toe. This seems to comfort Ally in some strange way.

Georgia is intelligent and sensitive enough to work out that Billy and Ally were more than just friends in the past, and confronts Ally about it at her apartment.

Office Gossip: Ally imagines Elaine's head expanding as she talks, and suggests that people like Elaine tell you what has been done, not so you know that it has been done, but so as you know that *they* have done it. She's probably right.

DA Renee: Is introduced in a lovely bitchy little scene as Ally gets ready for work, noting that for 'going to work with the ex-boyfriend' Ally has added a whole half-hour to her make-up schedule. She bluntly tells Ally to stop being in love with Billy.

Girl Talk: Two great Ally/Renee scenes, and the fantastic Georgia/Ally discussion in Ally's apartment, where both women resolve to hate each other.

Fantasy: Ally and Billy making love in a huge vat of cappuccino. Hmm, creamy. When Billy tells Ally he's married she's pierced through the heart by a whole flight of arrows. At one point she's crushed by a huge bowling ball falling from the sky. When in a conference-room meeting, she imagines herself as a tiny little girl in a vast chair. Looking in the mirror, Ally wishes she had bigger breasts, and the audience gets to watch them expand until her shoulder straps snap.

Song: Vonda Shepard performs a number of her own, original songs in this pilot episode including 'Maryland' (Shepard), 'Wildest of the World' (Shepard/Landau), 'Drown In My Own Tears', 'Baby Don't You Break My Heart Slow' (Shepard/ James Newton Howard), 'Like a Hemisphere' (Shepard), plus a snatch of 'Psycho Theme' (Bernard Hermann). We are also introduced to Vonda's renditions of 'Neighbourhood' (Leiber/ Stoller/Sembello/Dino), a beautiful number that'll become mostly associated with Billy, and 'Tell Him' (Bert Russell Berns).

An indication of the way the music and drama will begin to interact is given when Billy manages to interrupt the incidental music to talk to Ally, showing the song to have been in her head all along.

Fashion Victims: Ally's horrible, horrible neckerchief in the opening scene, which makes an unfortunate reappearance in the last third of the episode. Richard draws attention to Ally's micro miniskirt. 'Hemline's a little high but who am I to notice?' Ally's dungarees in the college flashbacks are nasty.

The Case: The 'Reverend Kessler vs Man-Made Magazine', which has apparently printed a story by a nun who claims to have had sex with him. He's sued for an injunction, and Ally is defending the magazine.

Separately we are given snippets of Ally's discrimination case, where one of the senior partners of her old firm squeezed her butt, causing her to sue him. He argues that he's a victim of an obsessive-compulsive disorder and couldn't help himself.

Ally wins Cage & Fish a contract with a major airline by arguing that tax laws discriminate against airlines.

The Defence: The magazine had every right to print such a story, if they believed it true. Ally believes this to be a First Amendment issue.

Guilty?: As Ally says, 'The judge had an opinion contrary to law.' The magazine, Hopkins admits, has every constitutional right to publish the article, but he pleads with them from doing so anyway. The case is about money, not facts. Much to her chagrin Ally loses, despite having the founding fathers on her side. She wins on appeal.

Judge Not: The initial Kessler/magazine hearing is presided over by Judge Hopkins, who's none too keen on trouser suits for women, according to Elaine. He seems to despise the whole case, and you can see his point.

Kisses: Many for Ally and Billy, all in flashback; from lip-play as eight-year-olds to their first full-blown snog as adolescents.

Toilet Humour: According to Richard the unisex 'helps men and women employees breed familiarity. As long as they don't come in here to breed.' A huge Billy/Ally discourse is interrupted by Richard stepping out of a cubicle. He rushes off, explaining that he can wash his hands later.

Hit The Bar: Whenever Ally is depressed Renee makes her go and dance. The dancing twins make their first appearance. In this episode the bar seems already to be a favourite haunt of Renee and Ally's, yet 'Compromising Positions' makes clear that the bar is situated underneath the offices of 'Cage & Fish'. Not impossible, but a hell of a coincidence.

Trivia: For this episode only the closing theme is Vonda Shepard's full vocal rendition rather than the instrumental arrangement used from #AM01 onwards. The episode has a caption card which reads 'Ally McBeal' separate to the normal season-one opening sequence. Some might argue that this makes it the title of the episode as well as the series. The incident with the unnamed 'pedestrian' will become significant in 105 'One Hundred Tears Away'.

The Verdict: 'The victim of my own choices, and I'm just starting.' It all starts here. It's been observed that if you miss this one, the whole series just doesn't make sense, so comprehensively does it introduce you to the characters and the rules of Ally's inner world. It's actually quite different to the subsequent series, smothered as it is in Calista Flockhart's voice-over, but it's a tremendous hour of television and really the only place to begin.

102
Compromising Positions

#AM01
15 September 1997

Written by David E. Kelley
Directed by Jonathan Pontell

Cast: Phil Leeds (Judge 'Happy' Boyle),
Dyan Cannon (Judge 'Whipper' Cone),
Tate Donovan (Ronald Cheanie),
Willie Garson (District Attorney Frank Shea),
John Cirigliano (Man#1), Robert Lee Jacobs (Greg Stone),

Betty Bridges-Nacasio (Clerk),
Steve and Eric Cohen (The Twins)
Special Appearance by Peter MacNicol

John Cage, Richard's as-yet-unseen partner, is arrested for soliciting a prostitute. Ally is assigned to defend him. Fish invites Ally along to dinner with a potentially lucrative client, Ronald Cheanie. The dinner is really a double date with Fish and his girlfriend, Whipper. Ally is initially enraged, but when Ronald turns out to be attractive and charming she begins to change her mind.

Everything Stops For Ally: She feels that using sexuality to get ahead is being unfaithful to 'love itself'. She is afraid of criminals. Which rather beggars belief given her choice of profession. Her rumination that love is about compromise, which is why people get themselves into compromising positions, is wonderful.

The Boy Next Door: 'Did you cheat on me?' Ally asks Billy. 'If I cheat, I'd lie about it,' he retorts, and then denies he ever cheated on Ally. This becomes significant in next season's 'Fool's Night Out'. Billy tells Ally that ex-girlfriends don't have rights, prompting her to reply, 'This one does.' Billy points at his groin and says, '*This* makes men stupid.'

Fishisms: 'A problem is just a bleak word for a challenge.' This is actually a good episode for Richard, as we see his obvious, real despair when Whipper betrays him. The same old Richard is in evidence earlier on, however: 'We started this firm with the same dream,' he says to John, prompting Cage to agree, replying, 'Money.'

Bygones: Rather sadly, Richard tries to invoke them after Ally tells him that Whipper kissed another man. He then immediately swigs his champagne from the bottle with a pained expression.

Smile Therapy: This is John's first appearance, and Peter MacNicol is outstanding. He delivers an amazing speech to the staff explaining why he picked up a prostitute, and then distributes questionnaires about his performance. He claims he wants 'candour' from the staff in their rating of his speech, but is offended when Ally rates him as a two out of five.

Georgia On My Mind: Georgia's little trick where she invites a complete stranger to have sex with her, just to prove that men are shallow when it comes to sex, is very funny, if a little cruel. And she kind of has a point.

Office Gossip: We see Elaine lurking in half-open doorways in order to gather gossip. She tells Ally about Billy's bachelor party where a hooker 'serviced' several guests, seemingly including both Billy and 'Happy' Boyle.

Girl Talk: Renee and Ally discuss Ally kissing her client. 'I saw a piece of cute meat and I said to myself you only live once, be a man,' says Ally. Unconvincingly.

Men: New client Ronald Cheanie, whom Ally ends up dating.

Fantasy: Hardly 'fantasy' but clearly imagined, we see Ally vomiting violently during Cage's speech.

Fetishes: It's here we first discover Richard's fascination with the 'wattle', the fold of skin on a more mature woman's neck. Ally is clearly confused and appalled by this.

Song: Vonda Shepard sings the old standard 'Pearl's a Singer' (Jerry Leiber/Mike Stoller) and 'Grain of Sand' an original song of her own. We also get to hear a snatch of the 'Leave It To Beaver' theme.

May I See Your Teeth?: First appearance of Judge 'Happy' Boyle. The card in front of him reveals his first name to be Dennis. He knows Billy well enough to have been invited to his bachelor party, where he probably indulged with a prostitute. Either because of this, or possibly the other way round, he's not very hard on consensual sex cases. He orders John to pay court costs and schedules probation. Elaine initially believes that Ally will get Judge Mack, who's even-handed but sometimes hard on young lawyers.

Whip-Lash!: First appearance of Judge 'Whipper' Cone, Richard's current girlfriend. Her explanation as to why she kissed Cheanie is devastatingly effective. She claims that twenty years ago she'd have slapped a man for coming up to her, telling her she's attractive and then trying to kiss her, but at her age . . .

Also Starring: Tate Donovan was the voice of Disney's *Hercules* (Ron Clements, 1997) and has appeared in *Friends*. Peter MacNicol (John Cage) is a prolific TV and film character actor, whose best-known roles are probably in *Addams Family Values* (Barry Sonnenfeld, 1993) and *Ghostbusters II* (Ivan Reitman, 1989).

Toilet Humour: We witness several major debates on the nature of love, and wattle-sex between Richard and Whipper within the walls of the unisex.

The Verdict: A slightly raw, painful episode in which all the characters we're only just getting to know are put through the emotional meat grinder. Despite strong suggestions to the contrary from both Billy and Georgia, it seems to be saying that love and passion make idiots of everyone, just sometimes in different ways. Writer David E. Kelley achieves a great moral equivalence here, where you can sympathise with all of the characters even as they're pitted against each other.

And it's nice to see Ally and Georgia getting on a little better.

103
The Kiss

#AM02
22 September 1997

Written by David E. Kelley
Directed by Dennie Gordon

Cast: Tate Donovan (Ronald Cheanie),
Richard Riehle (Jack Billings),

David Spielberg (TV Station Executive),
Alaina Reed Hall (Judge Elizabeth Witt),
Nelson Mashita (Foreperson),
Cissy Wellman (Secretary),
Eric and Steve Cohen (The Twins)
Special Appearance by Kate Jackson

Synopsis: Ally senses Cheanie is withholding something when he neglects to kiss her goodnight after their first official date. Georgia asks Ally to assist her in trying an age discrimination case when the opposing counsel turns out to be Jack Billings, the guy Ally tried to sue for sexual harassment at her old firm.

Everything Stops For Ally: 'All I ever wanted was to be rich and successful and to have three kids and a husband who was waiting home for me at night to tickle my feet. And I don't even like my hair.' Everybody say 'Aaaah' now.

Fishisms: Richard advances a rather bleak view of existence. 'I'm alone now, but I've got Whipper. Everybody's alone; it's just easier to take in a relationship.' He also advises Ally that love is 'an equation'. Apparently a 'Me' and a 'You' derive a 'We'. If the 'Me' is still a work in progress then you shouldn't start building the 'We' yet.

Girl Talk: 'I am a sexual object; he couldn't just give me a little grope?' whines Ally after Cheanie kisses her on the cheek. Renee and Ally have a brilliant conversation about the nature of dating, where Renee rubbishes Ally's reliance on books of 'rules for dating' and generally talks a lot of sense. 'The problem with playing games,' she says, 'is that somebody loses.'

Ally and Georgia bond a little, which Billy doesn't seem to like much. This case affects them both more than they'd like. 'Everything you think you are can disappear with a wrinkle. We both get mileage out of our looks, and it's temporary,' Georgia admits, 'We've got to win this case for peace of mind if nothing else.'

Song: Somewhat unsurprisingly we get 'It's in His Kiss' (The Shoop Shoop Song) here performed by Vonda, alongside her rendition of 'Let's Stay Together' (Al Green, Al Jackson, Jr. and Willie Mitchell). The soundtrack also uses pieces of 'The Dance of the Sugar Plum Fairy' from *The Nutcracker Suite*.

Fashion Victims: Richard presents us with his first major fashion error: a really unpleasant tie.

The Case: Barbara Cooker, a local news anchorwoman with eleven years' experience, has been fired because of a memo, that estimated that less than half the male audience wanted to have sex with her. She's won a Peabody Award and two local Emmys, but this is apparently not good enough in a modern climate. According to the station executives, 'Crunching the demo's, only six per cent of the 18–30-year-old men would care to sleep with her. The number's only slightly higher for the 18–45 guys. Basically the only men who get a rise out of her are no longer capable of rising.' Essentially the news service is being perverted by the need for ratings. Ally and Georgia argue that this is unfair, and despite strong comeback from Billings they win a total of $930,000 for their client.

Trivia: There's a bizarre reference to Hong Kong recently becoming a 'free country', as if democratic free rule under a British Colonial Government was in some way less 'free' than being absorbed by Communist China.

The Verdict: 'Today, sadly, when we shop around for an anchorperson we look more for a model than a journalist.' Kate Jackson gives a dynamite guest performance in this simple but effective episode. For a change the actual case is the main focus of the episode; Ally and Georgia fight side by side on a case that they deserve to win and succeed in both cementing their friendship and winning a case that's worth winning. Excellent all round.

104
The Affair

#AM03
29 September 1997

Written by David E. Kelley
Directed by Arlene Sanford

Cast: Kathy Baker (Katherine Dawson),
Tate Donovan (Ronald Cheanie),
Brett Cullen (Professor James Dawson),
Jerry Hardin (Minister), Jenjer Vick (Secretary),
Alexis Klayla (Cara Dawson aged 8),
Holliston Coleman (Cara Dawson aged 4)

James Dawson, a Harvard law professor who taught Ally, Billy
and Richard Fish, has died whilst out jogging. His widow,
Katharine, asks Ally to be a pallbearer. Ally panics and confesses to Billy that she had an affair with Dawson whilst in her
final year. Billy is appalled, but supports her, and agrees to
attend the funeral with her. This unnerves both Georgia and
Ronald, who are both feeling threatened. Georgia confronts
Billy, and Cheanie confronts Ally, dumping her. Ally performs
the eulogy at the funeral, telling not the truth, but what
Katharine most needs to hear.

Everything Stops For Ally: In her third year at Law School
(and after Billy left) Ally had a five-month affair with the
married Professor James Dawson. She loved him, and it's suggested that he loved her.

The Boy Next Door: Billy is the best cushion in town – as
Cheanie notes, Ally always turns to Billy when she has a
problem. Billy and Ally spend a lot of this episode together,
discussing Ally's difficulties with James Dawson's death. Ally
Freudian-slips wonderfully, telling Billy that there are many
ways in which Ronald Cheanie is not him, when she means to
say he's not right.

Fishisms: 'We're all going to a funeral, join us, it'll be fun.' He claims of Dawson, 'I simply loved the man, the word is so overused these days.' Which is doubly ironic considering Ally's feelings towards the dead man. 'One of the keys to life is the Fast Forward button.' Simply, you fast-forward your emotions to the point in time when whatever concerns you no longer hurts. This is apparently a double Fishism.

Georgia On My Mind: Billy says that Georgia's libido always rises when she's feeling insecure, and that a part of him wants her to be insecure for ever for this reason alone. The two of them have a wonderful conversation where Georgia states that Ally makes her uncomfortable for the simple reason that she knows she and Billy will have bad times, because everyone does, and that she doesn't want Ally in the next room when they experience problems.

Office Gossip: This is where Elaine invents her face bra; one of the most ridiculous notions of all time.

Girl Talk: Ally and Renee have another of their epic heart-to-hearts. This time whilst cleaning their teeth.

Men: (For the last time) Ronald Cheanie, who walks out of Ally's life, telling her 'I know it's my loss but there are some victories I'm not equipped to deal with.'

Fantasy: Ally imagines being guillotined. Pretty graphic. When Cheanie dumps her we see her being thrown out of a metaphorical dumper truck.

Song: 'You Belong To Me', a hit for Johnny Mathis, that Billy and Ally dance to in silence.

Fashion Victims: Cage in a very nice brown three-piece suit. Elaine in a sexy diagonal-checked grey minidress. Georgia power dresses in blue.

Also Starring: Jerry Hardin played Deep Throat in the first season of *The X-Files*.

Kisses: Ally and her late professor, James Dawson. Billy and Georgia.

The Verdict: 'The thing about funerals – the guest of honour is always dead.' A slow episode in which there's no actual case and only one plotline. Good Ally/Billy scenes do not save what is the least rewarding and most linear season-one plot. Strong character moments aside, it isn't one you'll want to watch all that often.

105

One Hundred Tears Away

#AM04
20 October 1997

Written by David E. Kelley
Directed by Sandy Smolan

Cast: Phil Leeds (Judge 'Happy' Boyle),
Dyan Cannon (Judge 'Whipper' Cone),
Keene Curtis (Judge Johnson Hawk),
Carol Locatell (Judge Henrietta Fullem),
Audrie Neenan (Mrs Clarkson),
Zeljko Ivanek (Judge Marshal Pink),
Betty Bridges-Nacasio (Clerk),
Daniel Hutchison (Officer Kenter), Gerald Emerick (Johnson),
Vonda Shepard (Singer)

After an altercation in a supermarket, Ally is arrested for aggravated assault and attempted shoplifting. Renee bails her out of jail and Billy swiftly clears her in criminal court, but Ally is then ordered before the State Bar Review Board. A litany of her recent travails is read aloud, and Ally suddenly finds herself on trial for her professional life.

Everything Stops For Ally: 'How did I get to be such a mess so soon in my life?' Ally ponders. Fair question. Her little fight in the supermarket is absolutely not her fault. The aggressive and unpleasant woman with whom she fights for the snacks frankly deserves all she gets, especially after she accuses Ally of 'playing the sex card' by asking a man whether she or Ally is in the right. As Ally quite reasonably puts it, 'Why are you being so mean?'

Her lengthy romantic fantasy about Omar Sharif and one-night stands is sweet, but confused. As Renee points out, it's probably best not to mention any of this in the witness box. Ally considers becoming a street person, but rejects the idea on the grounds that she wouldn't get to wear her outfits.

The Boy Next Door: Elaine states in court that Ally is still in love with Billy, and neither of them expresses real surprise at this suggestion. Billy's lengthy and impassioned speech about how special Ally is indicates the depth of his affection, romantic or otherwise, for his oldest friend. The story about Ally accidentally using toothpaste instead of spermicidal jelly, and Billy liking it, claiming it made her taste 'minty', is a weird little anecdote that Calista Flockhart and Gil Bellows somehow manage to make into a silly, warm and strangely romantic remembrance simply by playing it in a very sweet way.

Fishisms: 'You can't attack someone over a snack treat; that's not a Fishism, that's just common sense.' After a particularly bizarre conversation with his co-workers Richard comments that he is 'nothing if not surrounded'. He has a point. He displays another moment of humanity, angrily reassuring Ally, 'They go after one of us, we go after all of them.' Also brilliant is his outburst in court, saying of Billy, 'As much as I constantly stress the need for civility, he continues to have this reaction to witch hunts, especially when they're *so* blatant.' As Billy points out, 'It's not like you to be human, Richard, much less show it.' Fish remembers that a friend of his refused to take a urine test on the grounds that they didn't give him time to study for it. He's probably lying.

Bygones: Richard accuses Ally of being in the same room but on a different planet, and then quickly puts it down as a bygone. Ally snaps at him, 'Not everything's a bygone.'

Smile Therapy: The Biscuit is in Syracuse, a place that it is implied he has been in since 102 'Compromising Positions'.

Office Gossip: Richard and Ally panic when Elaine is subpoenaed to appear before the Bar Review Board. It is suggested that Elaine told Whipper that Ally was 'two thirds of a rice crispy'. She'd snapped, crackled and 'was ready for the final pop'. Elaine tries to save face by claiming that Ally is her favourite boss, and admitting that she says things to convince people she's a wordsmith. Elaine describes herself as in constant preparation to be a mother. Suffer little children . . . Oh, and she's sold her Face Bra to an Infomercial company. Shame she feels the need to tell the court this.

Snappish!: Billy and Ally become 'Snappish stereo' much to Elaine's horror. Apparently sometimes Ally simply 'looks snappish'.

Men: Cheanie has given evidence to the board implying Ally is unstable. Ouch!

Fashion Victims: We won't mention Georgia in a sexy nightie. Ooops. We did.

The Case: Ally McBeal versus the world, effectively.

The Defendant: The star.

The Defence: 'I am human, I am temperamental, I am guilty,' but so, goes the argument, is everybody else.

Guilty?: They let Ally continue to practise (yay!) but largely out of fear of seeing her in front of the board again when she inevitably appeals against any decision not in her favour.

Judge Not: Richard describes Judge Pink with a shudder: 'A conservative, no sense of humour, a Christian.' One of the review panel is a friend of Jack Billings (see 1 'Pilot/*Ally McBeal*') and Richard rightly interprets this case as his revenge.

Let Me See Your Teeth: Happy Boyle tells Whipper he has 'penile atrophy'. There are some details where 'too much information' is just an insufficient response. Happy fails to recognise Ally until he stares at her teeth, and then suddenly knows who she is. He agrees that she's a 'pretty little thing', the patronising old letch.

Whip-Lash!: Whipper accuses Ally of not having two feet on the ground, causing Ally to express surprise that some people do. It was Whipper who, in part, prompted the investigation of Ally by reporting Elaine's comments about her to the review board. She did this out of a sense of legal responsibility, not malice, and tries to intercede on Ally's behalf towards the end of the hearing.

The Verdict: 'This would actually be funny if justice wasn't truly this arbitrary.' Truly terrific. Not simply funny, but bursting with great character moments and with loads for the entire regular cast to do. The way it functions as a collection of consequences to earlier, seemingly minor details from previous episodes, is brilliant, and Ally's walk home in silent tears is one of the series' most powerful moments. One of the best episodes of the season.

106
The Promise

#AM05
27 October 1997

Written by David E. Kelley
Directed by Victoria Hochberg

Cast: Jay Leggett (Harry Pippen),
Rusty Schwimmer (Angela Tharpe),
Jamie Rose (Sandra Winchell),
Michael Winters (Judge Herbert Spitt),
Michael Bofshever (Judge Allen Stephenson),
James Mathers (Dr Carpenter), Landry Barb (Clerk),
Joyce Greenleaf (Bystander #1),
Kenneth Zanchi (Bystander #2),
Mary-Margaret Lewis (Jury Foreperson),
Brooke Burn (Jennifer Higgin)
Special Appearance by Peter MacNicol

Ally defends a friend of Whipper, Sandra Winchell, who has been brought up on solicitation charges. She serves as second chair to John Cage, whose idiosyncrasies become increasingly apparent. Meanwhile, our heroine saves a fat man's life and finds herself pursued, slowly, by him.

The Boy Next Door: Billy is described by Elaine as the office's 'designated sensitive male'.

Fishisms: Richard wants Ally to second chair the prostitution case because the purity she exudes might help them win.

Smile Therapy: This is the first time we get to see John in action in court. He pours water into his glass at inappropriate moments, calls witnesses up to the stand, introduces himself to them and then dismisses them without asking any questions.

At one point he answers a question that Ally only thinks, indicating just how closely in tune with her thought processes he is. Despite them being roommates, John feels that as Renee is opposing counsel it is inappropriate for Ally to lunch with her. Technically he's absolutely right.

In court he argues successfully that to condemn prostitution in an age of cinema sex, and in a world where women don't consider men marriage material unless their income is in a certain bracket, is hypocritical. When Ally objects to this line of defence, John explains that there's a reason why he made the arguments he did in court. It's that he was paid to.

We learn that John sings to himself to control his stutter, and sometimes the sound of his singing accidentally drops out.

He tells Ally that the world is no longer a romantic place, but that some of its people still are. 'Don't let the world win, Ally McBeal.'

Office Gossip: Elaine condemns the men of the office for being 'Neanderthals' every time Jennifer Higgin enters the room. So, in fact, do Georgia and Ally. The basic hypocrisy that underlies this is explored in 112 'Cro-Magnon'. Elaine opines that Jennifer is probably very stupid and that gravity will get her in the end.

Snappish!: Ally slams a door in Elaine's face, which Elaine claims is 'Door Snappish!' The next time Ally slams the door in her face, she shouts that she 'resents this side of the door'.

DA Renee: Renee's court technique is, compared to John's, boringly orthodox. She just sticks to the letter of the law, repeatedly referring to exact, strict interpretations that aid her case. 'You ruled him out in an instant on looks,' Renee says of Harry Pippen, and she's right. But you can't blame Ally for not wanting to date him. In her defence it's true that Pippen is himself being as shallow as everyone else by preferring Ally over Angela.

Men: Harry Pippen, the enormous lawyer whose life Ally saves. He falls for her despite the fact that he's due to be married at the end of the week. Ally convinces him that he should go ahead and marry his fiancée, even though she knows he doesn't love her.

Song: 'Goodnight My Someone' from *The Music Man*, performed by Calista Flockhart, Lisa Nicole Carson and Vonda Shepard. Ally and Renee listen to the words and suddenly realise that it's a very sad song about somebody who has nobody. 'Ask The Lonely' (another very sad song) is performed by Vonda Shepard, who also gets to sing the more upbeat 'I Only Want to be With You' (Hawker/Raymond).

The Case: Initially Ally is fighting a case that concerns two different ice-cream parlours having similar names. The opposing counsel in this case is Harry Pippen, whose technique consists of beginning to argue as he enters the room and speaking without pausing.

Withdrawn: Ally objects to testimony from her own client because it doesn't tally with her personal beliefs; which is unorthodox, even by John's standards.

Judge Not: Herbert Spitt, who's so thoroughly sick of Winchell firing lawyers and asking for continuances that he tells Ally to either be ready for trial today or he'll continue it for a year, and revoke bail. He refuses to allow Ally to withdraw her unorthodox objection, and sustains it.

Kisses: Ally gives the kiss of life to the unbreathing, uncon-scious Harry Pippen, and can taste his Spanish omelette. He, rather pathetically, describes this as a kiss unlike any he's ever experienced before.

The Verdict: 'You can't win a raffle without at least buying a ticket.' An utter mess, 'The Promise' gets caught out by what it's trying to say. By the series' normal logic, Harry should leave Angela and wait for his ideal 'someone' who makes his 'heart bounce', as Ally does. The only reason Ally tells him that he should marry Angela is basically because he's very, very fat and he has no other options. 'People like me and Harry, we don't get the partners of our dreams,' Angela says, following this up with, 'Sometimes when you hold out for everything you end up with nothing'. This is true, but very sad. Strangely nobody comes out with the sensible suggestion that Pippen should just simply try to lose some weight.

107
The Attitude

#AM06
3 November 1997

Written by David E. Kelley
Directed by Michael Schultz

Cast: Steve Vinovich (Jerry Burrows),
Jason Blicker (Rabbi Stern), Andrew Heckler (Jason Roberts),
Brenda Vaccaro (Karen Horwitz),
Brooke Burns (Jennifer Higgin)
Special Appearance by Peter MacNicol

Ally represents a Jewish woman who needs her rabbi to grant her a spiritual release from her marriage to her comatose husband. Ally decides to tackle the unyielding rabbi person-ally. Meanwhile, Georgia is the target of a senior partner's wife's insecurities.

Everything Stops For Ally: Ally absolutely goes off on one when faced with Rabbi Stern's inflexibility with regards to Horwitz's divorce. We can see that she does this because, as Elaine points out, she's prone to overreaction when issues involve matters of the heart. Ally's comments about Judaism do border on the genuinely insulting, and you can't blame Stern for being upset. Ally knows that she gets rid of her clients' problems by creating bigger ones for them.

The Boy Next Door: Billy bumps into Jennifer, and Georgia drags him away by his tie. Billy sees Georgia and Ally in the same toilet cubicle and looks confused. 'You might think there's an explanation,' Ally says, 'but you would be wrong.'

Fishism: 'Helping people is never more rewarding than when it's in your own self-interest.' This is the first Fishism Georgia hears as a member of the firm, and Richard hugs her.

Smile Therapy: When Burrows offers John a drink he replies, 'I actually had a small Sprite in your lobby. It refreshed me.' He excuses himself from his first meeting on the grounds that he's troubled, and he's less responsive to compromise when he's troubled. He tells Georgia that if she sues Burrows she'll win, and get money, but that she'll be 'unhireable'; he knows this isn't a real word, but he uses it anyway.

In conference he takes Georgia's hand and says, 'As a woman I'd say sue, but I'm not a woman . . . That's not where I was going, I got boxed in by my poor choice of syntax.' When preparing for his second meeting with Burrows, John hears his 'Bells', an excerpt from the soundtrack to the film *Rocky* (Gene Kirkwood, 1976).

John wins Georgia the case by effectively threatening to ruin the good reputation of the firm she works for by making this case loudly public. He wins, but it really is fighting dirty, even given how unreasonable Burrows' treatment of Georgia is.

Georgia On My Mind: Georgia is going to be moved from one department to another within her firm, because her boss's wife feels insecure about her husband working alongside so beautiful a woman. Georgia sues her firm for sexual discrimination, having retained the Biscuit to act for her.

Office Gossip: Elaine describes Horwitz as looking rather like her dog did just before they put it down for having rabies.

Men: Jason Roberts, the cute DA with the appalling eating habits, and Rabbi Stern whom Ally unwittingly serially insults. He very nicely assumes that Horwitz's hiring of Ally is some kind of joke, having eventually seen the funny side of Ally's behaviour. He asks her out on a date. She initially refuses, but eventually acquiesces.

Song: John plays a lengthy bagpipe solo. 'This Guy's in Love' (Burt Bacharach) is performed by Vonda Shepard as Jason and Ally have dinner. It stops and starts every time Jason gets salad dressing smears across his face. As Ally waits in the lift we hear the theme from the popular US game show *Jeopardy*.

The Verdict: 'They say it's all in the attitude, and mine has changed.' A slim but fun episode which basically serves to move Georgia from her old firm into Cage & Fish, and initiates a shift in Ally's behaviour, from looking for the love of her life to looking for a fun way to spend a Tuesday night.

108
Drawing The Lines

#AM07
10 November 1997

Written by David E. Kelley
Directed by Mel Damski

Cast: Cristine Rose (Marci Hatfield),
Stan Ivar (Jason Hatfield), Mark Metcalf (Hatfield's Lawyer),
Sandra Bernhard (Caroline Poop), Brook Burn (Jennifer Higgin)
Special Appearance by Peter MacNicol

Billy and Georgia are faced with a crisis of confidence in their marriage. Elaine threatens to sue the firm for sexual harassment if Fish and Cage don't meet her demands for improved working conditions. Ally, Georgia and Cage take on a lucrative divorce case. Fish uses some tactics, which causes a debate between the two parties as to which side is the most amoral.

Everything Stops For Ally: Ally needs four cups of coffee in the morning before she is even remotely capable of work. The coffee machine breaking down sends her into a flat panic. Later she feels depressed and eats two whole cartons of ice cream. Renee tells her, not unreasonably, that she's an emotional idiot.

The Boy Next Door: Whenever Billy has a problem he can't resolve he stares at his reflection in the mirror. Ally and Billy discuss being friends, which prompts Ally to say, 'When you say we're friends you say it as though it's the consolation prize.'

Fishisms: Perhaps the ultimate Fishism comes from this episode: 'If you want to be rich, you'd better have the money before the scruples set in.'

Bygones: Richard at his rudest and silliest. 'I miss you at every opportunity, Elaine. Kidding. Bygones. Go away.' 'We made a lot of money, and we won ugly. You should be thrilled,' Ally tells Richard. He presumably is.

Smile Therapy: During an important meeting with Marci Hatfield, John picks his nose. Richard understandably attacks him for his 'impromptu excavation project'.

Office Gossip: Elaine pushes forward with the sexual discrimination claim she made in the previous episode. She argues that the men's letching over the mail girl contributes to a hostile working environment, and that this constitutes $8,000 each and three extra vacation days. Elaine also says that if you can word things cleverly it's more meaningful. Apparently this is a Jesse Jacksonism. She feels that the lawsuit is in the spirit of Richard Fish.

When Richard calls Elaine's bluff with his speech about making work fun, you suddenly realise that he means what he says, and that part of the point of Cage & Fish is to enjoy practising law. Ally feels that there is something desperate about Elaine. 'She feels the need to be in the middle of things'; the suit is a way of putting herself there.

Snappish!: Elaine accuses Ally of disguising being snappish in a soft tone.

DA Renee: Renee tries to dance with John and tells him he's a 'cute little enigma'. He seems somewhat disturbed by this.

Fantasy: Both Ally and Billy fantasise about dancing together in formal dress in the unisex. At one point Ally's hair leaps up in electric shock horror.

Fetishes: Coffee – lots of coffee; Ally's attitude to her first cup of the day borders on the erotic. Here are some highlights of her talking Georgia through her morning cappuccino. 'Just knowing it's close . . . close your eyes. Just think about tasting it. Smell it. Pull it away . . . tease yourself a little. Slow, slow, slow.' Strangely this seems to turn Billy on.

The Case: The entire firm gets behind Richard's acquisition of a juicy divorce case for two reasons, 'First off, money. Secondly, money.' Marci Hatfield is leaving her husband, Jason. A pre-nuptial agreement limits her divorce settlement to $600,000. Mr Hatfield is worth $18,000,000 and Cage & Fish have been offered a third of everything they gain for Mrs Hatfield over and above the offered $600,000.

Also Starring: Mark Metcalf played 'The Master' – Buffy the Vampire Slayer's nemesis in her first season.

Toilet Humour: Ally and Billy have a really nice conversation where he admits that he misses her. John and Elaine negotiate the terms of her sexual harassment suit from separate, closed cubicles within the unisex.

The Verdict: What would in other circumstances be a very silly episode is given extra gravitas by the lengthy Billy/Ally conversation and the passion of Gil Bellows and Calista Flockhart's playing of it. 'Drawing The Lines' breaks new ground for the series in its portrayal of how the two ex-lovers relate to each other. Ally and Billy's decision not to create boundaries for how their friendship functions but to free-fall without rules and see how it plays out will have very serious consequences in the future.

109
The Dirty Joke

#AM08
17 November 1997

Written by David E. Kelley
Directed by Daniel Attias

Cast: Keene Curtis (Judge Johnson Hawk),
Brooke Burns (Jennifer Higgin), Nate Reese (Clerk),
Steve and Eric Cohen (The Twins),
Sandra Bernhard (Caroline Poop)

Worried about 'turning into Mary Poppins' Ally bets Renee
that she can tell a dirty joke to the audience at the downstairs
bar. Attorney Caroline Poop, who recently represented Elaine,
returns to Cage & Fish, this time representing Jennifer Higgin,
who is now serving Richard and John with a lawsuit which
claims Elaine's previous suit constituted same-sex sexual
harassment.

Everything Stops For Ally: Ally watches *Whatever Happened to Baby Jane?* (Robert Aldrich, 1962). Ally hates Julie
Andrews, both as Sister Maria in *The Sound of Music* (Robert
Wise, 1965) and Mary Poppins. Renee mentions but can't
remember the title of *S.O.B.* (Blake Edwards, 1981). It turns
out that Ally's hatred of Julie Andrews comes from being
voted 'most likely to turn into Mary Poppins' at high school.

Ally's reaction to Renee's dirty joke borders on the psy-
chotic, as she gives the disabled character a huge back story
and demands to know what Renee's doing laughing when the
poor woman is drowning.

Ally buys a new outfit for her date with the rabbi. She
claims she's never dated a rabbi before, but that she hopes he's
more fun than the priest.

Renee asks Ally what kind of person goes to Freud to understand limericks, uses words like 'ribald' and dates rabbis. The
answer the rest of the table come back with is 'Julie Andrews'.

The Boy Next Door: Billy gets angry when he discovers that Richard touched Georgia's wattle.

Fishisms: When staring at Jennifer he claims he had a great-aunt who told him that if he stared at a beautiful woman for long enough he'd go blind. He now knows her to have been partially right.

Sick of being the named party in lawsuits, Richard announces a new company policy. 'Listen up, anybody who sues this firm, or me personally, we all drop whatever cases we're working on, and devote all our creative efforts to ruining that person's life . . . I do not want to stop short with just getting even retribution. Not strong enough. Ruin, that's the goal: irreversible, irreparable, irrational ruin.'

Georgia On My Mind: Georgia initially refuses to be first chair on the Caroline Poop case. When Richard demands to know why, she claims that it's simply because Jennifer Higgin feels oppressed because she's too sexy, and she relates to this. Richard wants to know what her second reason is, and when she tells him that she doesn't have a second reason he's amazed. 'The first one stinks; you must have another one,' he insists. She eventually admits that she is convinced Caroline Poop is hitting on her. When she challenges Poop about this, accusing her of giving her a 'let's get together and watch *Ellen* sometime' look, Caroline tells Georgia that the reason she keeps looking at her is not because she wants to seduce her, but because she is amazed by Georgia's close resemblance to Barbie.

Office Gossip: It isn't in Elaine's nature to try to hurt people; she can't resist trying to help. The problem is that that's when she does the most damage. She describes Jennifer Higgin as walking around in a 'slutty little way' but insists that she has no personal acrimony towards her.

Guy Talk: Renee informs Ally that men don't like telling dirty jokes in the presence of women. The way to break into this clique is apparently to tell a really dirty joke yourself, then you'll get handed a (metaphorical) cigar.

Fashion Victims: Billy's blazer. No, no, no! Jennifer's jumpers? Oh, yes.

The Case: Ally blows the Higgin/Poop case apart at the hearing stage, pointing out that as Jennifer didn't feel oppressed until Elaine and the other women brought the lawsuit, she has no case. A previous complaint cannot be the basis of another sexual discrimination complaint, because any sexual harassment case gives the plaintiff qualified immunity from prosecution based on it.

Song: Vonda Shepard sings The Bee Gees' 'I Started A Joke' (Gibb/Gibb/Gibb), a lyrically and musically gorgeous little number that even the authors have failed to explain the meaning of.

The Verdict: 'Dirty jokes are supposed to be sick, that's the point.' This episode would be great but for one simple fact. The dirty joke isn't. Maybe it's television censorship, but not only is it far from the dirtiest joke either of us can think of, it's also a censored version of that joke. Still, at least Renee's joke is funny – Ally's is just dumb. The final Ally/Billy scene is very good though.

110
Boy To The World

#AM09
1 December 1997

Written by David E. Kelley
Directed by Thomas Schlamme

Cast: Wilson Cruz (Stephanie/Steven Grant),
Dyan Cannon (Judge 'Whipper' Cone),
Armin Shimerman (Judge Walworth),
Amy Aquino (Psychologist),
Niles Brewster (Attorney Ken Banks),
Ronald Hunter (Detective Greene),
Harrison Page (Reverend Mark Newman),

Danny Wantland (D.A. Corbett)
Special Appearance by Peter MacNicol

Ally defends 'Stephanie Grant', a thrice-convicted transvestite prostitute, and is desperate to avoid prison for this fragile, beautiful young man. Richard's uncle has died, and there are legal difficulties with the funeral service.

Everything Stops For Ally: Ally claims that all the things that upset her during the rest of the year don't affect her at Christmas time. Ally tells Stephanie she has a way with Freudian slips; 'So do I,' she deadpans, 'I'm wearing one.'

Fishisms: Richard's Uncle Kevin has recently died. He hated short people (apparently he was bitten by one at six years old) and the minister at the local church won't let this aspect of his life be celebrated at his memorial service. Richard points out that his uncle was 'a kook', someone known to eat the occasional caterpillar and to dye the hair in his ears. Richard instantly knows that Stephanie is really a guy, due to the shape of his neck. He claims to know every neck in the room.

Richard's funeral oration for his uncle is beautifully done. He claims the dead man told him not to 'paint me a saint' and not to let the congregation cry. He says that his uncle was a father figure for him, who was 'good, bad, caring, insensitive, loud', that he 'liked some people for silly reasons, disliked others for sillier reasons' and that his philosophy was simple: 'Life's just a stupid game, it doesn't matter what you do or what you have, if you're loved in the end then you win.'

Smile Therapy: 'Do you find me short?' John asks Ally. 'You're not tall,' she replies, 'but I wouldn't consider you short.' He also asks her if she would consider dating him. She demurs, saying that she wouldn't because he's her boss and they work together, but otherwise, yes she would. John sadly points out that 'would is a subjunctive word, contrary to fact', but Ally fails to understand him. She later regrets turning him down, but she decides that she'd really like to go to dinner with him, and tells him so.

Office Gossip: Elaine doesn't want too much green in the Christmas decorations at the office. This is apparently because the majority of the decor in the office is blue and blue co-ordinates poorly with green. She very obviously tries to hit on Stephanie: 'All of your office needs, I'll take care of them.'

Girl Talk: There's a lovely scene with Ally, Renee and Stephanie at Ally's apartment, where Stephanie demonstrates his obsession with make-up and offers to bleach Ally's teeth for her.

Fashion Victims: Stephanie makes clothes. Ally jokingly tells him that the only reason she's pursuing his case with such vigour is because she wants him to give her a wedding dress he's made.

Judge Not: Judge Walworth is clearly a very wise man, who defiantly puts the interests of the plaintiff ahead of what could be interpreted as a personal attack on him. He's played by the amazing Armin Shimmerman who was smothered under heavy make-up as Quark through seven interminable series of *Star Trek: Deep Space Nine*. More interestingly he was School Principal Snyder in the first three seasons of *Buffy: The Vampire Slayer*, where he ended up being eaten by a giant snake for his pains.

Whip-Lash!: Whipper hands Ally a case which has no one to defend it, saying 'The Commonwealth thanks you.'

The Case: Ally defends Stephanie by arguing insanity and gets Whipper to suspend his sentence for a year provided he has a job.

Also Starring: Wilson Cruz was Rickie Vasquez in *My So Called Life* with sometime Juliet, Clare Danes.

Toilet Humour: John intrudes into Ally's cubicle to see if she's OK. As she's been in there for twenty minutes he's correctly assumed she's there for solitude rather than to take advantage of the facilities.

Kisses: Ally gently kisses John under the mistletoe.

The Verdict: 'The reason I left home is because everybody called me sick.' At times beautiful, and blessed with a guest performance of genius from Wilson Cruz, this tragic, intelligent, sensitive episode is a painful but brilliant highlight of the first season. The sheer comic madness of Richard's plotline ameliorates the pain somewhat, but ultimately you'll come away from this brilliant episode both cold and unhappy.

111
Silver Bells

#AM10
15 December 1997

Written by David E. Kelley
Directed by Joe Napolitano

Cast: Eric Pierpoint (James Horton),
Amanda Carlin (Mindy Horton),
Katie Mitchell (Patti Horton),
Dyan Cannon (Judge 'Whipper' Cone),
Bailey Thompson (Jean Horton),
Steve Cohen and Eric Cohen (The Dancing Twins),
Peter Roth (as himself),
Renee Goldsberry, Vatrena King and Sy Smith (The Ikettes)

Three people want the firm to argue for them to be allowed to be married as a group. A kind of ménage à trois polygamy. Elaine puts all her efforts into organising the office Christmas party, and persuading as many of the colleagues as possible to go up on stage during it and sing.

Everything Stops For Ally: The polygamy case upsets Ally and violates her sense of romantic idealism; she clearly hates arguing it, and her instincts prove correct when Mindy reveals that she's only agreeing to the idea in order to keep her family together. Effectively James is subtly abusing Mindy, by putting her under pressure to accept a situation that really only he is happy with. The true meaning of Christmas for Ally is Santa and being allowed to believe in something she knows isn't real.

She admits to Georgia just how much she admires her. 'Here's to you, Barbie.'

The Boy Next Door: Billy concludes that his and Ally's friendship 'makes us both stronger' with Ally snapping back, 'It's just a coincidence that we used to be lovers.' Whenever Ally feels insecure or unsteady she grabs hold of the things that steady her, and Billy is one of the things that does that. Ally tells Billy and Georgia point blank that 'husbands, wives, ex-girlfriends' is 'not a combination that calls for honesty' but 'a combination that calls for pretending'.

Fishisms: Richard is very enthusiastic about the polygamy case for one reason: 'piles, piles and piles of money'. He claims he'd argue it himself if the judge and he weren't fornicating. Both Ally and John refuse to take the case, but Richard tells the Hortons that the firm will take the case regardless.

Elaine hassles Richard about proposing to Whipper, pointing out that she wants a ring, not a song. She's also annoyed that Richard is choosing to sing a love song rather than a Christmas carol. 'I paid for this party, Elaine,' he points out, 'I can sing whatever I want.' He doesn't think much of her attempt to advise him on his love life either. 'Imagine my comfort having you for emotional counsel,' he retorts, and wonders whether he should dye his roots in order to truly profit from her wisdom.

Later, when trapped between a bickering trio of Ally, Georgia and Billy he comments, 'I'm in the middle and clueless, I feel like Elaine.'

Talking to Whipper he admits that he's afraid of his parents, and turning into them. As a child he constantly listened to music on headphones to drown out the sound of his parents screaming at each other. He says his heart would actually quicken as the gaps between songs came nearer, as for that brief moment he'd be able to hear them argue. He equates marriage and dependency with fear for that reason.

Smile Therapy: John emerges from the toilet cubicle without his trousers. He later confesses to Richard that he's drawn to Ally, and he wonders whether he should ask Ally to go to the Christmas party with him. As his date.

Later he charges up to Ally to ask her, his mind echoing with Marvin Gaye's 'Let's Get It On', and ringing with the bells, and then he realises that he's left his flies undone. John tells Ally that his mother tried to get him to not believe in Santa by telling him he sexually fondled the elves. She did this because her therapist had told her the first step was to dis-illusion the boy, and undermine his admiration for Saint Nick. A year later she told him Santa had died of a heart attack. John blamed himself for this, as he'd always left Santa a plate of Oreo cookies and a glass of whole fat milk on Christmas Eve.

Georgia On My Mind: The case reflects aspects of our heroes' private lives (surprise) as Georgia sees the parallels between the ménage à trois that they're arguing a case for, and the fact that Billy has been a better husband since Ally came along. Georgia knows that this is because Billy can reach certain pockets of intimacy with Ally that he can't with her. This isn't because there's actually anything sexual going on between them, but is simply a result of the close connection they have from growing up together.

Ally points out that whilst she never exactly planned to break up Billy and Georgia's marriage, she isn't thrilled to be the best thing that ever happened to it. She insists that she, Ally and Billy get into a room and discuss 'them'.

Once there, Billy demands to know what Georgia is angry about, and she tells him, 'I am angry that in order to have a meaningful discussion about our marriage I gotta have her in the room, I am angry because I don't even know who to blame, I am angry because I like you better since she came back into your life, I am angry because somehow she has managed to make you and I closer, I am angry because I'm not sure I want her out of your life, I am angry because I don't know how to handle this, and on top of it all I like her, damn it! I'm angry about that too!' Ally very sensibly gets the hell out of there.

Georgia later confesses that whatever the successes and failures that she and Billy share, she doesn't want Ally to be any part of them.

Office Gossip: Elaine describes the Ikettes as black, sexy and coinciding with her sensuality. Richard and Renee agree that if she, Elaine, caught her mother kissing Santa Claus she'd tell her father in a second. Ally describes Elaine singing as '70s Slut Rock'.

Girl Talk: Ally and Renee discuss how society is made up of more women than men, and how if they all tried hard enough the women could change society's perceptions of their obligations towards motherhood, career and marriage. 'I plan to change it,' Ally rants, 'I just want to get married first.'

Fantasy: Ally imagines Whipper shooting James Horton dead in the witness box. The discussion of the three-way relationship leads her to momentarily visualise the three of them asleep in the same bed. When John asks Ally on a date she literally turns to ice.

Song: There's a bevy of Christmas songs in this episode. Elaine (Jane Krakowski) sings 'I Saw Mommy Kissing Santa Claus', while Lisa Nicole Carson and Vonda Shepard perform 'Santa Claus Is Coming To Town' and Vonda sings 'Please Come Home for Christmas' solo.

The musical highlight of this episode is when Richard sings 'More Today Than Yesterday' (Spiral Staircase) to Whipper at the Christmas party. Greg Germann may not be technically as good a vocalist as some of the other regular cast members, but he 'acts' the song brilliantly.

. . . And Dance: Slow dancing isn't really dancing at all, Ally opines, it's just two people leaning on each other as if they'd fall down without the other one.

Fashion Victims: Elaine is cute in a Santa hat.

Whip-Lash!: Happiness is going to bed at night with something a little more secure than a Fishism. Richard offers to marry her. 'What's the big deal?' he asks, they're together and they love each other, so what's the point of marriage, what does it mean? Whipper points out that it must mean something for Richard to be so afraid of it. Whipper pages Richard with the verdict of the polygamy case during the party, which Richard feels she has done deliberately in order to ruin his party. She denies the plaintiff's motion saying 'Your timing may be right on this issue, but you picked the wrong judge.'

Also Starring: The man who, whilst dancing with Renee, tells her he runs a network is actually FOX President Peter Roth, making a cameo appearance. Eric Pierpoint (James) is perhaps best known for playing George Francisco in FOX's short-lived but repeatedly revived (and really rather good) *Alien Nation*.

Trivia: This is Cage & Fish's third annual Christmas party, which means the firm had been established for about two and a half years before Ally joined.

The Verdict: 'Sometimes people just need to surrender.' Brilliant from top to tail, 'Silver Bells' is often fraught, fractious, very funny and very sweet. This episode touches on deep character issues in a yuletide setting, without ever resorting to sentimentality – quite an astonishing achievement. It even manages to deepen Richard without damaging his potential as a 'devil-may-care' comedy character. The ending is very superb, with Ally trying to draw John out of his shell, Billy and Georgia happy and Richard singing his heart out. We don't give out ratings, but if we did this one would get full marks.

112
Cro-Magnon

#AM11
5 January 1998

Written by David E. Kelley
Directed by Allan Arkush

Cast: Michael Easton (Glenn), Eddie Mills (Clinton Gil),
Henry Woronicz (Austin Gil),

Michael Winters (Judge Herbert Spitt),
Lee Wilkof (District Attorney Nixon),
Barry Livingston (Dr John Emburg),
Derk Cheetwood (Dwayne Stokes), Nicolette Vajtay (Jill),
Sharon Omi (Bailiff), Karen Elyse (Foreperson)

Ally considers dating a nude model for a very 'obvious' reason, and defends a teenager on an assault and battery charge. Billy begins to get paranoid about one particular aspect of married life.

Fishisms: Whilst watching boxing with Elaine, Billy, John and Georgia, Richard yells, 'Somebody kill somebody' at the screen. Somewhat disturbingly.

Smile Therapy: Ally has developed enough faith in John as a litigator that she defends him when Austin Gil criticises his unorthodox behaviour in court. John tells a story about being thirteen years old and waiting in line at a movie theatre. A bigger boy pushed into the queue in front of him and when John objected he said, 'What are you going to do about it?' Of course John could do nothing. He was afraid to physically stick up for himself. Many years later a drunk man was obnoxious to him in a bar, and threatened him physically. This time John was not afraid and, to his own amazement, knocked the man to the floor with a single blow. Of course, the whole story might all be made up to acquire the jury's sympathy.

John had a hallucination that recurred for two years, in which his dead aunt wanted to have tea with him. He finally stopped it by having tea with her. He once again demonstrates the ability to notice when Ally is hallucinating.

Georgia On My Mind: Billy just suddenly comes out with the question, 'Do I satisfy you in bed?' in the middle of a different conversation with Georgia. She tells him she's 'a very satisfied woman. I am very, very happy in the bed. Trust me.' Later that day Billy, er, fails to rise to the challenge and whilst he's deeply embarrassed, Georgia claims to be happy about it happening just the once. 'The idea of you being insecure with me instead of me being insecure with you' is something she finds endearing.

Office Gossip: Elaine smokes cigars, loves boxing and clearly believes that 'size' is everything. Nothing we couldn't have worked out for ourselves there.

Guy Talk: In the unisex, Billy and Richard discuss the women's recent obsessing over Glenn's penis. Billy asks Richard if he's ever measured the size of his penis, to which Richard replies, 'All the time.' He says he knows he's good in bed because he's always satisfied.

Men: Glenn, the professional snowboarder/artist's model with the enormous . . . reputation. Ally goes to be with him in the full knowledge that he's leaving the country and that there's no possibility of a relationship, which is something of a shift away from her normal attitude.

Oogachaka!: The big one. The dancing baby appears to the strains of Blue Swede's twisted classic, 'Hooked On A Feeling', a record reintroduced into the public consciousness through its use on the soundtrack to *Reservoir Dogs* (Quentin Tarantino, 1992). Ally eventually gives in to the baby and dances with him. As Ally begins to dance the music changes from the original version of 'Hooked On A Feeling' into a Vonda Shepard cover. Irrelevant, but interesting.

Shrink Wrapped: John says he has a therapist who advised him to confront his hallucinations. Given her later advice to Ally it's probable he's talking about Dr Tracy.

Fashion Victims: Richard's waistcoat is ace. Georgia's ripped jeans and tight, old sweater suit her. So there.

The Case: Ally is defending Clinton Gil, a nineteen-year-old man who physically assaulted another, breaking his cheekbone in the process. He did this because he was angry. The boy's father refuses to allow him to plead *guilty* because he doesn't want him to have a criminal record when he applies to medical school.

The Defence: Clinton was defending his date, an ex-girlfriend of the boy he assaulted, who was verbally abusing both of them and had refused to leave despite being repeatedly asked to go.

Guilty?: Not. Of course, thanks to John Cage's brilliant summing-up.

Withdrawn: Ally tells the judge that she finds herself troubled, and requests permission to take a moment. John is both astonished and pained by this blatant theft of his technique; Judge Spitt simply looks pained. John pulls his trick of asking the witness to state their name and then not asking them any questions.

Kisses: Ally fantasises about kissing Clinton Gil. Immediately afterwards she upbraids herself for this: 'He's nineteen!' Silly girl. She later kisses, and manages far more with Glenn the model.

Song: Vonda Shepard sings the magnificent 'I Could Have Danced All Night' (Lerner/Loewe) from the musical *My Fair Lady*.

The Verdict: 'We're women, we have double standards to live up to.' A thematic sequel to 106 'The Promise', 'Cro-Magnon' is one of the most famous episodes of *Ally McBeal*, even if only because of one of the series' most enduring images: the dancing baby. It's also rather good in other ways: John's summing-up (with accompanying flashbacks) is one of his best ever, and the 'Sex & Violence' montage is amazingly well put together, smothered as it is in Mascagni's wonderful 'Cavalleria Rusticana'.

113
Blame Game

#AM112
26 January 1998

Written by David E. Kelley
Directed by Sandy Smolan

Cast: Michael Easton (Glenn), Harry J. Lennix (Ballard),
Susan Merson (Judge Stoller), Adrian Sparks (Katz),
Elizabeth Ruscio (Cynthia Pierce),
Daniel Mahar (Michael Lamb), Ben Siegler (Hoverless),
Dale Weston (Reporter), Vince Brolato (Foreperson),
Dean Purvis (Man), Christopher Michael (Bailiff),
Renee Goldsberry, Vatrena King and Sy Smith (The Ikettes)

John, Georgia and Ally represent the adult children of a man
who died in a plane crash. Glenn, the one-night-stand from the
previous episode, returns without warning, much to Ally's
alarm. She decides to take revenge: although what for is a moot
question.

Everything Stops For Ally: In the pre-credits sequence Ally
dreams that she and Georgia are in a plane crash, which she
survives and Georgia doesn't. Renee finds this funny as it's
so obviously partially a result of a subconscious desire to get
Georgia out of her way. Ally tricks herself into going out
with Glenn again, by telling him that she didn't intend him as
merely a one-night-stand (which she did) and then blames
him for tricking her into dating him. She realises that she
actually likes him, and they have sex again, but by this
point Glenn is worried about being used and gets quickly out
of her life. Which is again explained by Ally as being his
fault.

When Ally asks Renee if she unfairly blames everyone else
for her problems she gets angry when Renee repeatedly replies
in the affirmative. She possibly tells us far more than we need
to know when she says of Glenn that she 'bit his hook, line and
swallowed his sinker.'

We see a lot of the more shallow, selfish side to Ally here,
which the Ally critics of the series believe is always on show.
This doesn't make her bad of course. It just makes her
complex. There's a massive contradiction when she goes
straight from feeling sorry for herself about being alone to
turning down the offer of a dance from a perfectly acceptable-
looking, perfectly nice-seeming guy.

The Boy Next Door: Billy tries to talk to Ally about Glenn but she refuses, claiming it as a boundary. He gets angry about Ally's sleeping with Glenn, which he then apologises for. As an ex-boyfriend he gets jealous. He shouldn't, and he knows he shouldn't, but he does.

Fishisms: 'Don't bring the law into this, somebody's dead, there's money!' Richard goes on TV and lies about his feelings on the case in hand. 'A case like this is why I started this firm, to answer the call to human anguish, to perhaps make air travel safe for all people in the process. Too often today we hear the adage "Law is business". It's not a business to me or the other fine attorneys of this firm; it's a calling.' See, lies.

When Lamb and Pierce decide that apportioning blame is more important than receiving a settlement he's unimpressed: 'This is what happens when the justice system is perverted by principles', he whines.

Richard tells Georgia that if they lose the case he'll vomit and then dive into it. He's actually brought his snorkel into court with him for just such an eventuality.

Smile Therapy: John does isometrics to alter his blood flow in the evenings. Whatever. He asks Ally to postpone the concept of them dating until Glenn is out of the picture, as 'being the jugglee' troubles him.

Office Gossip: Elaine monitors Ally and Billy's conversations using a sound-enhancing microphone dish and headphones. Are there no depths to which this woman will not sink?

Men: Glenn, who's given a bit of personality this time and winds up being treated rather badly for his pains.

Fantasy: Ally burns red (with appropriate sizzling sound effects) as the rest of the girls in the office giggle about her second one-night-stand with Glenn.

Oogachaka!: The baby dances away happily as Glenn and Ally have sex again.

Song: As Richard is given the verdict, and the notice of the $1.1 million settlement, we hear the beginning of 'Tell the

World How I Feel About 'Cha, Baby', the opening line of which is 'You're the reason I want to live'. Nice.

The Verdict: 'It's not you, it's me.' After the second time they have sex Glenn is afraid of Ally treating him as a 'boy toy' (which is of course exactly how she wanted to treat him) so he walks away. Ally deliberately misinterprets his reticence to be mistreated as an excuse, and a ploy to stop her thinking badly of him. She's at her least sympathetic *ever* here (although Billy is equally out of line) as she spectacularly misunderstands the situation, and conspires with Renee to humiliate Glenn. Yet, the fact is that if one of the men in the firm behaved in the way that Ally and Renee do in this episode, they'd be rightly vilified for cruelty, usery and insensitivity. At least that's how we interpret it.

114

Body Language

#AM13
2 February 1998

**Written by David E. Kelley,
Nicole Yorking and Dawn Prestwich
Directed by Mel Damski**

Cast: Kathleen Wilhoite (Janie),
Lawrence Pressman (Judge Smart),
J. Kenneth Campbell (Yorkin), John Thaddeus (Michael),
Evan O'Meara (Policeman),
Carrie Stauber (Policewoman),
David Doty (Minister),
Jeffrey von Meyer (Attorney Skroot),
Bill Dwyer (Band Leader), Annika Brinbly (Tory),
Eric Mansker (Bailiff), Nancy Stephens (Dr Karp),
Dyan Cannon (Judge 'Whipper' Cone),
Linda Gehringer (Attorney General Janet Reno),
Steve and Eric Cohen (The Dancing Twins)

Ally and Georgia are attempting to argue for a woman who wants permission to marry a maximum-security prisoner. Ally comes up with a brilliant argument, which should allow their client to marry her beau: if he donates some sperm that Janie can use to conceive, then she, as a woman pregnant with the child of a convict, has a legally valid reason to marry him.

Everything Stops For Ally: Ally and Renee attend a wedding where they fight – literally – over who gets to catch the bridal bouquet. This leads to Ally both punching, and then knocking to the floor, her closest rival – a middle-aged woman with false teeth – in order to seize this symbolic prize. She then imagines Renee dropping a big rock on her head.

She tries to flirt with Judge Smart in order to get what she wants. Billy is unimpressed with Ally's solution to her legal problem, leading her to comment, 'We're lawyers, that's our job: distort the law beyond all common sense.'

Fishisms: Richard spots the Attorney General at the bar, and goes up to talk to her, fingering her wattle in the process. Unfortunately, while he's getting his jollies, Whipper walks in. As Ally says, 'The Whip and Janet Reno, now there's a cat fight.' Richard tries to defend himself against Whipper, 'like I'm really gonna hit on someone who can have me attacked by the FBI', but she dumps him anyway. John tries to cheer him up, but Richard points out that the fact that Whipper has dumped him means he doesn't want to smile. He suggests that if John has a problem with this he should stand on a railway line and take a moment.

Bygones: 'I couldn't help but overhear, probably because I was eavesdropping. Bygones.' When Richard attempts to win Whipper back she knees him solidly in the groin. This isn't strictly a bygone, but we're sure Richard wants to forget it. The next time he talks to her he wears a protective cup in case she knees him again, which Whipper finds extremely funny but John sees it as merely sensible. So do we.

Smile Therapy: John claims to be in Smile Therapy the morning of the case. He says he's prone to sternness, and that there's some evidence to suggest that smiling is not a one-way process. You smile because you're happy, but perhaps you can make yourself happy by smiling. He then accidentally leaves the unisex without his trousers.

John teaches Richard how to hear 'the bells' – a chiming sound that gives him confidence and allows him to feel better about himself. John's bells are a section from 'Going the Distance' by Bill Conti from the *Rocky* soundtrack. Richard's bells are a ringing, 'dinging' cow-bell noise.

DA Renee: 'Richard and Whipper [splitting up] is another set-back for love, and you take that personally,' Renee points out.

Judge Not: Billy thinks Judge Smart is 'all mood'. Some days he says yes, some days he says no. It's worth going back into court with some new evidence because of the real possibility of a second opinion.

The Case: Janie decides that to bring a child into the world in order to take advantage of a legal technicality that will allow her and Michael to marry, is wrong. But the prison governor is personally persuaded by Ally's arguments about love, and decides to let them marry anyway.

Song: Janie sings 'For Your Love' (Ed Townsend) every night as a remembrance of her imprisoned boyfriend. We see her signing it alongside Renee as Ally dances with the inflatable man. Vonda performs the Leiber/Stoller standard 'Don't'.

The Verdict: One of the series' few co-written episodes, this lacks coherency but has a couple of brilliant scenes, chiefly Ally and Georgia nearly being arrested whilst ferrying 'the merchandise' from prison to hospital, and John's attempt to teach Smile Therapy to Billy and Elaine. (Billy thinks it's stupid, whilst Elaine fears it will cause wrinkles.)

115
Once In A Lifetime

#AM14
23 February 1998

Teleplay by David E. Kelley
Story by David E. Kelley and Jeff Pinker
Directed by Elodie Keene

Cast: Richard Kiley (Seymore Little),
Steven Flynn (Sam Little), Brigid Brannagh (Paula),
Phil Leeds (Judge 'Happy' Boyle), Bruce Nozick (Attorney),
Renee Goldsberry,Vatrena King, Sy Smith (The Ikettes)

Celebrated artist Seymore Little, whose work Ally studied at college, wishes to marry. The problem is that he's been declared legally incompetent, and his son, Sam, is now his guardian. Sam won't let him get married because he believes his intended bride is a gold-digger.

Meanwhile, John prepares for his second date with Ally, as Ally's obsession with Billy continues to grow.

Everything Stops For Ally: Seymore Little feels that no real lawyer would dress the way Ally does, and repeatedly refers to her as 'skirtless'. Ally is still clearly very much in love with Billy and does her best to put John off her without hurting him. When John realises that the reason she was continually gabbling about hair care during their date was in order to incur his disinterest (as he puts it), she tells him about 'The Ick' – the theory she and Renee have about knowing that dating someone isn't right even when they don't know *why*. It's very difficult to sympathise with Ally at this point because it's clearly groundless self-justifying rubbish designed to excuse the fact that she basically doesn't think John is good enough for her, when any idiot can see that they'd make a terrific couple.

The Boy Next Door: 'Every time we get by this, something comes along to tear the lid off.' The Little case, with its inevitable discussion of love eternal, of course reflects on the Billy/

Ally relationship, leading to some frank discussion between the two of them. 'Will you ever forgive my letting go?' Billy asks her, to which she replies that she forgives him, but can't understand why he left her.

'This one love forever thing is silly, somebody else can always come along,' says Billy, talking about the case. 'Somebody did,' Ally snaps back, clearly meaning Georgia; and then pretends she was talking about Seymore's fiancée Paula. Billy cuts off the conversation with Ally saying, 'It's not right to talk about a thing that I can't also talk about with Georgia; and I can't talk about *this*.'

Fishisms: Richard is concerned for the obviously upset John but attempts to hide it. 'I won't pretend to care what's bothering you but I do care very much as to how it affects me.' Richard's extensive list of different ways women like to be kissed is very funny, and reasonably comprehensive, but provides John with more issues than he is prepared to deal with.

Smile Therapy: John has a remote control for flushing the toilet. He uses this to ensure that the bowl is fresh whenever he decides to visit the unisex, as he finds remnants extremely distressing.

Georgia On My Mind: Georgia is understandably *very* unimpressed by how irritated Billy is that John is going on a date with Ally. Correctly surmising that Billy's real reasons for his objection are distinct from his stated 'he's a founding partner, she's an associate' smokescreen.

Office Gossip: According to Elaine, when Richard hired Ally he expected her to bill two hundred hours a month, so by those criteria, which Elaine insists are not her own, Ally is currently a failure at Cage & Fish. Elaine tells Richard and John that she was 'known as a giver' at high school, meaning that boys always went straight for second base. The three of them discuss men who slobber excessively during kissing, and once she's realised that Cage is one of these people, tries to be nice about the problem, offering the solution of sucking heavily on your date's tongue, and swallowing both your own excess slobber and some of theirs. She then snogs John's face off as a demonstration. Richard pays far more attention to this than he really should.

Guy Talk: Loads of it, as Richard tries to help John through the difficulties of trying to date Ally. 'If you don't kiss a girl on the first date you're a gentleman. If you don't kiss her on the second, you're gay', is Richard's considered opinion on the issue of whether Cage should kiss Ally. He also argues that 'All that stuff about feminism, autonomy, gender equality . . . women don't really want that, they want to be taken.' He reveals that on his first date with Whipper she called the police, although we're mercifully spared any details.

Fantasy: Ally hallucinates an elephant sitting between her and Billy. Presumably this symbolises how she can never forget their love. Seymore Little can see and talk to his late wife. (See 316 'The Boy Next Door'.)

Oogachaka!: Renee and Ally discuss the idea of Ally trying to get back with Billy, with Ally denying she'd try for it. Billy is married and 'I gave up adultery for Lent'. She does concede that she feels herself falling backwards into love with Billy again. Renee is unimpressed, saying that 'that damn Oogachaka will come out again and you'll be on the floor with him'.

Song: This episode contains two of the lengthy montages so beloved of the series. The first is to 'You Belong To Me' and largely consists of a conversation between Billy and Ally in the office, intercut with footage of Georgia waiting for him at home. The second is to 'The End of the World' (written by Dee/Kent and performed by Vonda Shepard) and emphasises Little's love for his dead wife, Billy and Georgia, Ally's obsession with Billy, and John's reflections on having blown it with Ally.

. . . And Dance: Barry White's 'Can't Get Enough of Your Love, Baby' is played as John performs an extraordinary dance number to ready himself for dinner with Ally.

The Case: It seems that Little and Paula don't really want to marry for love; it's a pretext to get round the son's legal responsibility for the father, so that Seymore can open a gallery and exhibit his paintings of his dead wife. The reason

Sam doesn't want his father to open the gallery is because he believes that such an exhibition of inferior works would damage his father's reputation in the history of art. He sees this as protecting his father for posterity.

Let Me See Your Teeth: Happy's back! He's appalled by Little's dentures and keeps obsessing over the fact that Seymore bought his dead wife a boat. Nevertheless he is wise enough to set up a new form of guardianship for the Littles that will allow the older man his gallery, without giving him full legal control of his estate.

Kisses: Ally fantasises about kissing Billy outside Happy's court. John kisses Ally, knocking her to the floor in the process. She's unimpressed.

Hit The Bar: Ally and John dance in the bar after dinner, with Ally imagining John as a man dressed in appalling 70s retro clothes who's dancing like a mad thing. She feels she's stuck in 70s hell.

The Verdict: 'There are some loves that just don't go away.' The case dovetails thematically with what's going on in the lawyers' lives beautifully, and the regulars play the whole situation to the hilt. Richard Kiley's performance is superb, and the whole neatly avoids sentimentality, instead demonstrating real, and quite painful, emotional depth. That said, there's far too little Fish in here for our tastes.

116
Forbidden Fruits

#AM15
2 March 1998

Written by David E. Kelley
Directed by Jeremy Kagan

Cast: Dina Meyer (Anna Flint),
J. Patrick McCormack (Senator Foote),

Elaine Giftros (Nancy Foote), Marty Rackham (Joe Bepp),
Gary Bullock (Judge Kenneth Steele),
Andrew Bloch (Mr Colson), Jeff Sanders (Court Clerk),
Helen Duffy (Foreperson)

Senator Foote is being sued by his new wife's ex-husband, who claims that Foote deliberately and cynically destroyed his marriage in order to win his wife, Nancy, for himself. John and Richard are determined that the case should not be tried. They feel that to sue a public official while he is in office will impact on time he should be devoting to his public duties – and they don't care if the Supreme Court itself disagrees!

The Boy Next Door: The combination of their shared history and how closely they're currently working together has given Ally and Billy the ability to finish each other's sentences. Everyone in the conference rooms finds this distracting, and it winds Georgia up. After Ally gets up in court and delivers an argument that more fits her situation with Billy and Georgia than the court case, Billy gets very angry with her. 'Whatever the hell's between us and whatever isn't you leave it out of the courtroom. That was unprofessional what you did in there and it was out of line,' he says. And he's right.

Fishisms: A great deal is made out of this being Richard's first appearance in court in a long, long time. Everyone panics and John gives him a few tips, such as remembering to call the judge 'Your Honour', but no one could be prepared for what follows: Richard getting to his feet in front of Kenneth Steele.

Richard begins his address to the court by stating his citizenship of the United States, and claiming that 'as such I am appalled that the machinery of our government can be hampered by these cheap lawsuits'. When it's pointed out that the Supreme Court has recently declared that the President himself can be sued whilst in office, the judge asks Richard why a senator should be exempt when the head of state is not. 'I'm glad you asked me that, Your Honour, because it will allow me to comment on a very small detail so far ignored with respect to the Clinton/Jones ruling. They screwed up.' 'Who did?' enquires Judge Steele. 'The supreme court,' responds Richard. 'Bad ruling.' 'The supreme court screwed up?' asks the incredulous judge, as the other members of the Cage & Fish legal team simultaneously take a moment. 'And you would like me to substitute your judgement for theirs?' 'Yes,' Fish comes back. 'Do I win?' He doesn't but this just unleashes a torrent from Richard who points out that the supreme court's judgement was 'based on their conclusion that the President being sued wouldn't take up much of his time or hamper his ability to do the work. Hello? How out of it are they? Not gonna be a burden, not gonna take up any time? Let me tell you something, Judge, the supreme court, they're old; and the media, pick up a newspaper, any newspaper, what do they cater to: dirt, sleaze, gossip, crap!' When the relevancy of this line of argument is challenged, Richard, amazingly, has a valid answer. It's apparently relevant for two reasons: 1) 'The American public, stupid people!' and 2) 'Lawyers like me, I'll sue anybody. Merits? Hah! Who cares? I'll go after senators for the fun of it. And don't tell me I can't cripple a congressman's ability to do his work. With today's media it's not like they go out and check the facts. I could say something about you having sex with a goat, totally untrue; so what, all I've gotta do is say it!' Then, the argument goes, Steele would spend his life performing spin control rather than trying cases. Richard finishes, 'I'll say it to you, I'll say it to them. Bad ruling, bad, bad ruling.' For his pains he gets a round of applause from the courtroom, and surprisingly measured response from the judge. 'Despite your zealous and scholarly analysis I have decided not to overrule our highest court.'

Later that day Richard appears on televison and again argues his point. 'We make special exceptions all the time. Young men are sent to war, to their deaths, for the sake of the country, the national interests are put before their lives, but they can't be put before the simpering little wimp who cries all day because his wife left him? Got a country to run!' Ally informs an appalled Renee that Richard has said that he'll only stop speaking when his fifteen minutes of fame are up.

Smile Therapy: John is drawn to prosecuting attorney Anna Flint, who has an amazing smile (and nice hair too). Determined to win her, he decides to act more like Richard. He touches her wattle and, realising what he's doing, she calls him a pervert. Poor Biscuit.

Georgia On My Mind: Ally goes to talk to Georgia at the bar and asks her if she thinks that Ally is trying to break up her and Billy's marriage. 'Do I think you're trying?' Georgia replies. 'I think you can do things without trying, Ally.' Ally tells Georgia that she is competing with history but that history is all she's competing with. Georgia doesn't believe her, and it's fairly clear that Ally's not convinced of it herself. To make matters worse Ally finishes the conversation by obviously lying to Georgia, telling her that if she and Billy were alone on a desert island, and no one would ever find out, they'd still not have sex because neither of them could betray her. Georgia shrewdly baulks at the very 90s 'frankness' of their conversation: 'This dialogue is just a little too "healthy" for me.'

Oogachaka!: The dancing baby returns, throwing a spear at Ally. Later it appears at the foot of her bed and waves at her, but she's able to banish the image by concentrating.

Song: John plays the Supremes' amazing 'Someday We'll Be Together' in court and feels compelled to dance to it there and then.

Shrink Wrapped: When Renee tells Ally to get help she refuses. 'Even if I get past all my problems I'm just gonna go out and get new ones.'

The Case: The case is a pure MacGuffin, a way of creating a moment when the Ally/Billy/Georgia triangle tensions can reach boiling point.

The Verdict: 'I like being a mess, it's who I am.' An interesting case reflects on the lives of Ally, Billy and Georgia and brings so many issues to a head. We didn't think for a second that Ally and Billy would take Georgia up on her offer to let the two of them have one adulterous night to work it out of their systems, but it shows how desperate Georgia is getting.

Gil Bellows and Courtney Thorne-Smith excel in all their scenes together, this episode giving them far more substantial and emotional scenes to play than any previous instalment. Calista Flockhart delivers Ally's courtroom speech brilliantly, pulling the episode's improbable conclusion off by sheer force of performance. Bravo!

117
Theme Of Life

#AM16
9 March 1998

Written by David E. Kelley
Directed by Dennie Gordon

Cast: Dyan Cannon (Judge 'Whipper' Cone),
Linda Gehringer (Attorney General Janet Reno),
Jesse L. Martin (Dr Greg Butters),
Paul Guilfoyle (Harold Lane),
Liz Torres (Hanna Goldstein),
John Fink (President of Brigham Health Management),
Dawn Stern (Jeanette), Sally Wingert (Tour Guide),
Don Perry (Foreman), Tracey Ullman (Dr Tracy Clark)

A woman is suing Dr Greg Butters for temporarily transplanting a pig's liver into her body. He did this because there was no human organ available for transplant at that time. An incident with the attorney general leads Whipper to reconsider her relationship with Richard.

Everything Stops For Ally: Ally repeatedly falls over in this episode. She blames her shoes, takes one off and throws it across the room. It hits John.

The Boy Next Door: Billy tells the office that some men shy away from a woman they're in love with. The 'freefall' scares them. With the rest of the office staring at him, Billy says that he read this somewhere. Yeah, right.

Fishisms: Billy has a philosophical problem with how Cage & Fish works. He feels the firm takes too many cases devoid of legal merit. Fish insists that it is not their place to decide this, they are not judge or jury, but advocates. Richard lectures Billy about this, but when he's interrupted by a phone call he simply presses a button and makes Billy listen to a tape recording of his exact speech.

When talking about his relationship with Whipper, Richard asks Elaine and Georgia, 'You're both women, what kind of lie works here?'

Richard describes himself as 'upper-ordinary' rather than 'extraordinary', which indicates a self-awareness you might not normally associate with him.

Smile Therapy: The way that John is continually on hand through the first half of this episode, handing out Dr Tracy's card, is a simple but very funny visual gag that Peter MacNicol really pulls off well.

DA Renee: It says far too much about Renee that she, Ally and Georgia go to her kickboxing class; she's getting more and more aggressive and her advice to Ally is becoming of less and less use.

Office Gossip: Elaine offers to have sex with Richard should he want it.

Girl Talk: Well, not 'talk' but the kickboxing match between Ally and Georgia deserves a mention. Billy is sensitive enough to not like it at all, but Elaine's enjoyment is as twisted as it is obvious.

Doctor's Orders: Introducing Dr Greg Butters, played with charm and calm authority by Jesse L. Martin. Butters has performed unauthorised transplant surgery on a woman to save her life; and is she grateful? No.

Whip-Lash!: 'Any woman who would let a strange man finger her wattle in public has a problem.' Whipper goes for Janet Reno, whose wattle Richard has secretly been dusting with his finger. In a very tender scene she dumps Richard, telling him that he's sick. Hmm . . . maybe not that tender.

Fantasy: Ally imagines herself swimming through the office.

Oogachaka!: The dancing baby roller-skates around Ally and Greg as they walk through Boston.

Song: Ally considers 'Searchin' My Soul' (the theme song to her TV series) as the theme song for her life, before settling on 'Tell Him'. Dr Tracy's theme song is 'Tracy' by 'The Cufflinks'.

Shrink Wrapped: 'You're a cracker.' She's here! Ally's unpleasant, aggressive, sarcastic new therapist, who laughs at her, tells her to hit Georgia and orders her to get a 'theme song'. Understandably Ally wonders whether she's on a hidden camera TV show.

Fashion Victims: Dr Tracy, whose clothes defy the term 'vile' and need a new word entirely of their own.

The Verdict: With the introductions of both Greg and Dr Tracy this episode should really be more of a big deal than it is. Hannah Goldstein is a dreadful human being, whose suit is motivated by physical revulsion at the idea of a liver taken from a pig whom she closely resembles. It doesn't help that the performance of the woman who plays her is so bad, thereby pushing us into feeling even more sympathy for Dr Greg who's clearly a decent man who did what he had to do.

118
The Playing Field

#AM17
16 March 1998

Written by David E. Kelley
Directed by Jonathan Pontell

Cast: Tracey Ullman (Dr Tracy Clark),
Jesse L. Martin (Dr Greg Butters),
Josh Evans (Orin Coolie),
Miriam Flynn (Karen Coolie),

Christine Dunford (Eva Curry),
Wrenn T. Brown (Mr Stone), Shea Farrell (Mr Tyler),
Jerry Sroka (Joel), Michael Winters (Judge Herbert Spitt)

Ally and Dr Greg are involved in a road accident, which inevitably has repercussions both legal and personal. Georgia finds herself fighting a sexual harassment case she's personally unimpressed with, whilst Richard outs himself as a closet feminist.

Fishisms: Informed that their case has no basis in law Richard demurs, 'Don't talk to me about boundaries, we're pioneers, upwards and onwards.' Criticised by Georgia he tries to fight her on her own terms, 'I can't tolerate that kind of gender bias. If I were John I'd be taking a moment right now.' Billy knows that the case is serious when Richard confesses that he even consulted the law with regards to it.

In court again, Richard claims to hate sexual harassment laws, believing the impetus for them comes from disgruntled lesbians angry that they don't have the same opportunities to get ahead as straight women. Although he is willing to concede that some of the clamour for them might have come from ugly women who were sick of seeing pretty girls get ahead. At least according to Mr Fish, most people who bring sexual harassment suits are ugly. Fact. Richard does have a point that harassment laws are premised on the notion of 'women as victims' and that this can therefore be used to support their case.

Smile Therapy: John has located a word that helps him control his stutter: 'Poughkeepsie', a part of upstate New York. John insists the phrase is strictly phonetic, and that there's nothing 'geographic' about his choice. He's developed a new 'courtship smile' with which to demonstrate his adorability; unfortunately it makes him look like a serial child murderer. Having said that, Elaine seems to like it.

Georgia On My Mind: Georgia hates the case Richard is making her fight, and asks Billy if it's the most ridiculous thing ever. Apparently it isn't; the most ridiculous thing is that they might win. The essence of the case is thus: Eva Curry works in an office where several women who have had sex with the manager have later been promoted. Although there is no question of quid pro quo, and she admits that he never initiated any of the encounters, she feels that the only way to get ahead in that workplace is to get to know the boss by having a sexual encounter with him. This makes Georgia very angry as she quite reasonably sees it as a perversion of a valid law. She's unimpressed when Richard points out that it's no more of an abuse of a technicality than her own case against her previous employers. The judge rules that he can't be sure that Curry hasn't been discriminated against and allows the case to go to court.

Oh, her new hair is great, too.

DA Renee: Renee locates her esteem in her breasts, because that's the part of her that men are initially drawn to. Ally tells Renee that her best feature is her eyes, leading Renee to comment that 'men don't go for eyes; that's a big lie'. Oi! No it isn't. Dr Tracy feels Renee to be both strong and stable. Considering the events of 120 'The Inmates', this doesn't say much for the Doc's deductive skills.

Doctor's Orders: 'This could be someone.' In our considered opinion Dr Greg is a sweetie and a hero. Ally noticeably relaxes around him, and he finds her more bizarre personality traits endearing and amusing as opposed to frightening. He also has the ability to tell when she's having one of her 'episodes', something only John has previously demonstrated.

Fantasy: Whilst dancing with Dr Greg, Ally imagines herself swimming free of the pool of water that has haunted her recently.

Oogachaka!: Tracy tells Ally that the baby is her subconscious mocking her, and that she needs to get out there and kick its butt. Or something. Later, when pint-sized, ten-year-old lawyer Orin Coolie walks into the office, Ally mistakes him for the baby and physically attacks him.

Shrink Wrapped: 'I don't need to pay a therapist to give me crap – I have a roommate who does it for free.' Dr Tracy takes the 'theme song' concept to another level, insisting Ally imagine she has back-up singers behind her whilst performing it.

The shock Doc comes to the bar, insults both Ally and Georgia.

Dr Tracy admits that she skipped a lot of psychiatry classes. That's a shock. Georgia quite sensibly asks, 'This is the woman in charge of your mental health?'

The Verdict: Much better. Tracy's advice, whilst still off the wall and often useless, seems to have some application at times. Josh Evans, who plays Orin Coolie, is tremendously good, and gets the balance between monstrous and sweet just right.

119
Happy Birthday, Baby

#AM18
6 April 1998

Written by David E. Kelley
Directed by Thomas Schlamme

Cast: Barry Miller (Henderson),
Harriet Sansom Harris (Cheryl Harris),
Alaina Reed Hall (Judge Elizabeth Witt),
Jesse L. Martin (Dr Greg Butters), Danny Borowicz (Stripper)

It's Ally's birthday (she's twenty-eight) and to celebrate she's defending foot fetishist Mark Henderson against a charge of sexual assault, plus breaking and entering. Meanwhile, Elaine is organising Ally's birthday celebrations in her own inimitable style.

Everything Stops For Ally: 'I had a plan, my whole life I had a plan: when I was twenty-eight I was going to be taking my little maternity leave but I would still be on the partnership track, I would be home at night, cuddled up with my husband reading "What To Expect When You're Nursing" and trying cases. Big home life, big professional life, and instead I am going to bed with an inflatable doll and I represent clients who suck toes. This was not the plan.'

Smile Therapy: John is drawn to Renee even more after she performs her raunchy song and dance number at the bar. When she tells the jury that she likes to have her toes sucked, his nose whistles audibly.

Georgia On My Mind: Georgia asks Ally a valid question: 'What makes your problems bigger than everybody else's?' Amazingly Ally has a sensible answer. 'They're mine.'

Office Gossip: Elaine makes a ham-fisted attempt to seduce Dr Greg, and then claims that his not wanting to sleep with Ally has made her depressed. She hires a stripper for Ally even though it's obviously the last thing in the world that Ally would want as a birthday gift. She then gets up in the bar and sings a song for her, persuading both Renee and Dr Greg to do the same. Elaine asks Georgia for help with an ethical dilemma. If you invite a dozen or so men to go home with you from a bar, and the majority of them show up, are you morally obliged to have sex with all of them? Ally tells Elaine that everything she does is based on a desire for attention. Ally asks her how long she'll continue in this vein. ''Till I'm noticed,' Elaine replies sadly. Elaine then tells a bizarre story from her childhood: Elaine's best friend was bought a new bike; Elaine also wanted a bike, but her parents couldn't afford one. By selling herself to boys at recess for a nickel (really!) she made enough to buy herself a bell, which she would put on the bike when she got one. She reveals that while she never actually got a bike, she made a great deal of noise with the bell.

Fetishes: The whole episode revolves around Mark Henderson's foot fetish. Barry Miller plays Henderson with a twitchy depravity, which declines into subtlety once the script's decided he's all right really. He honestly believes that Richard is mocking him when he tells him of his wattle fetish, unaware that this is actually Richard 'sharing'.

Doctor's Orders: 'If I'd known you stayed out late on school nights I never would have hired you,' says Dr Greg after he and Ally have a big date the night before a trial. When he refuses to 'come upstairs for coffee' with her because he has early morning rounds the next day, she speculates that he might be gay. Which is a bit dumb and unfair. Ally finds out that Greg's been offered a senior ER post in Chicago. He's going to take it as it's such a great opportunity, but this of course means that he and Ally can't take their embryonic relationship any further.

Song: Jane Krakowski and Lisa Nicole Carson join Vonda to sing 'I Am a Woman'. Our response can only be 'lousy song, nice performance'. Elvis Presley's 'Love Me' (the one that begins 'Treat me like a fool'.) performed by Jesse L. Martin (Dr Greg) as a birthday present for Ally is sweet and seems to be going rather well until Renee interrupts, joining him on stage, singing along and distracting attention away from Ally, for whom this is supposed to be a celebration. The episode ends with Elaine packing up the office to Vonda Shepard's rendition of 'Que Sera Sera'.

. . . And Dance: The stripper dances to Tom Jones 'It's Not Unusual', growling at Billy and throwing his trousers at Richard, who seems more than unusually interested. Ally boogies around her and Renee's apartment to the fast version of 'Tell Him'. She then kills the inflatable man by sitting on him.

Shrink Wrapped: John tries to give Mark Henderson Dr Tracy's business card, but Ally stops him. Frankly, Tracy is the last thing Henderson needs. The last thing anybody needs, to be fair.

Trivia: With this episode the title sequence changes again, adding clips of all the principal cast to go with their credits. These replace the montage of Calista Flockhart that has run on the previous seventeen episodes.

The Verdict: In many ways this is an old, old idea. The central character hates their birthday, and in fact rather than being a celebration of the best things in their life it becomes one of the worst days of the year. Renee is very unsympathetic here, as she clearly, on some level, is attempting to attract Dr Greg even while denying it, but Elaine's speech (which seems to come out of nowhere) is funny, clever and sad.

120
The Inmates

#AM19
27 April 1998

Written by David E. Kelley
Directed by Michael Schultz

Cast: Donna Murphy (Mrs Hanson),
Kelly Connell (Dr Peters),
Michael Brandon (District Attorney Dawson),
Paul Jenkins (Detective Kale),
Daniel Dae Kim (Police Officer), Al Pugilese (Joel Hunt),
Isaiah Washington (Michael Rivers),
George Cedar (Judge Jonathan Harker),
Alaina Reed Hall (Judge Elizabeth Witt),
Tony Amendola (Judge Walter Swan), David Burke (Harry),
Steve and Eric Cohen (The Twins),
Renee Goldsberry, Vatrena King, Sy Smith (The Ikettes)
Special Appearances by:
Dylan McDermott (Robert G. 'Bobby' Donnell),
Steve Harris (Eugene Young),
Lisa Gay Hamilton (Rebecca Washington),
Kelli Williams (Lindsay Dole),
Camryn Manheim (Ellenor Frutt)

Marie Hanson, a wealthy civil client, is accused of murdering her husband and wants Billy to defend her. Such is the seriousness of the case that John advises they call for outside help. Enter Bobby Donnell and Eugene Young from a firm more experienced in this kind of thing. In a separate case, Georgia finds herself defending a restaurant owner who's fired a waiter for being heterosexual. Meanwhile, Renee is arrested.

Everything Stops For Ally: Ally is terrified by the possibility of meeting a criminal. The corpse seems to her to be 'even more dead than I thought', and upon seeing their client, Marie Hanson, her first reaction is 'there's the killer'. As Marie gives Billy and Ally her angle on the case, Ally chews on Billy's shoulder seemingly as some form of comfort. She explains the philosophy of Cage & Fish as 'there's more to life than being a lawyer and I don't mean golf'. There's a sweet moment where she challenges Billy's desire to do bigger, nastier criminal cases with the question: 'Why can't we just stay tucked away in our little sheltered . . . what's so great about the real world?'

The Boy Next Door: After seeing the cast of *The Practice* Billy decides he wants to be in a less frivolous law firm. 'This firm is a joke. We do stupid cases. We look like clowns. We get a big case and look how we act: Ally faints at the crime scene and calls our client a killer. You [Richard] go on TV and say it's the wifely thing to pick up the hatchet, and you [John] keep blurting out "Poughkeepsie" and flushing toilets by remote.' You've got to admit that he has a point.

Fishisms: This is a great episode for Richard, in which he says and does more stupid things than ever before, such as 'What's inside doesn't count, Georgia, it's how things look. Fishism.'

When told that Marie Hanson doesn't remember murdering her husband, he offers, 'Killed her husband, slipped her mind. It happens.' He initially feels that they should take the case, because 'She did it! If we win – we're heroes, we pulled off a miracle. We lose – the whacko goes to jail, justice is served. Win win.' After a discussion with John, he changes his mind: 'High profile losing, not good,' he says. He decides to refer it out, on the grounds that he'll do less work and 'still get to split the fee'. His reasoning is that 'The more I thought . . . in the long run crime doesn't pay, at least not for the lawyers.'

Richard is interviewed on television about the Hanson case, and unfortunately lets his mouth run away with him. 'I am not denying that marriage is an insidious institution. I don't dispute that love dies in the short run leaving only hate and contempt to fester. What I do object to is that every time a husband is found chopped to pieces we automatically say,

"Had to be the wife". Marie Hanson is a rich woman. If she wanted her husband dead she'd have hired somebody. It's common sense.'

When asked if his firm is a joke Richard replies that, in fact, it's just that outsiders don't get the joke.

Bygones: Richard to Eugene: 'Client. Husband. Hatchet. Bygones.' Ally tells Bobby, 'You sound like Jack Webb,' i.e. the Dragnet guy. He looks quizzical and she declares it a bygone. Not strictly a bygone, but Richard's comments upon first meeting Bobby deserved repeating: 'You know what the world thinks of criminal attorneys? Bottom-feeding scum suckers. Can't have that image running to the firm, although it looks good on you.' He then advises them to fumigate their office and repaint it.

Smile Therapy: John pulls a tricep when Richard yanks his arm, pulling him into a lift. After this he uses an artificial aide to take his moment. John had a cousin who was convinced she was a reincarnation of Helen Keller. She was the most contented woman John has ever met. She spent her life wandering around shouting out 'I can see', 'I can hear'.

Georgia On My Mind: Georgia defends a restaurateur who has fired a waiter for not being gay. 'We caught your client at a hockey game – how gay can he be?' asks Richard. The argument is that gay waiters create a better atmosphere, and generally have a better knowledge of food and wine. 'This is a French bistro – we need somebody fey to move the crème brûlée,' argues Richard.

Office Gossip: Elaine pretends to be Ally by hiding in a cubicle in the unisex and listens in to advice that John intends for her. She immediately begins to spread John's confessional around the office. 'Did you know John's afraid of chickens? They make him faint,' she tells anyone who will listen. She later ambushes Bobby Donnell in the unisex, and tells him, 'I had a dream last night that you and I had unprotected sex. I'd tell you more if I knew you better.'

The Practice

'Axe Murderer'

(TP-219) 27 April 1998

The plot of 'The Inmates' was concluded in that night's episode of *The Practice*. Just as 'The Inmates' had had substantial roles for *Practice* characters, Bobby and Eugene, Ally and Billy play a major role in 'Axe Murderer'.

Dr Peters, while still reluctant to testify, has agreed to go on the stand. Cross-examined by Billy he tells the court he hypnotised Marie because of her constant sleepwalking. Under hypnosis she told him she was Lizzie Borden. He began asking her complex questions about the Borden case and she answered them all correctly, giving him information about Borden that had been rarely published. The DA cross-examines Dr Peters, and forces from him the admission that he and Marie were lovers. Bobby is furious that Peters didn't reveal this information to him earlier. Ally theorises that Marie and Peters conspired together to commit murder, but Bobby rules this out. Despite the lack of any real supporting evidence Bobby plans to suggest to the judge that Peters killed Hanson. Ally is angry at this, but Bobby tells her that his primary duty is to acquit his client.

In court Bobby claims that while it is possible that Marie killed her husband in a trance, it is also plausible that Dr Peters killed Hanson while Marie was blacked out. At this suggestion Dr Peters stands and produces a gun. He then calmly shoots himself in the head.

Later, Ally tells a weeping Bobby that Dr Peters really did kill Mr Hanson. The police have traces of Hanson's blood in Peters' car; plus Peters left behind a note explaining everything. Ally apologises for some of the things she said to Bobby, and he tells her, 'You didn't say anything I haven't heard before.'

Fantasy: Looking at Bobby, Ally transforms into a panting dog, chanting: 'He's so yummy!'

The Case: Murder One. Marie Hanson is accused of murdering her husband with a hatchet.

The Defence: Hanson's hypnotherapist, Dr Peters, believes that Mrs Hanson either is, or believes herself to be, a reincarnation of Lizzie Borden, a nineteenth-century woman accused, and later acquitted, of killing her parents. Richard, incidentally, feels that Lizzie Borden did kill her parents and that she only got off because the jury took pity on an orphan.

Shrink Wrapped: 'I have pips and I have a theme song, the last thing I need to do is see your shrink,' Ally curtly informs Marie Hanson.

Withdrawn: Richard's amazing speech about PC culture and the right to work is breathtaking in both its asinine audacity and solid legal basis. After he's finished Georgia tells him that she's never going into court with him ever again.

DA Renee: This episode provides one of the series' most contentious and intelligently handled plotlines. Renee, in typical fashion, gets all predatory on a guy (Michael Rivers), demanding that he ask her out, and then practically ripping his clothes off on the dance floor. She takes him home, heavily implies that they're going to have sex, and then refuses at the last minute. He assumes that this is a game, and carries on kissing her. She slaps him, he slaps her back, and then she beats him up, climaxing with a kickboxing move to the chin, which breaks a bone in his neck. Defending her actions to Ally, Renee wants to know why it isn't possible for her to take a guy home for coffee without expecting to be mauled. Ally explains that by attracting Michael's attention in the overtly and deliberately sexual way that she did, Renee led him to reasonably expect that sex was in the offing. She had every right to refuse when she did, and the moment that Michael carried on, he *was* the one in the wrong. Nevertheless she was wrong to deliberately provoke him for so long, and the violence of her reaction was disproportionately strong. Consequently she has to share the blame. 'You can lead a man by the penis but it's the wrong way to tame him,' Ally comments.

Also Starring: Kelly Connell was a regular in David E. Kelley's *Picket Fences*, playing Carter Pike. All the cast members credited as 'Special Appearances' are regulars in David E. Kelley's *The Practice,* another legal series set in Boston. Michael Brandon was Dempsey in tacky 80s cop show, *Dempsey & Makepeace*. Daniel Dae Kim played John Matheson in the short-lived *Babylon 5* spin-off series *Crusade*.

The Verdict: 'You think we're all from Mars here.' 'I never said which planet.' This episode has three plots, all of which are terrific. It mixes the funny and the very serious skilfully and without ever being tasteless; most importantly it allows us to realise just how much we've become embedded in Ally's world by showing us the shocked view a group of outsiders have of the world of Cage & Fish. Quite simply brilliant from start to finish.

121
Being There

#AM20
4 May 1998

Written by David E. Kelley
Directed by Mel Damski

Cast: Isaiah Washington (Michael Rivers),
Michael Easton (Glenn),
Eric McCormack (Assistant District Attorney Kepler),
Gibby Brand (Judge McCough),
Emma Nicole Dickerson (Yone Renee),
Shannon Welles (Elderly Woman),
Herb Corben (Elderly Man), Patricia Tate (Bailiff),
Earl H. Kim (Foreperson)

Renee's case goes to court, with Ally and John defending her. Back in the office, Georgia takes a pregnancy test, which comes out positive.

Everything Stops For Ally: Ally says she likes having all of her happiness ahead of her. She lives her life as one long Christmas Eve, which makes her 'happy, happy, happy' apparently.

Fishisms: 'Permit me to be avuncular here, since I'm likely not the father. Having a child, it's a selfish thing. Couples don't walk around wanting to "give life". They say "We want a child", "We want, we want". It's a selfish thing. Not that it's not a good selfish, but it's selfish. Don't punish yourself for not wanting to celebrate your greed here . . . Georgia, you're entitled to melancholy. Your body's about to swell, distort and, treadmills aside, it'll never be the same. [To Billy] The infant's gonna see way more of her breasts than you will, and when you finally do get a visit there's the big droop.' To this list of woes Richard feels he has to add 'sleep deprivation' and the fact that Georgia's face will age ten years in the first one.

Smile Therapy: John plans to use a 'please' summing-up. This consists of a regurgitation of the facts, a dismissive tone and saying 'please'. On this case he 'clicks' his objections due to a throat irritation. His strategy is to undermine the severity of the whole case.

He puts Renee on the witness stand and then dismisses her without asking her a question. He says he did this for three reasons: 1) Renee is so aggressive she'd make a lousy witness; 2) juries dislike defendants who aren't prepared to testify. Therefore he puts Renee on the stand to make it look as if she's prepared to testify and that he decides not to let her; 3) he needed the right moment to say that the prosecution have a terrible case. This is because they actually have 'a wonderful one and if we chose to put on a defence we might reveal that we don't have one'. Nevertheless John gets Renee off, of course. Other quirks of John's revealed here are that he has arch problems which means he wears orthopaedic shoes, and that he drafts his closing arguments in bare feet.

Georgia On My Mind: Georgia takes a pregnancy test, and it produces a 'pink line'. Convinced that she's pregnant, she decides to keep the baby unable to even consider abortion for

herself, despite being virulently pro-choice. Ally puts on a brave
face when she's told, but is clearly devastated. Later, Georgia
has a blood test, which shows that she isn't pregnant after all. A
revelation which, even after only a day of believing they were
expectant parents, Billy and Georgia find deeply painful.

Office Gossip: 'Ally wants me in the loop to snoop the scoop,'
says Elaine delightedly. Topping the 'face bra', Elaine has now
invented the 'cool cup': a large refrigerated pair of underpants
that keeps a man's genitals cool. This is because heat kills
sperm, and Elaine theorises that using the 'cool cup' can help
keep men more virile. Even John realises that this is just silly.

DA Renee: Renee spends the episode becoming more and
more angry at John's attempts to defend her legally shaky case.
'Your law firm is the big ship of fools,' she tells Ally, and is
furious when the jury seems to discount the possibility of
self-defence. 'It wasn't self defence; when are you going to
admit that?' Ally demands, saying that Renee attacked him out
of anger. Renee uses sex as a 'power thing', intimidating men
with her sexual aggression. The only men who respond to this
sort of tactic are people that both Renee and Ally know Renee
doesn't want. Renee is angry that Ally could even suggest this,
but the next morning admits that she knows Ally's right.
'Everything you said is true,' Renee says, elaborating that 'I
was the first girl in my class to get breasts' and that she was
teased mercilessly for it. One day she snuck into the boys'
toilets because she'd heard that there was graffiti about her.
She read it and was dreadfully upset by it, although she doesn't
tell Ally what it said. She went home crying and decided that
they 'teased me because they liked me'. This became an idea
she held on to all her life. 'I can't bear it if a guy doesn't want
to grab me a little. But if he does grab me I'm back on that
playground again.'

Men: Glenn returns, subpoenaed into testifying against Renee.
He tells the court about his brief 'relationship' with Ally. John
refuses to cross-examine the witness despite Renee's pleading
that he made her look stupid. 'He made it look like it was. You
penguined him, Renee, that's what happened.'

Fantasy: A cannon blasts a hole in Ally when she finds out that Georgia is pregnant.

Song: This episode uses Bill Conti's 'Going the Distance' and Vonda performs Michael Jackson's 'I'll Be There', a wonderful ballad from which this episode takes its name.

. . . And Dance: Everybody in this office performs an epic dance number to 'Wedding Bell Blues' performed by the Fifth Dimension and written by Laura Nyo.

Toilet Humour: After discussing their baby with them in the unisex, Fish dismisses Billy and Georgia by walking into a toilet cubicle and saying 'Bran.' There are some situations where the words 'too much information' aren't sufficient.

The Verdict: A slight, but intelligent episode that is far less silly than normal. Lisa Nicole Carson gets to play Renee in a much more serious vein than normally, and it's impossible not to feel sympathy for her. Gil Bellows and Courtney Thorne-Smith really make the most of Billy and Georgia's subplot, giving both their characters, and our perception of their love, more depth than ever before.

122
Alone Again

#AM21
11 May 1998

Written by David E. Kelley
Directed by Dennis Dugan

Cast: Dyan Cannon (Judge 'Whipper' Cone),
Dabbs Greer (Vincent Robbins),
McNally Sagal (Mary Halliday), Michael G. Hagerty
(Michael Huttle), Jocko Marcellino (Prison Guard),
Neal Lerner (George Pullman),
Gibbt Brand (Judge McGough), Landry Barb (Clerk),
Bill Bishop (Foreman), Bill Finkelstein (William),

Renee Goldsberry, Vatrena King and Sy Smith (The Ikettes)
Special Appearance by Cynthia Stevenson

John has to defend a man charged with trying to break out of
prison when he had only a month of his sentence left, and finds
himself fighting it against an old friend from law school,
Hayley Chisholm (Cynthia Stevenson). Georgia and Richard
represent a jilted bride looking for damages. Unfortunately the
judge is Richard's recently jilted ex, Whipper Cone.

Everything Stops For Ally: A good episode for supporters of
the theory that Ally and John are inevitable soulmates. Ally
instantly knows that John is/was in love with Hayley. She tells
him, 'Just like you can tell when I'm seeing something, I can
tell what's going on with you.' 'Most people look at me like
I'm "odd strange" not "odd special"; you were the first person
since Hayley to,' John tells Ally.

The Boy Next Door: Ally claims she is 99 to 60 per cent over
Billy. Which just about sums her up, really.

Fishisms: When advising his client he tells her, 'In every person's life there comes a time when you have to go forth and be
vicious.' When she has second thoughts about pursuing
damages, he's appalled: 'Never trust second thoughts. Where
there's two there's three; you'll be thinking for ever.'

Smile Therapy: 'Who better to go in with nothing than John
Cage?' asks Elaine, summing up the Biscuit's amazing series
of nonsensical court victories; a tally to which he adds in this
episode. There's something both beautiful and tragic about
John's friendship with Hayley, a woman whom he loves but
who can never see him as more than a friend; who never
understood that he wanted her as more than a friend. 'There's
something to be said for platonic friendships, they never disappoint,' she says, showing just how much she doesn't get it.
There's a very *When Harry Met Sally* vibe to Hayley and
John's friendship, but without the happy ending. John tells
Ally about the one time he told Hayley that they ought to be a
couple, phrasing it as if it were a joke so he could back out if

necessary. John was heartbroken when she considered John's 'joke' to be the funniest he ever came up with. 'I opened the door,' he explains, 'the door came back to strike me in the nose.' He never raised the idea properly because 'the beauty of not knowing' enabled a small amount of hope to exist within him. 'I was afraid that I would spoil it,' he says of their friendship. 'That's not some bell you get to un-ring.' As a part of his closing statement John tells the jury the story of a 'friend' of his who was in love with a woman who was also his best friend. This finally makes Hayley realise how John feels, but she still doesn't seriously consider the possibility of a relationship with him.

Office Gossip: Elaine has recorded 'All the sounds of a spousal relationship' on to a CD. This, she claims, gives the experience of a 'virtual husband'. She repeatedly demonstrates the CD to the recently jilted-at-the-altar Mary Halliday, giving a new definition to the term 'hard sell'.

Fetishes: Richard demands Georgia give him her shoe. She refuses.

Song: Another episode named after a song, this time Gilbert O'Sullivan's 'Alone Again (Naturally)'. Watching the final montage, where the song accompanies scenes of all the characters alone, can result in tears before bedtime.

The Case: Vincent Robbins, who attempted escape from prison when he had only one month left of his sentence to serve, having spent eighteen years inside for armed robbery. John successfully argues that Robbins' escape attempt was not that at all; it was the final stage of an escape plan he'd been arranging for eighteen years, which he executed for the thrill of seeing it work, not because he intended to leave federal custody. Bizarrely, the jury go with John's argument.

Richard and Georgia seek damages on behalf of a woman jilted at the altar. Despite Judge Cone's reluctance to 'legislate for love', Richard appears to win the legal argument. Unfortunately their client, after seeing the way Fish operates, and having seen him reduce 'marriage' down to 'money', is so disgusted that she drops the case.

Withdrawn: Hayley has as many courtroom quirks as John, including pretending to cry at testimony, mentioning guns as often as possible and shouting 'Bad jury!' She claims she once offered to adopt a defendant during cross-examination.

Whip-Lash! Richard and Whipper clash badly in court, with Whipper arguably letting her anger at John damage her objectivity. She later claims that her bias is 'against the legitimacy of the suit', but admits that 'the one bringing it doesn't help'. Richard argues for 'fairness'. He feels that 'the duty of a court, a judge, is to see wrong and try to right it. That doesn't change when you've had sex with one of the lawyers! Underneath that robe as well as a phenomenal body is a great judge. Behave like one.' Whipper sees the sense of his argument, and excuses herself from the case, knowing her objectivity is damaged.

The Verdict: 'What do you want us to do?' 'Whatever it is you usually do that makes juries ignore the law.' A simply beautiful episode. Hayley is John's female equivalent and it's both inevitable and tragic that she can't see that they're perfect for each other. Equally sad is that while Ally tries to push John and Hayley together she fails to see that so much of what John says about him and Hayley could be applied to John and herself.

123
These Are The Days

#AM22
18 May 1998

Written by David E. Kelley
Directed by Jonathan Pontell

Cast: Willie Garson (Alan Farmer),
Richard Schiff (Bernie Gilson), Bob Gunton (Michaelson),
Albert Hall (Judge Seymore Walsh),
Lee Wilkof (Attorney Nixon),
Phil Leeds (Judge 'Happy' Boyle),

Rhonda Dotson (Julie Martin), Ken Abraham (Hendrix),
Gerry Vichi (Foreman)
Special Appearance by Dylan McDermott

Bobby Donnell returns to Cage & Fish (see 120 'The Inmates' or start watching *The Practice*) because he has a case for which he needs help from an outside counsel. Due to the nature of the suit (a poor man, Bernie Gilson, who has a healthy heart wants to switch it for that of a rich man, Willie Garson, who has a diseased heart) he feels that Ally would be ideal to second-chair to him.

Everything Stops For Ally: 'Whenever I get depressed I raise my hemlines. If things don't change I'm bound to be arrested.'

Georgia On My Mind: Billy and Georgia argue, seemingly because they both wanted to have an argument. They feel they've already become stuck in a rut. They always have sex on Tuesdays and Saturdays, and it always lasts for seventeen minutes, give or take a few seconds. Billy concludes that they have to start acting more their own age, by behaving in a younger and more irresponsible manner. Yay!

Office Gossip: Elaine offers to take minutes for Georgia and Billy's little bout of marital distress. When they tell her to get out, she tells them they're both rude and snappish. She implies that she'll have casual sex with Richard at any time he should want it. At school the boys apparently knew her as the 'human window of opportunity'.

Men: 'For the sake of our relationship let's not have one.' Bobby says he can't have a relationship with Ally right now because he'd mess it up. He has issues and 'baggage' in his life and he doesn't want what is a potentially phenomenal relationship to be soured by that. The undercurrent that runs all the way through the scene is that basically Ally and Bobby can't have a relationship because they star in separate TV series.

Fantasy: Ally imagines shooting out an extendable tongue and spinning Bobby round with it. When Bobby asks Ally 'Will you do it with me?' (meaning the case) Georgia and Elaine's tongues extend down to the floor.

Song: The episode, and indeed the season, ends with a montage of clips from previous episodes set to Vonda's rendition of 'Neighborhood'.

. . . And Dance: Ally asks Bobby when was the last time he danced. She then makes him dance around the office with her in silence. 'You just need to hear the music in your head. You can do that, can't you?' she tells him. As they dance, the audience and Ally hear 'Just One Look' (Payne/Carroll) again performed by Vonda Shepard.

Fashion Victims: Georgia walks into Billy's office wearing nothing but a pair of new 'sexy shoes'. 'Did you get a good price for them?' Billy deadpans.

The Case: John's second cousin has taken to assaulting people with a sawn-off paddle if they strike him as being too happy. John defends him, allowing him to testify that he 'accelerates love'. He attacks people knowing that the shared adversity of being attacked will push them closer together. John presents the jury with a typical Cage closing argument, which features references to, among other things, his mother's death. Against all expectations, including his own, John finally loses. And quite right too.

Judge Not: Albert Hall makes Ally come to a decision in court. 'In your client's best interests, make the call,' he tells her, pushing her into the position that she and Bobby have pushed him. She denies her own motion, finally realising that it is not in Gilson's best interests to give his heart away. Garson then tells Gilson that he never would have taken his heart. He let the case go this far for two reasons: one, because he knew it would increase Bernie's self-esteem to be allowed to pursue the idea, and two, because he believes a man should be judged by the devotion of his friends. He likes the idea that after his death his children will grow up knowing that he was a man for whom his best friend was willing to sacrifice his heart.

Let Me See Your Teeth: Happy is trying John's 'paddle' case, and is appalled when one of the prosecution witnesses in his case has 'a small piece of spinach caught in an incisor'. 'When oral decay starts to build up between the tooth and the gum, bacteria starts to build colonies; even the most nutritious vegetable can turn into Vietnam,' he explains to a perplexed jury. Nobody has any idea what relevance this has.

Kisses: 'I have a great imaginary world, but sometimes I just need things to happen for real,' says Ally, and then kisses Bobby for a long, long time. Ally tells Renee all about it, commenting that sometimes first kisses misalign, and you get a little 'tooth on tooth'; this kiss, however, featured 'full alignment, upper on upper, lower on lower'. Ally's judgement of its quality is a simple 'Oh My God'.

The Verdict: 'I've got green hair and I'm due in court.' This is a satisfying, intelligent and sufficiently moving conclusion to the first season. It's clearly structured so that it works both as a coda to season one, and a conclusion to the whole series should the show not have been renewed. Dylan McDermott once again clearly relishes the more light-hearted material he's presented with in this show, and subtly alters his performance to reflect the shift in emphasis.

Season Two

Regular Cast

Calista Flockhart (Ally McBeal)
Courtney Thorne-Smith (Georgia Thomas)
Greg Germann (Richard Fish)
Lisa Nicole Carson (Renee Raddick)
Jane Krakowski (Elaine Vassal)
Portia de Rossi (Nelle Porter)*
Lucy Liu (Ling Woo)*
Vonda Shepard (Vonda Shepard)
with
Peter MacNicol (John Cage)
and
Gil Bellows (Billy Alan Thomas)

Created by David E. Kelley

* Portia de Rossi and Lucy Liu initially appear as guest stars in the series and join the regular cast from 210, 'Making Spirits Bright', the first episode to feature both actresses in the title sequence.

The Episodes

201
The Real World

#2M01
14 September 1998

Written by David E. Kelley
Directed by Jonathan Pontell

Cast: Caitlin Dulany (Laura Jewell),
Richard Lee Jackson (Jason Tresham),
Susan Krebs (Judge Kensington), Tracey Ullman (Dr Tracy)

Ally finds herself defending Laura Jewell, a thirty-seven-year-old woman charged with the mandatory rape of Jason Tresham – a teenager similar to one she has had dreams about; he has similar dreams himself. Is Ally really looking for a man – or a boy?

Meanwhile, Fish wants to expand the firm by recruiting attorney 'Sub Zero Nelle' Porter. Beautiful, blonde, successful: the women at the firm hate Nelle from the off, but nonetheless she joins the firm. John Cage is drawn to her – even though Nelle can't even remember his name.

After a closing argument by John, he and Ally win their case, leaving Laura free and Jason glad his first love hasn't been convicted. Jason and Ally go on a date, but Ally realises that she is using Jason to relive memories of Billy, and decides not to continue the relationship.

Introducing: Nelle Porter, the new lawyer at Cage & Fish.

Everything Stops For Ally: The case feeds straight into Ally's self-obsession. When Jason says in the witness box that Laura's sadness seems worse than loneliness, Ally snaps: 'What could be worse than being alone?'

The Boy Next Door: Is Billy the same as the boy Ally fell in love with, or has part of him died over the years? (Oddly, we're never asked whether this happens to girls when they become women.) Billy and Ally have a heart-to-heart where they look back at their time together. Billy thinks that so much of their romance came from the fact that 'we were kids'. When Ally says, 'Maybe I'm meant for a boy,' Billy replies, 'Maybe you're meant for *this* boy.'

We Got It Together, Didn't We?: John and Nelle meet; he's drawn to her but doesn't think he stands a chance. She makes his heart go 'boom' especially when she lets her hair down. However, he wants her around so he can 'flex his romantic muscles'.

Nelle, on the other hand, can't even remember John's name. Not a good start.

Fishisms: Richard admits to getting aroused by his stock portfolio, and finds women who break the law to have sex 'extra sexy'. Although he has a great life, he says he wants 'more . . . more money'. Good to see he's just like the rest of us . . . in that respect, if no other. His lascivious description of Laura's case – right in front of her! – is a classic moment of tactlessness: 'Laura here is a statutory rape client. Slept with a sixteen-year-old boy. It's rich, it's fresh, it's delicious.' The firm's philosophy according to Richard is 'selfishism, everybody looking to get ahead'.

Bygones: Richard handing Laura's case over to Billy and Georgia: 'I'd do it myself if I knew the law. Bygones!'

Smile Therapy: John disturbs everyone with his description of his adolescent lust for actress Jennifer O'Neil. As he says: 'I put a padlock on my bedroom door that summer.'

Georgia On My Mind: Ally asks whether Georgia fantasises about boys. We never get her answer, as they start talking about Billy (see **Girl Talk**). She *hates* Nelle.

Sub Zero: 'Sub Zero Nelle' Porter is looking to leave rival law firm Goodman-Dale. And has 'serious portables'. We presume John means an impressive list of movable clients. Yet . . .

According to Elaine she was profiled in Boston magazine *Hot Women Lawyers*. When Nelle shakes hands she doesn't put hers out very far because she wants the other person to meet her more than halfway. Clearly a woman to keep an eye on. When Fish asks if Nelle cares about potential resentment from her co-workers, we never hear Nelle's reply.

Office Gossip: Elaine says Nelle is, 'Such a bitch.' When asked to back this up she advances that Nelle is 'smart and she's pretty. What else do we need to know?' She then sends Nelle to talk to Ally on the grounds that Nelle will hate her. Ouch!

DA Renee: Renee, never the most subtle of people, seems somewhat overzealous in her prosecution of Laura, more or less attempting to force her into admitting paedophilia to secure a conviction. We think she's jealous.

Guy Talk: Richard and Billy discuss predatory older women and liking being led in bed – until they realise Georgia is listening.

Girl Talk: In the unisex, Ally and Georgia discuss Billy's 'size' to wind him up (they believe he's in the cubicle and listening). Actually Billy is standing behind them, and Cage is in the cubicle. As Cage says, 'That kind of frank dialogue disturbs me.'

Men: Jason Tresham, a subpoenaed and unwilling prosecution witness in the case Ally has to defend. When they first meet, Ally stands open-mouthed, staring. We think this means she likes him. She makes an even weirder noise when they're in the lift together. They go on a date, and get through all the bases – literally, on a baseball diamond.

Quotes: Jason: 'Lonely people have hope' and 'Some people find love permanent, some are just meant to be alone.'

And another moment of cheer from Ally: 'The last thing you want is to be in love with someone you can't have; that is something I know.'

Fantasy: The episode begins with Ally dreaming of an encounter with a beautiful young man reaching out to touch her hand. We later discover that prosecution witness Jason had the same dream at the same time – the beginning of a drift away from reality this season. In court she fantasises having sex with Jason.

Fetishes: Richard 'likes puppets', whatever that involves. 'I had a thing for Sheri Lewis growing up. That little puppeteer act.'

Song: When John looks at Nelle he hears 'You Can't Hurry Love' – a hit for Diana Ross and The Supremes. As Ally says goodbye to Jason, Vonda sings the ballad this episode is named after.

Shrink Wrapped: Another sledgehammer-subtle attack on Ally's obsessions by Tracy: 'Ally, with you everything is about you. Narcissism is a wonderful thing.'

On Ally's 'unpure sexual thoughts': 'As opposed to philosophical impurities. Gee. Thanks for clearing that up.'

'For a woman to think about an eighteen-year-old boy once in a while, this is not something to get therapy for.'

Then there's Tracy on morality: 'If it weren't against nature then they wouldn't have to pass the laws, would they?'

Is it any wonder Ally responds, 'I'm not finding this helpful'?

Thankfully there's Tracy's closing moment of wisdom: 'It can't last for ever but who made up the rule that the best loves do?'

While we're on the subject, it's worth mentioning Jason's own potential – with such a gift for cod-psychology and a knack for making older women feel better about themselves, we feel he has a great career as a therapist ahead of him.

Fashion Victims: Nelle's very severe look here – green-grey suit, black-rimmed glasses – gives no hint of the fashion terrors to come.

The Case: It's Ally vs Renee again, with the state prosecuting a woman in her late thirties for the statutory rape of a sixteen-year-old boy.

The Defendant: Laura Jewell, a rather sad middle-aged woman charged with statutory rape.

The Defence: Cage argues she plead insanity: 'Thirty-nine-year-old woman with a sixteen-year-old boy – she'd have to be crazy.' His closing argument seems to involve romanticising the case, referring to old movies and his teenage fantasies.

Guilty?: They deserve to win, not on the insanity defence but because it's a victimless crime. What teenage boy *wouldn't* want to be educated in the ways of l-ur-ve by an older woman? We feel the only threat to this lucky lad is a potential kicking from his less fortunate, jealous peers.

Kisses: The little nibble between Jason and Ally in her boat-house fantasy seems a bit tame to us – but not to Ally, who makes an odd whinny as she imagines it.

Toilet Humour: John feels he knows more than he wants to about Billy (see **Girl Talk**). Billy is left open-mouthed when he finds Nelle changing her top – needless to say, Georgia isn't pleased.

Hit The Bar: Ally tries to put Nelle off by telling her the firm would never make a woman a partner.

The Verdict: 'Here we go again.' 'Oh God, I hope not.' The second season starts as it means to go on, with Ally sliding into a typically doomed romance, defending a completely ludicrous case (especially from a European perspective, from which the American approach to their teens' sex lives seems incredibly draconian), and trying to hold her ground against scene-stealing one-liners from the supporting cast. The big newcomer here is Portia de Rossi. She makes an instant impression as Nelle, whose glacial charm brings a delightful rogue element into the office, setting up frictions that will run for the rest of the year. In terms of the actual plot and the apparent 'moral' of the episode, it's hard to agree with the idea that teenage boys – the horrible, hormone-driven little wretches – are deep romantics compared to adult men or that such a boy getting some action is a victim. But then, with Jason and Ally's shared dream blurring the line between Ally's fantasy world and the 'reality' around her, anyone watching for gritty social commentary is clearly in the wrong place. A great start to a great season, and one which leaves you gagging for the next episode.

202
They Eat Horses, Don't They?

#2M02
21 September 1998

Written by David E. Kelley
Directed by Mel Damski

Cast: Tim Thomerson (Mr Daley),
Wayne Newton (Harold Wick),
David Ogden Stiers (Judge Peters),
Mark Metcalf (Walden), Albert Hall (Judge Seymore Walsh),
Stuart Pankin (Mr Handy)

Ling Woo, one of Nelle's most profitable and litigious clients, decides to sue radio 'Shock Jock' Harold Wick for contributing to sexual harassment in the workplace via his vulgar and sexist broadcasts. Nelle and Ally manage to get Judge Peters to let the case go to trial, but quit while they're ahead, making a public statement implying Wick is impotent. Ally, who thinks this is grossly unfair, goes on Wick's show as a guest.

Cage gets squeamish as he and Georgia defend Paul's Bistro, a French restaurant being sued for serving horsemeat. Can they really defend people who eat 'Mr Ed'? His summation, though less than enthusiastic, wins the day.

Ally is worried that the firm is going to hell, engaging in dirty tactics against people who don't deserve it. John agrees with her, but says that as long as they have Ally, the firm will keep its moral centre.

Introducing: Ling, the litigant from hell.

Oops!: When being made up for her appearance on Wick's show, Ally seems surprised it goes out on cable TV – even though she was watching it earlier in the episode.

Everything Stops For Ally: Our lead is at her most sympathetic and least self-obsessed here, her appearance on Wick's show contradicting her occasionally prissy image. The way she helps John with his self-doubt is rather sweet.

The Boy Next Door: Billy seems disturbed, then later amazed, by Ally's turn on the Harold Wick show.

We Got It Together, Didn't We?: John's heart goes 'boom' as he watches Nelle apply lipstick. He's gutted when he finds out Fish told her that he was 'drawn' (see **Bygones**). However, in the same conversation he finds that she 'understands' his desire for a fresh bowl, and that she doesn't entirely rule out dating men she works with. Later, when he asks whether she's eaten horse Nelle takes that as a dinner invitation, and tricks John into asking her out. They dance at the bar.

Bygones: John confronts Richard about revealing his feelings for Nelle, but Richard has other things on his mind than breaking a confidence, and gets out of it with 'Bygones' and 'Bygones squared'. As he says, Ling's case is 'an excellent chance to boost our profile and erode the first amendment in the process . . . I'm not about to take time out just because I breached some little "trust" thing you and I had going.' Richard is on top form here, sparring with Ling from the off: swapping insults, touching wattle . . . It must be love.

Smile Therapy: John hears voices telling him the horsemeat case is wrong. He has a stuffed-toy horse from childhood called Frawlie, who he used to pretend kicked the bullies at school. Smile therapy itself comes into play when Ally accidentally shouts at him.

Grrr!: Introducing Ling, who makes an instant impression. We soon find out that she's aggressive, hates change and 'newness', especially Nelle's new firm. Her reference to killing Wick through sex is the first allusion to her legendary prowess, which will be referred to later in the season. She thinks Richard Fish is 'a man without any nice qualities'.

Office Gossip: Elaine describes Ling as 'Vicious Ling' – in her presence.

Girl Talk: Ally and Renee discuss why Ally wears such short skirts, and the extent to which they're noticed by the men.

Quotes: Renee: 'She'll probably end up on the cover of *Time*.' This is the first, and by far the most subtle, in-joke alluding to the appearance of Calista Flockhart as the face of 90s' feminism on the cover of said magazine. In the context of the show it's a reference to Ling.

Song: Vonda sings the self-penned 'Will You Marry Me?', one of the tracks on her first 'Songs from *Ally McBeal*' soundtrack CD. Cage and Ally sing the theme tune to *Mr Ed*. Badly.

Fashion Victims: Nelle's rather severe spectacles, and Wick's horrid shirt.

The Cases: A hearing for a ludicrous sexual harassment case, and a trial for an equally ludicrous case involving horsemeat.

The Plaintiff: The hearing: Ling, who considers a radio broadcast to be sexual harassment.

The Defendant: The trial: Mr Handy, proprietor of a French restaurant.

The Defence: The trial: 'We don't treat animals too well,' says John. 'We're human beings: this is glue.'

Guilty?: In the hearing, Ling's case against Harold Wick clearly deserves to go down in flames. It's totally groundless and represents an attack on free speech. In trial two, in spite of John's reservations, their victory in the horsemeat case is well deserved. People intolerant of other cultures' eating habits really shouldn't go to foreign restaurants – especially when they don't understand the menu!

Judge Not: The horsemeat trial is conducted by Judge Seymore Walsh, who shows little tolerance for John's courtroom tricks. He's very defensive of Elizabeth Taylor. The free speech case is presided over by Judge Andrew Peters, probably the most sympathetic and humane of the judges.

Also Starring: The prolific Tim Thomerson played Jack Deth in the low-budget, cult-film series *Trancers*, and has an occasional role in *Xena: Warrior Princess*. Mark Metcalf played the evil Master in the first series of *Buffy The Vampire Slayer*.

Toilet Humour: Nelle gets introduced to the remote control.

Hit The Bar: Ling doesn't seem to like the bar; Vonda 'bugs' her. However, that doesn't stop her dancing with Richard there later.

The Verdict: 'I just know I want to take you home and make you my nasty little whore.' Addressing issues most shows wouldn't touch with a twenty-foot pole, 'They Eat Horses, Don't They?' questions our attitudes to sex, free speech and animals, though thankfully not in the same context. The cases here are untenable but not implausible, and both represent attacks on freedom by intolerant people. After Nelle's scene-stealing debut the previous episode, this time it's Ling's turn to tear through the regular cast like a cyclone, leaving the old guard alarmed at the changes in their workplace. It's an episode low in character moments for most of the established regulars, with Billy and Georgia barely present, but so full of great jokes and serious, well-expressed arguments that it's almost impossible to complain.

203
Fool's Night Out

#2M03
28 September 1998

Written by David E. Kelley
Directed by Peter MacNicol

Cast: Jennifer Holliday (Lisa Knowles),
Harrison Page (Mark Newman), Lydia Look (Leigh Woo),
Gerry Becker (Stone), Kayrenn Ann Butler (Jody)

Mark Newman, the preacher at Fish's church, has a problem. He recently ended a relationship with the lead singer of his church choir, Lisa, and now she only sings songs about broken hearts and shattered relationships. The congregation seem to like it, but Mark doesn't think it's right. Ally is sent in to talk to Lisa, and ends up thinking about how men leave and why Billy left her. She realises that he had met Georgia the day he visited Michigan, shattering Ally's illusions about their break-up. This leaves Georgia wondering if Billy might change his mind once more, especially as Nelle's presence is making her feel insecure.

Ling is disappointed with the breast implants she bought for her sister, Leigh. With the surgeon unavailable to sue, Ling wants to sue his assistant, whose breasts the surgeon claimed as his own work – even though they were, in fact, natural. Billy decides the only way they can solve the problem is to examine the breasts in question . . .

Everything Stops For Ally: Ally is chosen to mediate with Lisa because she 'speaks the language of loneliness'. Ouch!

The Boy Next Door: In the pilot we found out that Billy broke up with Ally when he decided to finish his law studies in Michigan. Now we discover that he had already met Georgia when he made that decision. He was in love with her from the moment they met and this occasioned his splitting up from Ally. This revelation leads to a frosty silence between Ally and Billy, and a tearful showdown shortly after.

We Got It Together, Didn't We?: Nelle demands to know when she and John are going to go out – that is, somewhere other than just the bar. John takes Ally's advice that 'you only die once', and decides to date Nelle.

Bygones: 'I'd promise you satisfaction if you were the least bit capable of happiness,' John tells Ling, but later he reveals how much he really likes her.

Smile Therapy: John considers wearing platform shoes to date Nelle, but thankfully Fish talks him out of it.

Grrrr!: Ling's breasts are reputedly 'beyond reproach'. In reference to the surgeon's work on Leigh's breasts, Ling says, 'My uncle slit his wrists with more finesse.' We see here that

Ling is an unpopular person who reacts to her own unpopularity with aggression, to give herself control over the situation. In spite of his endless stream of one-liners at her expense, Fish tells Ling he likes her, and even rolls a secretary across the room to make room for them to talk alone.

Georgia On My Mind: On closing down the breast case: 'It's over, Ling. Hard "L", hard "G", hard times.'

Office Gossip: Seeing Ling is in a bad mood, Elaine wonders if 'perhaps her gynaecologist pulled the wrong tooth'.

Fetishes: Fish goes straight for the wattle with Ling, the dirty devil.

Song: Several songs from Lisa: 'Political Science', 'Fools Fall in Love', and 'I'm So Tired of Being Alone'.

. . . And Dance: Ally seems to shake as if in a religious frenzy while at church. Cage does his Barry White dance in the unisex, and (beginning of a season-long running joke) Elaine sneaks up behind him and joins in.

Fashion Victims: Various gaudy choir outfits at the church. Off-duty Mark wears a horrid burgundy jumper – with shirt and tie underneath. Lisa had a lucky escape.

The Case: The case of the cold hard breasts. As Georgia says, the case is ridiculous, and she stops it going to court. Her intervention sparks a row between Ling and Nelle about Ling litigating the world.

Toilet Humour: Georgia says she hates Nelle because she's used to being the most beautiful – which Ally overhears. Elaine comes in and wants to know what she missed.

Hit The Bar: Ally's solution to Lisa's problem partially involves Lisa singing her more personal songs in the bar, accompanied by Vonda, and sticking to the hymns in church.

The Verdict: 'Why is it great with men right until they run?' 'Fool's Night Out' goes back to the pilot, and Ally and Billy's original break-up. The discovery that Georgia didn't come along in Ally's absence, but that Billy in fact made his choice all those years ago, shatters many of Ally's fantasies about her one great love. The scenes between Billy and Ally are quite painful to watch, with a tangible sense of betrayal. Georgia's fear that one day Billy might move on from her seems convincing, when paralleled with both the cosmetic surgery plotline and Lisa's heartbreak. The twin themes of much of the series – the question of whether there can be a true, everlasting love and the role of women in professional life – are neatly intertwined through the episode, a case of the show firing on all cylinders and hitting the mark every time.

204
It's My Party

#2M04
19 October 1998

Written by David E. Kelley
Directed by Jace Alexander

Cast: John Ritter (George Madison),
Shaun Michael Howard (Ben),
Albert Hall (Judge Seymore Walsh), Lee Wilkof (Nixon)

Ally's preparing for a dinner party, and everything has to be right, so she practises her dancing. Of course, there might not be a party at all if she can't get out of jail . . .

Ally takes the case of George Madison, a boyfriend of Elaine's who has been fired as editor of a feminist magazine on the grounds that he's a Baptist, and that Baptist teachings place the woman in the home. Judge Walsh objects to Ally's short skirts, and when she refuses to stop wearing them in his court he throws her in jail for contempt, even though she wins George his case.

The lawyers turn up en masse to Ally's hearing, and Nelle argues for her release, saying that the focus on hemlines suggests that sexually attractive women can't be taken seriously. Judge Walsh frees Ally and the party goes ahead, but not without the odd argument, and some special tension between Ally and George . . .

Introducing: Stefan, John's pet frog.

Everything Stops For Ally: 'Once in a while,' Billy tells Ally, 'it would be nice if life was more than just your party.'

Ally lets her dress sense get in the way of the good of the firm and, as Billy notices, she doesn't seem too grateful that they turn up to support her. As she says, 'I don't even say sorry when I am.' Ally again claims to be allergic to criminals.

The Boy Next Door: Billy and Ally have a bust-up over dinner: Billy doesn't think she appreciates her friends enough, especially in light of their support for her, and he finds cheap cracks describing all men as Neanderthals offensive. Things are icy between them, although matters thaw a little when Ally explains that she 'cherishes' all her friends.

We Got It Together, Didn't We?: As John watches Nelle he dreams of them together, her pregnant. The dream – which features his and her children – ends when John trips down the stairs.

Fishisms: Another great Fishism: 'Men and women, friction. Friction, friction, friction, friction, orgasm. Fishism.'

Fish suggests Ally gets back at Judge Walsh by wearing tight jeans. He is seen reading a Chinese phrasebook, presumably a nod to his relationship with Ling. He invites Ling as his date to the party, and hears the cowbell when he talks about it. In one of his occasional displays of loyalty, he insists all the lawyers turn up for Ally's contempt hearing – 'One for all, and all for me.'

Bygones: Ally asks if Judge Walsh would ever throw a man out of court for the way he dresses. Richard replies: 'He would if he dressed like that – Bygones!'

Smile Therapy: John's owned Stefan the frog for six years, which Richard points out is three years longer than he's gone with a woman.

Grrr!: Richard and Ling have been out on three dates, but she hasn't let him kiss her.

Sub Zero: Nelle is fully aware the women of the firm hate her, but doesn't seem too bothered about it.

Office Gossip: We meet Elaine's 'non-exclusive' boyfriend, George, whom she met at the patent office. This leads us to another of Elaine's inventions: personalised condoms (see box). At Ally's party, she says it'll be weird associating Ally with fun.

Condoms

Those Elaine personalised condoms for each character, in full:

Richard:	'Bygones.'
John:	'Enjoy the moment.'
Georgia:	'Pay the bill.'
Elaine:	'Come Here Often?'
Ally:	'Take A Number.'
Nelle:	'Caution: Frostbite.'
George:	Initially 'Been There', then later 'Reinstate Me'.

Guy Talk: Richard asks John to ask Nelle if Ling likes him, possibly not the most direct way of finding out.

Men: George Madison, the Baptist magazine editor Ally just can't stop herself spilling coffee over. He allows his own case to be put at risk so Ally can defend her hemlines.

Fantasy: Ally fantasises that she jumps on George's shoulders, burying his head between her legs. What on earth could that mean?

Song: At the party, the guys sing Edwin Starr's 'War', the girls sing 'Double Shot of My Baby's Love' and both sexes sing 'Neither One of Us'. Earlier in the episode Ally sings along to early pop standard 'Please Mr Postman'.

. . . And Dance: Ally practises her dancing to Rick James' 'Superfreak'. At the end of the episode Ally dances with Renee's friend Ben, while George dances with Elaine. George and Ally exchange glances as the episode ends.

Also Starring: John Ritter (George Madison) is one of those ubiquitous actors, having appeared in everything from *Buffy The Vampire Slayer* to *Veronica's Closet*. He's perhaps best known for his role in the *Problem Child* series of sadistic comedies.

Fashion Victims: Ally's bright orange prison uniform.

Judge Not: Judge Seymore Walsh (Albert Hall), whose intolerance for the antics of Cage & Fish's lawyers extends to Ally's dress sense.

The Cases: Ally and Georgia represent George Madison, who has been fired from his job editing a feminist magazine because of his Baptist faith. Ally is dragged up before Judge Walsh for contempt of court after refusing to wear longer skirts.

The Defence: At Ally's contempt hearing, Nelle argues that saying a risqué skirt destroys the credibility of the court reinforces a myth that sexually attractive women can't be taken seriously. She emphasises her point by taking off her jacket and letting her hair down.

Guilty?: We're torn – George clearly doesn't believe a woman's place is in the home, but his attachment to a faith does damage the credibility of his magazine. As for Ally and her short skirts – that's for the judge to decide. It's his courtroom.

Kisses: Ling places a lot of importance on the first kiss, and indeed her first long, slow, kiss with Richard leaves him shellshocked.

Trivia: John and Stefan are practising for the 'New England Regionals'.

The Verdict: 'She won her case, and you're still judging her by her hemlines.' Connected thematically rather than by coherent plotting, 'It's My Party' spins wildly around the screen trying to get to the point. That the second half of the episode is dominated by the party scene doesn't help, as it's a slight departure from the usual intercutting of cases and plot-threads. However, this confusion is probably little more than a reflection of the complexity of the issues involved. The role of women in the workplace and the home, expressed through Baptist beliefs, John's fantasies and the snappy exchanges at the party, are not likely to be wrapped up neatly in forty-two minutes. Thankfully, Kelley knows better than to try to resolve anything, and instead lays out all sides of the debate with wit and sympathy.

205
Story of Love

#2M05
26 October 1998

Written by David E. Kelley
Directed by Tom Moore

Cast: John Ritter (George Madison),
Natasha Gregson Wagner (Hannah Puck),
Josh Evans (Orin Coolie), Kristin Dattilo (Laura Payne),
Latanya Richardson (Yvette Rose),
Eric Christmas (Judge Maynard Sniff)

Ally gets into a fight with Hannah Puck, a girl she finds crying in the street. As they cool off in a jail cell together, Ally is persuaded to defend Hannah in court: Hannah's best friend, Laura, stole her boyfriend, so she dumped Laura in a garbage bin. The case parallels Ally's own feelings for Elaine's boyfriend, George Madison. It also brings her head-to-head with her old adversary, ten-year-old midget genius Orin Coolie.

Meanwhile, John accidentally flushes Stefan the show frog down a toilet. Can the rest of the firm get through a frog's funeral without laughing?

Everything Stops For Ally: 'You're Elaine's boyfriend: that's the end of the story.' Ally chooses to put friendship before her chances of happiness with George, staying loyal to Elaine all the way. Just shows our heroine can be selfless occasionally. To ease the pain, she gets George to do his wiggle walk as he walks away from her.

Ally also scores points for hugging John when he's upset about Stefan, and pep-talking him back into the room when he's offended by the laughter at the memorial service.

We Got It Together, Didn't We?: Nelle's frog fear, and her whacking of Stefan all over the place, get between her and John. Things thaw a little when she tells him about her own loss of a pet, and buys him an American Tree Frog. He names the new frog Milly (see **Sub Zero**). John says Nelle is a kind person and promises not to tell.

Smile Therapy: Believing himself to have killed Stefan, John crushes his toilet remote. He has a frog whistle to call Stefan, and cries over his loss. He plays the bagpipes while in mourning and manages to make a memorial speech even more absurd than his colleagues previously imagined: 'I can only hope the bowl was indeed fresh when he fell into it.'

Sub Zero: Nelle's hatred and fear of frogs comes, as she tells John, from when her beloved pet hamster, Milly, was eaten by an Argentine Horned Frog. Nelle's obvious childhood adoration for Milly, her desire to spend all her time with the hamster and her pain at losing her best friend touches John, and the audience.

Fishisms: One of Richard's greatest moments of wisdom: 'Men love any woman they want to sleep with, it's the ticket to admission. Fishism.'

Office Gossip: Elaine asks Ally to stay away from George. She reads a rehearsal memorial speech, which she and Richard feel covers the kind of absurd things John is likely to say, to try to get the laughter over with in advance. 'You can have any man you want, Ally, please don't take mine,' says Elaine in a heartfelt moment.

Cruelty To Animals: Stefan the show frog begins the long road to death when he gets flushed down a toilet by John. Before this he gets batted across the office by Nelle, and caught by Fish – who sniffs the frog. The worst is yet to come.

Men: A return for George Madison, Elaine's 'non-exclusive' boyfriend.

Fantasy: Ally fantasises about licking coffee foam from George's face.

Fetishes: Fish sniffing Stefan the frog. Is there anything he won't take a deep breath of?

Song: 'The Red Red Robin' plays whilst Ally is happy, only to grind to a halt when she finds Hannah crying in the street. George wiggle-walks away to 'Nobody But Me'. Vonda's cover of 'What Becomes of the Broken Hearted?', showcased here, appears on the second *Ally McBeal* soundtrack CD.

Fashion Victims: Elaine's ill-advised burgundy tight-top and cardigan combo. Her velvet coat is lovely, though.

Judge Not: Hannah's case is presided over by Judge Maynard Sniff, who refuses to let Ally withdraw from the trial when she finds out Hannah fired her previous lawyers. In a nifty reference to Judge Walsh's ruling in the previous episode, Judge Sniff tells Ally she can dress however she likes.

The Case: Hannah Puck, on trial for taking her boyfriend-stealing-friend Laura out with the trash.

Withdrawn: Plenty of stunts from the despicable Orin; crying, complaining Ally 'hurt his feelings'. His very presence is used to discredit Ally by bringing up her previous assault on him.

Guilty?: The $1 damages awarded to Laura are about right: obeying the letter of the law, but acknowledging that Hannah shouldn't be punished further for her understandable reaction to betrayal.

The Verdict: 'The trashcan she threw you in: did it fit?' A simple story about humour in the face of loss, and the way absurdity and tragedy can go hand in hand, 'Story Of Love' is full of moments and anecdotes that seem both silly and meaningful. Although George seems a bit of a creep to us, Elaine and Ally's tug of love over him is raw and uncomfortable. John's eulogy for Stefan is one of the series' most painfully funny moments. All this, and one of Richard's best Fishisms: good stuff.

206
Worlds Without Love

#2M07
2 November 1998

Written by David E. Kelley
Directed by Arvin Brown

Cast: Dyan Cannon (Judge 'Whipper' Cone),
Richard T. Jones (Matt Griffin), Kellie Waymire (Chrissa),
Jessica Harper (Sister Helen), Shea Farrell (Priest),
Lee Wilkof (Nixon)

John and Ally represent a nun who broke her vow of celibacy but wishes to return to the convent, Whipper makes a disastrous bid for Richard's affections, Renee meets an old love who is unhappily married, Stefan re-emerges from the depths but ends up in a coma, and Ally makes one confession she may regret . . . It's just another day at Cage & Fish.

Everything Stops For Ally: Ally steps into the confessional and can't stop talking – 'I covet all over . . . you have no idea.' She's understandably alarmed when she later finds the priest has run off to sell tapes of confessions in the form of a TV show: *World's Naughtiest Confessions*. Her self-awareness is touching: 'Getting dumped isn't exactly a show of penance. If it were I'd be Mother Superior.' There's a great bit of slapstick as a shoe-challenged Ally hops into a wall – the kind of little touch that can make a potentially dull scene interesting. Ally's intervention in Richard and Whipper's lives results in Fish bringing Ling back to his place – only to find a naked Whipper lighting candles around the apartment. When Whipper is upset the next day, Ally helps her through it by getting Whipper to imagine having to live with Richard's habits, his friends, his jokes . . .

DA Renee: Renee takes centre stage for once as she runs into Matt Griffin, the lost love of her youth. As she says: 'That was my Billy.' She meets him for coffee and finds out he has a bumpy marriage. As they discuss old times, things get too intense and she runs off. Later, she changes a dinner date to a meeting at the bar, so Ally can chaperone. The next day Renee takes time off work and Matt comes to the apartment to visit her; they kiss.

Fishisms: Personal questions don't bother Richard – he just lies. When Ally tells Richard that Whipper misses him, he says it's over. His lack of conviction leads Ally to tell Whipper she thinks Richard misses *her*; with disastrous results. Richard's repeated use of the word 'alive' while telling John about Stefan is inspired, playing up the survival and almost subliminally saying 'coma' while doing so.

Whip-Lash!: Whipper is the judge presiding over the case of the wanton nun. She uses Ally's sniffling in court to call Ally to her chambers, ostensibly to examine her illness but really to ask after Richard. Later, having quizzed Richard, Ally tells Whipper it isn't too late for the two of them, leading Whipper to make her nude intrusion on Fish and Ling's evening.

Grrr!: Ling shows the power she has when Fish, Billy and Georgia retreat en masse beneath the terror of one of her stares. She has problems with newness – it doesn't make her feel sexual. The morning after finding Whipper in Fish's flat, Ling wants to sue Richard for 'intentional infliction of emotional distress'. When told by Nelle she can't sue Richard, Ling storms out declaring her 'need to shop'.

Georgia On My Mind: Georgia wants Ling to answer one simple question: 'Does anything nice come out of your mouth?' It's a fair point.

Cruelty To Animals: Poor old Stefan. He re-emerges from the toilet alive, only to make the ill-advised move of jumping onto Nelle's head. The poor little dear is then batted between Nelle and Georgia, until Georgia throws him hard into Richard's cubicle door, and he slides unconscious to the floor. He's then left in a coma and on a respirator. Ling's rather callous comment on Stefan's condition counts as cruelty in itself: 'A frog is not a vegetable, it's meat.' This somewhat foreshadows Stefan's final tragic demise.

Smile Therapy: John takes Milly, the frog Nelle gave him, to meet the comatose Stefan, and sings a song about the importance of being a frog.

We Got It Together, Didn't We?: Nelle's involvement in Stefan's latest injury could seriously damage her chances with John – she doesn't tell him, and lets him believe Stefan surfaced in a coma rather than being bashed about the place by her and Georgia.

Office Gossip: Elaine claims to be very good at flirting with clergy: 'At communion, I always got the extra wafer.' She smuggles the comatose Stefan past John by stuffing the injured frog down her top.

Girl Talk: Ally and Renee discuss her planned meal with Matt, and what it signifies: as Ally says, 'No one goes to dinner to have dinner.'

Quotes: Ally sums up the series: 'Is it me or do we seem to be a magnet for strange cases?'

Ally tries to get Whipper to feel better about her getting naked and waiting for Richard by suggesting no one would criticise a man for doing that. Whipper's response to this is blunt but truthful: 'Ally, he'd be arrested!'

Richard telling John about Stefan's survival: 'It's a miracle: maybe it's because you've been hanging out with a nun.'

Fantasy: When she finds out her confession may be on TV some day soon, Ally is literally drained of colour.

Song: Vonda's covers of Roy Orbison's 'Crying' and the Paul McCartney penned 'World Without Love' appear; both are on the second soundtrack CD. John Cage sings 'Be A Frog' to Stefan. Vonda sings 'A Love So Beautiful' as Renee and Matt dance.

The Case: A fairly silly one: Chrissa Lang is a nun who had an affair, and now wants to rejoin the order. The Church, in the form of the forthright Sister Helen, argues Chrissa should have restrained her urges, and only showed penance when she was dumped by the man involved.

Guilty?: It's a pretty dumb case, and religious orders aren't really something the court can intervene in. Of course, the distraction of a priest taping confessions and trying to sell them on a TV show allows the Church an excuse to back down, so nothing is really resolved in court.

Kisses: The kiss between Renee and Matt: the tension between her love for him and the knowledge that he's a married man adds to the moment.

Toilet Humour: Nelle catches Ally hip-thrusting in the unisex.

Trivia: The FOX network, home of *World's Naughtiest Confessions*, is in real life the channel *Ally McBeal* is on. Other FOX shows include, according to Sister Helen, *Deadliest Car Crashes* and *The Oral Office*. Classy.

The Verdict: 'There's no sin in loving men, only pain.' Love, separation and the barriers that keep those who love apart are explored in a neat little episode. The conclusion of Chrissa's case is a typically nifty dodging of the issue – an outside event, in this case the priest taping confessions, causes one side to back down before a resolution can be reached. Most notable, however, is Lisa Nicole Carson getting her teeth into a really juicy plot for Renee, demonstrating a range of emotion beyond Renee's usual sly one-liners. With such a strong cast it's easy for the minor players to get lost, so it's nice to see Renee get her moment in the sun – and some heartbreak of her own.

207
Happy Trails

#2M08
9 November 1998

Written by David E. Kelley
Directed by Jonathan Pontell

Cast: Phil Leeds (Judge 'Happy' Boyle),
Dyan Cannon (Judge 'Whipper' Cone),
Rob Schneider (Fitzy), John Fleck (Spicer),
Jennifer Holliday (Lisa Knowles),
Melanie Chartoff (Joanne Poole)

Billy and Georgia are in the middle of representing a woman fired for being orange when the presiding judge, Happy Boyle, dies. Thoughts of mortality and loss at Cage & Fish are heightened when Stefan, after a brief recovery, is accidentally eaten in a Chinese restaurant.

Meanwhile, Ally has troubles of her own – how can she get rid of Fitzy, the date from hell?

Let Me See Your Teeth: The late Phil Leeds' last appearance as Judge 'Happy' Boyle is a tour de force. Boyle wants to know if there are other orange people out there, and muses on how he always thought aliens would end up in his court asking for their rights. He says that some people think he's an alien and call him Yoda – but he tries to rise above it. He thinks Billy and Georgia's client is a very pretty colour, and that he wishes his wife glowed in the dark – it would help him see what he is doing. He appears to fall asleep, but when Billy steps forward to check on him, he's dead.

Everything Stops For Ally: Ally's complete lack of cruelty leads her astray as she constantly fails to get rid of Fitzy. Her desperate attempts – pretending to be dead, pretending to be a lesbian – don't work, showing that she just has to be cruel to be cruel. Eventually, she manages to dump him, saying that she never wants to see him again. EVER. Later, Ally winces at just the *presence* of Nelle and Ling.

The Boy Next Door: Billy seems surprised himself by how hard Happy Boyle's death hit him, and regrets the fact that Happy used to invite him to lunch and he never used to find the time to go. He gives a eulogy at Happy's funeral about the importance of spending time with people while you still can and ends on an upbeat note: 'The man lying there – show him your teeth.'

Georgia On My Mind: Georgia never knew Billy cared so much about Happy Boyle and suggests Billy has issues relating to his late father – Billy denies this.

Fishisms: When Richard talks to Whipper about how 'people come, people go' he can be interpreted as referring to both Happy's death and the fact that Richard has moved on from Whipper to Ling.

Bygones: Richard on the comatose Stefan: 'This Thanksgiving he's the vegetable. Bygones.'

Cruelty to Animals: Stefan comes out of his coma, only to be accidentally swatted out of the window by John. He's tempted back in from the window sill, and John takes him to dinner with Richard, Nelle and Ling. Unfortunately, the restaurant staff misunderstand their instruction to feed the frog – instead they make him the main course.

Sub Zero: Nelle's terror of Stefan is almost tangible in one scene – a neat bit of reacting from Portia de Rossi. She gives John a little speech about God hating frogs, that causes him to ask her to leave him alone. 'For what it's worth,' she tells him, 'I didn't find him delicious at all. I thought he was a little tough.'

Smile Therapy: While in the restaurant Richard is informed of Happy Boyle's death via his mobile – John asks that they all take a moment. After Nelle has left his office he starts to laugh, and when Ally comes in they both laugh hysterically over the absurd series of disasters that befell Stefan. John then turns on

Ally for laughing, stunning her with a tirade about losing his 'best little friend', and how sick people are for laughing at tragedy.

We Got It Together, Didn't We?: In spite of all the conflict above, after Happy's funeral John and Nelle end up standing outside her door. Nelle invites John in, but he politely refuses. She kisses him, saying she's not going to wait any longer for him to make the first move. As John walks off he hears Barry White – and dances in the street.

Whip-Lash!: Whipper apologises to Richard for her naked intrusion, and gives Richard back her key to his apartment. Losing Happy hits her hard: 'Now why did you go and do this, Happy?' She makes the funeral arrangements and gives a eulogy. (We're not sure how appropriate to Happy Boyle's character a riotous gospel funeral is, but never mind.)

Grrr!: When Whipper arrives Ling says: 'The naked woman is here. She's disguised in clothes.' Ling refers to John as 'the strange one' in Chinese. When the staff at the Chinese restaurant tell Ling what they did with Stefan, she tells the others that John is 'going to be taking a big moment'. She takes another bite after she knows they're eating Stefan: 'Tastes like chicken.'

Office Gossip: Elaine tells Ling she knows she's hurt and that she just wants to be a part of it. When Ling replies that it 'helps just not being you', Elaine concedes this is a good comeback, and that Ling is her 'favourite vicious person in life'. When Whipper comes to the office to apologise to Richard, Elaine wants to gather everyone to watch. Most importantly of all in this episode, she encourages and helps Ally to get rid of Fitzy, including telling the man himself to 'stop and take a big bite out of reality'.

Guy Talk: Fish gives John kissing advice, advice he was given by Ling.

Girl Talk: Ally and Renee discuss how weird people are and Ally suggests that maybe they're making a mistake in overlooking the freaks: 'We're brainwashed into believing the best people are normal and attractive and maybe they're not. The

John Cages and the Happy Boyles; maybe they're the real nuggets, and maybe we're missing out skipping over all the Fitzys.' Admirable as these sentiments are, they're hard to square with Fitzy himself!

Men: The utterly vile Fitzy; he calls Ally 'Alison', he has itineraries for their dates, he fills whole rooms with flowers, he sings karaoke while wearing an open-chested shirt, and he never, ever gives up.

Quotes: When Fitzy asks if Ally judges people on personality, Ally snaps 'Great – get one.' But she clearly regrets it (see **Fantasy**).

Ling breaks the news about Stefan gently to John: 'The bad news is, Stefan is back. The good news is he's delicious.'

Fantasy: Having told Fitzy to get a personality, Ally imagines being tiny. When he brings her an 'itinerary' for their date, she imagines running away like Road Runner – Beep! Beep!

Fetishes: Happy Boyle's vast wattle made him the most likely person for Fish to have had a homosexual experience with, apparently.

Song: Rob Schneider (as Fitzy) delivers a truly appalling and cheesy version of 'Puppy Love'. At different points in the episode Fitzy is accompanied by the intros to 'Puppy Love' and Tom Jones' 'It's Not Unusual'.

. . . And Dance: After Stefan's final death, John does his angry dance to 'Gimme Dat Ding'. The old people at the funeral wave their walking frames in the air.

Shrink Wrapped: John describes Stefan as suffering from a little 'separation anxiety'.

Fashion Victims: Fitzy's open-chested, puff-sleeved shirt that he wears at the karaoke bar.

The Case: The case of a woman sacked for being orange. It never reaches a conclusion due to Happy Boyle's sudden death, but Billy's argument that the law doesn't allow for discrimination against someone because of the colour of their skin – whether it be black, white or orange – seems like a winner.

Kisses: Ally kisses Elaine to try to get rid of Fitzy. It doesn't work: 'You think you're the first woman I've dated who pretended to be dead or gay?'

Also Starring: Comic actor Rob Schneider played Sylvester Stallone's sidekick in *Judge Dredd* (Danny Cannon, 1995). John Fleck's many TV appearances include *Star Trek: Deep Space Nine* and a regular role in *Murder One*.

Toilet Humour: John, nervous about Nelle, climbs into Richard's cubicle to ask advice.

Trivia: John Cage's handkerchiefs are initialled.

The Verdict: 'People are sick. They laugh at tragedy.' Cathartic rather than tragic, this loving tribute to the late Phil Leeds finds the humour in sadness without ever becoming excessively mawkish. While Ally is off having a lightweight sub-plot with Fitzy, Peter MacNicol and Gil Bellows carry much of the weight of the episode as both John and Billy deal with personal losses – and both come out the other side stronger. Few series can juggle sadness and happiness, comedy and tragedy, cynicism and romance without ever dropping a ball, but at this stage David E. Kelley doesn't slip up once. Great stuff.

208
Just Looking

#2M09
16 November 1998

Written by Shelley Landau and David E. Kelley
Directed by Vince Misiono

Cast: Justin Theroux (Ray Brown),
Christine Ebersole (Marie Stokes),
Tony Plana (Judge Warren Figueroa),
Reese Silley (Male Stripper), Twni Graf (Jennifer)

Ally, Georgia and Elaine have a premonition of something bad heading towards them: it turns out to be Ling, who apparently owns a mud-wrestling club that the pressure group MOPE (Mothers Opposed to Pornographic Entertainment) wants to close down. Complications ensue for Ally and Georgia when counsel for MOPE turns out to be Ray Brown, an old friend – and old flame – of Georgia's. Georgia encourages Ally to date Ray – but is she just using Ally to live out her own fantasy? Can Ally even get to a date with Ray when she gets stuck in the toilet? Can Richard and John survive an undercover mission into the world of all-female mud wrestling?

Everything Stops For Ally: Ally can't understand how Ling could own a mud-wrestling club, and doesn't want to take the case. Richard criticises Ally for never thinking of anyone but herself (see **Fishisms**). When due for a date with Ray Brown, Ally gets stuck in John's remote control toilet. She seems very excited when, while she is stuck *in* the toilet bowl, Elaine activates the flush. Ally is rescued from the toilet by the fire brigade, who break the bowl. Ally turns Ray down when he asks to see her again, and is surprised he even asked. Later, she hears a klaxon when she sees Ray and Georgia moving together.

Georgia On My Mind: Like Ally, Georgia can't relate to Ling's ownership of the club and doesn't want the case. When Nelle suggests they send Billy to check the place out, Georgia refuses. Her attraction to Ray Brown is understandable – although they're supposedly contemporaries, he seems to be five years younger than her. Perhaps she just wants the secret to his youthful looks? After Ally turns him down for a second date, Ray talks to Georgia who confesses her interest. She makes clear she wouldn't actually do anything, and Ray says the problem is they never kissed, leaving unresolved tensions. Later Ray stops a lift they're alone in and they almost kiss. But not quite.

Also Starring: Justin Theroux, appearing here as Ray Brown, has recently appeared as one of Patrick Bateman's friends in *American Psycho* (Mary Harron, 2000).

Fishisms: Of MOPE's case, Richard says they'll probably go for 'that women/degradation cliché'. He puts Ally, Nelle and Georgia on the case, in spite of protests. His attack on Georgia and Ally is classic Fish, delivered at a machine-gun pace by Greg Germann: 'This is a client with whom I'm still trying to reach sexual fruition. For once I'll ask you to think about someone other than yourselves. Can you do that, Georgia? Can you think about the senior partner who signs your pay cheque? How about you, Ally? Could you possibly consider somebody other than yourself? I realise it involves using a new muscle, but to me any job is meaningless unless it offers the opportunity for personal growth. Off we go, be lawyers.'

While investigating Ling's club with John, Richard successfully bids for the chance to have a wrestle with one of the girls, Jennifer. Later, when Nelle can't do the summation due to her inability to comprehend or appreciate the club, Richard is drafted in to give a closing. He hears the cowbell as he goes into the courtroom, and when they actually win that cowbell rings madly.

Bygones: Talking about Ling's club, Fish wants to know how she could 'keep it a secret. Bygones.'

Grrr!: Ling prefers being the plaintiff, but says being a defendant is nice too: it gives her a 'martyr glow'. In court defending herself, she is relentless in her assertion that the women's mud-wrestling club does not degrade women, and in fact empowers them: 'Go into that club, you come out with a lower opinion of men. Trust me.' Every question Ray asks her in his cross-examination leads to a speech. As Ally says of Ling: 'She's my hero! I disagree with almost everything she says, she treats me like dirt and somehow she's my hero.' She's our hero too.

Office Gossip: Elaine's latest invention is a complex toilet remote for John, which not only flushes but warms and lifts/lowers the seat. (She likes a warm seat, apparently.) This handy device almost immediately leads to Ally getting stuck in the bowl, a situation that has Elaine looking for her camera and making public announcements. At college Elaine went on a date with a quarterback, and to take off the pressure she went out with the whole team.

Smile Therapy: John says he once considered joining the CIA, and demonstrates his espionage skills throughout the episode. He insists that, 'field reconnaissance isn't to be trivialised'. He protests when the fire brigade want to break his toilet to free Ally and takes to carrying a section of broken porcelain around with him afterwards.

Sub Zero: Nelle refuses to do the closing argument for Ling's case, on the grounds that she doesn't believe in it. She bemoans that people have never seen her without her make-up, and that 'progress aside, women are still things to be looked at'. She doesn't believe that clubs like Ling's help the situation. She encourages Richard to do the closing and to speak from his 'dumbstick' on the grounds that she doesn't 'get it'.

We Got It Together, Didn't We?: Nelle tells John to 'be careful' as he heads off to investigate the bar – John clearly gets a kick out of this. While dancing at the bar Nelle tells him he would have made a great spy, and commiserates at the death of his toilet bowl.

Men: Ray Brown, an old friend of Georgia's whom she once dated. Ally is interested enough to go home and change her pants – she says Ray reminds her of Jack Webb from *Dragnet*, and that she had a crush on both Webb and Mr Ed.

Fantasy: Ally finds out Georgia told Ray she wanted to go for a drink with him, and her head shrinks into her pullover with embarrassment. When Richard and John see Jennifer, the mud wrestler, their tongues loll out a foot.

Fetishes: Richard touches waitress-wattle. Oh, and then there's the female mud wrestling and Richard's participation in it. We could write a whole essay on this – but we won't.

Ouch!: Fish twists his shoulder while wrestling, while Ally claims to have sprained her butt in the toilet. John nearly stabs himself with a paper knife when he bumps into Georgia. 'She just jumped out at you,' says Elaine. 'I'm a witness.'

Song: Vonda sings 'Secret Agent Man' as John infiltrates the wrestling club. As he spies around the office the *Hawaii Five-0* theme plays.

Fashion Victims: While the firemen rescue Ally from the toilet, Elaine tries on a fireman's helmet. John's trenchcoat is less than inconspicuous as he does his secret agent schtick.

The Case: Ling owns a female mud-wrestling club, which a local pressure group wants to close down. Ray Brown, representing MOPE and their acerbic leader, Marie Stokes, argues that the club is the equivalent of a strip joint and is dragging the neighbourhood downhill. Nelle argues with Stokes over censorship and where to draw the line. Stokes doesn't think women performing sex scenes in movies are being exploited because they're 'paid tons of money'. Ray's closing is persuasive, saying that places like Ling's club oppress women, reducing freedom and producing inequality. But Richard gains our sympathy with his passionate tirade for the dumbstick, and how vital it is for men to realise they are not alone in being testosterone-driven idiots: 'These places aren't just sex shops. They stand to preserve our mental health.'

Withdrawn: Nelle calls a male stripper as a witness, to present a comparison. As Ally says, it's a stunt.

Judge Not: Judge Warren Figueroa presides over the MOPE case.

Guilty?: It's a tough call, but we'll agree with the verdict in the episode – that Ling's club is fairly harmless and should be allowed to stay open.

Toilet Humour: Introducing John's new remote control, which causes Ally to get stuck in the toilet – resulting in the breaking of John's 'fresh bowl' to free her.

Hit The Bar: Georgia dances with Ray at the bar. Nelle dances with John, and Billy dances with Ally.

The Verdict: 'Sex is a weapon. We all use it.' It's hard to believe this is one of the series' few co-written episodes, so perfectly does it fit into creator David E. Kelley's agenda.

After a couple of rather serious episodes concerning love and loss, we're back to one of the show's other perennial themes here, a spiky examination of the relationship between the genders. Questions of voyeurism are addressed as we not only see Richard living out a fantasy by wrestling in mud with a beautiful woman, but Georgia using Ally to act out what might have been with Ray. Courtney Thorne-Smith gets a rare chance to excel as Georgia flirts with a path she knows, deep down, she will never take. With typically eccentric court performances from Richard and Ling and important issues raised, this is explosive, witty fun.

209
You Never Can Tell

#2M06
23 November 1998

Written by David E. Kelley
Directed by Adam Nimoy

Cast: Shawn Michael Howard (Ben),
Murray Rubin (Seymore),
Bob Glouberman (Wallace 'Wally' Beek),
Larry Brandenberg (Judge Raynsford Hopkins),
Neil Giuntolli (Whitton), Michael Reilly Burke (Wells),
Michael DiMaggio (Sean), Michael Davenport (Dr Herbert)

Ling sues an employee for having sexually charged thoughts about her, while Nelle tries to date John. Ally learns an important life lesson that the Fitzy experience should have taught her already: never, ever date someone recommended by Renee's friend Ben. Can Sappho herself save Ally from Wallace, who is a living expression of tedium itself? And with Thanksgiving coming up, will anybody have anything to be thankful for?

Everything Stops For Ally: Ally explains that cushion kicking is part of Thanksgiving, as she gives thanks for all the problems in her life. When Ling says she thought she and Ally were friends, Ally's response is to laugh out loud. She isn't pleased when Renee says they're going on a double date to a bowling alley with Ben and one of his friends: Ally doesn't think good men can be found in bowling alleys. Ally is lumbered with Ling's case and takes Georgia as second chair. When Elaine admits George dumped her, Ally says 'He did?' with rather too much enthusiasm. She invites Elaine over for Thanksgiving, to watch football and kick cushions. Ally is awful at bowling, claiming this is because the holes are too big. Seymore Martin, an old man, offers her his late wife's bowling ball to use. 'She too had little hands,' he explains. Unfortunately, the holes are a little too tight, and Ally gets the ball stuck on her hand. Because she doesn't want to break the old man's heart by having his most precious possession sawn in half, Ally keeps the ball on her hand for the next day: until it drops off of its own accord – right onto her foot. Ally tries to get Elaine to dump Wally for her when she finds she can't get him to go: 'Fifty-dollar raise if you get rid of him.' In the end she kisses Georgia to get rid of Wally – but accuses Georgia of slipping her the tongue.

Grrr!: Ling doesn't like Richard's pet names for her. When asked if he can call her anything apart from 'Ling', she replies 'Sugar. Or honey. Pumpkin. Anything food, you can call me food.' She fiddles with a Rubik's Cube while walking around Richard's office, and by the time she passes it back to him it's finished. She thinks the staff at Cage & Fish are 'a mean and spiteful group'. Ling claims to be penile psychic – she can tell when men are thinking with their dumbsticks. In court she describes the defendant as a 'gross pig'.

Fishisms: Having been told he's allowed to call Ling food items, Richard uses such unusual pet names as 'Bacon Bits'. Richard insists he doesn't take Ling's cases because he wants to sleep with her, he takes them because she's 'wealthy, and a potential cash cow the firm can milk in perpetuity'. In spite of this, he suggests that after this case is over Ling might want to have a rest from suing people for a while. She asks how he's going to milk her then, and Richard smiles when he realises

she made a joke for him. Richard thinks Nelle has 'unbeliev-
able legs'.

Bygones: 'John, you've got the biggest booger on . . . oh,
sorry, it's a frog. Bygones.'

Office Gossip: Ally realises something is up when Elaine
starts attention-seeking again, this time via another invention –
a dress that makes women appear pregnant. Great for queue
jumping and speeding, it's lightweight and has a water pack
that can be burst to simulate the real thing. Ally finds out that
George has dumped Elaine, and although she'll be fine she
doesn't like being alone at Thanksgiving: 'It makes it hard to
eat the turkey because you feel like one.' Elaine tells Ally that
George told her everything (see 205 'Story of Love') and that
'on Thursday, I'll be giving thanks that you're my friend'. She
wonders if she and Ally will ever get to be pregnant for real.
Elaine plays Barry White in the unisex to try to create a mood,
and tells John to take Nelle on the dance floor – grab her arm
and spin her close to him. Elaine tells John she finds happiness
easy to create – she acts happy, then sees herself how others
see her – but loneliness is harder to deal with. She claims to be
lonely every day of her life.

We Got It Together, Didn't We?: Nelle wants to move
things on: 'I'm beginning to really like you. Can we just go out
on a real date with a beginning and an end?' She knows he
wants to covet her from afar, but that's driving her a little
crazy. Nelle is reluctant to go to the bar for their date, but
agrees because John feels more comfortable there. At the bar
Nelle claims to be having a good time, but expresses a desire to
get John out of his 'cocoon'. When a guy called Sean tries to
chat Nelle up, even though she rejects the guy, John still calls
an early end to the date, claiming to be tired. (The fact that
Sean sniggers when told John is Nelle's date doesn't help.)
The next day Nelle walks in on Richard, Billy and John doing
a post-mortem on the date. She tells John she doesn't mind him
telling them what's going on, but would like it if he told her at
some point. John tells her he's afraid: 'I let my frog run free
and it ended up getting flushed down the toilet. I don't want

my hope to meet the same fate.' He's worried Nelle, getting hit on all the time, will find somebody else, someone who has the qualities she finds attractive in him but with better packaging. Nelle replies that she's losing interest as he speaks: 'I'm not drawn to victims.' In the unisex they both hear Barry White – because Elaine's playing it on a stereo while hiding in one of the stalls.

Sub Zero: Nelle, rather cruelly, tricks Ally into saying that she's fantasised about kissing another woman, then says she never has such thoughts herself. The others aren't impressed by this. Elaine's trick with the stereo makes Nelle think Ling was right: 'You're all nuts.' Nelle attacks Billy for presuming that she's as shallow as most men, and is only interested in looks. She tells Billy she really likes John.

The Boy Next Door: Billy ineptly tries to protect John from being hurt by Nelle. When he confronts Nelle in the unisex, and tells her John is a vulnerable guy and that he hopes she wouldn't date him out of 'curiosity or sport', Nelle uses John's spare remote flusher to make Billy think John was listening. She tells Billy that if he didn't want John to hear all that, he wasn't being very loyal by saying it at all. He later tells John he was probably more concerned about office soap opera than anything else, and that he really can't judge whether he and Nelle are right for each other. When Nelle appears behind him again, he explodes: 'Do you just sneak up on people?!'

Georgia On My Mind: Georgia asks Ling if 'sympathetic' is in her range, and suggests Ling doesn't mention being psychic while on the stand.

DA Renee: Renee calls Wally a 'walking HBO special', implying the worst kind of true life TV melodrama. She thinks Seymore the whinging widower is about as funny as Wally.

Guy Talk: Billy and John discuss the Nelle situation, and John admits he's a little scared he'll fall in love with her, and get hurt because it won't work out in the long term. When John asks Billy if he can see John and Nelle working out, Billy admits he can't.

Girl Talk: At the bar Nelle and Ling discuss the problems of beauty, of how awful handsome men are. Ling says that true happiness can only be found in one thing – shopping.

Men: Wallace 'Wally' Beek, a friend of Renee's friend Ben. Wally is a scary-eyed, humourless proto-serial killer, who won't give up because he believes relationships work through perseverance. He claims to be an excellent dancer, and when Ally gets the bowling ball stuck on her hand Wally asks if she's menstruating – menstruating women can swell up. He sends cards and flowers constantly, and turns up at the office saying he was up all night worrying about Ally and the bowling ball. Ally gets rid of him by pretending to be a lesbian, and Wally responds by saying that he can't see her any more, but gives her some scripture in case she wants to change her evil lesbian ways.

Fantasy: When Ally meets Wally, she imagines zooming out of the bowling alley like Road Runner – 'Beep, Beep!'

Song: Ally tries to play her theme song, 'Tell Him' in her head but it keeps winding down. Wally sings 'You Are My Sunshine' to Ally through her office door. Vonda sings 'You Never Can Tell' at the bar.

. . . And Dance: John does his angry dance to 'Gimme Dat Ding'. His attempt to spin Nelle into his arms on the dance floor results in them falling over. Renee, Ally and Elaine dance together at the bar.

Fashion Victims: Nelle wears a Ling-designed air steward-ess outfit, which renders John, Richard and Billy speechless. The latter two snap out of it when Georgia and Ally slap them.

The Case: Ling is suing one of her employees for having sexual thoughts about her, thereby creating a hostile work environment. Ling says she couldn't sack the man, Whitton, because he's union. On the stand, Ling tells the court how Whitton would look her up and down in a sexual way, and how the thoughts of him wanting to sleep with her gave Ling nightmares. He also used to say her name in a soft, sexual way: 'Woo'. He also said 'Hello' and 'Good morning' in a lascivious manner. Wells questions Ling's dress sense: he says it's provocative, she says it's contemporary. Ling claims she is suing not for her own sake, but to protect others in the future.

Judge Not: Judge Raynsford Hopkins presides over Ling's case. Twice he has to tell her that yes or no questions require a yes or no answer and to stop giving speeches.

Withdrawn: While Wells, Whitton's attorney, argues for dismissal, Ally pretends to be attracted to him to prove how you can act sexually with someone without actually doing anything. She explains that what she's signifying is that 'I want it. Right here, right now. Rough.' This takes the case one step further. Elaine tries to fit Ling with a neckbrace to make her seem sympathetic, but Ally's having none of these cheap tactics.

Guilty?: It's a stupid case, Ling deserves to lose, and she does. We don't even see her lose – it happens off screen.

Kisses: Ally kisses Georgia to get rid of Wally, who doesn't believe in homosexuality.

Toilet Humour: Numerous Nelle-related confrontations occur in the unisex, including Elaine's demonstration of how John should 'take' her.

The Verdict: 'Does he look like he beats being alone?' Low key but worthwhile, 'You Never Can Tell' doesn't really add up to much, but is a nice study in loneliness. Wallace is a grotesque but in a completely different way to Fitzy, and is played with suitable blank-eyed psychosis. The John and Nelle plotline aside – and their relationship goes through a pretty dark place here – the laughs are too broad for much else in this episode to be taken seriously and you won't feel much for the characters.

210
Making Spirits Bright

#2M10
14 December 1998

Written by David E. Kelley
Directed by Peter MacNicol

Cast: Mark Linn-Baker (Sheldon Maxwell),
Lee Wilkof (Nixon), Richard T. Jones (Matt Griffin),
Dyan Cannon (Judge 'Whipper' Cone),
Lara Flynn Boyle (Helen Gamble),
John de Lancie (Jackson Poile), Amy Castle (Young Ally)

It's Christmas again, and bond trader Sheldon Maxwell, a
major client of Richard's, has been dismissed from his job for
seeing a unicorn in the office. As it was Sheldon's money that
allowed Richard to set up the firm, Fish is quite keen to win
this one. Billy takes the case and brings in Ally as second chair
because he remembers when she saw a unicorn – an event that
initially Ally can't remember herself. While Matt comes back
to haunt Renee, Elaine prepares to do a number and John tries
to catch Nelle under the mistletoe, Ally wonders whether she
will ever see a unicorn again. Alone late at the office, she gets
her answer.

Everything Stops For Ally: Ally remembers seeing a unicorn
when she was seven, and at the end of the episode she sees one
again. Sheldon can tell that she saw one and asks her about it.
Sheldon's summary of the people who see unicorns sums up
Ally: 'They're lonely, with virtuous hearts.' The fact that she
petted the unicorn apparently indicates a person of pure spirit.
As Ally says, it's lucky the unicorn turned up when she was
seven.

Ally catches Renee in bed with Matt and, when faced with
Renee's excuses the next morning, babbles, 'Studies show that
when two people attracted to each other, take off all their
clothes and get into bed things just happen!'

Ally doesn't think anybody should be happy, after all, it's Christmas.

The Boy Next Door: Ally doesn't remember the childhood unicorn incident until Billy reminds her. He says he remembers everything, suggesting a deep affection for their time together. When he and Ally discuss Renee's predicament he asks, 'Is it the worst thing in the world for her to be with this guy?' Is this the same man who believes in monogamy and matrimony over everything else? He is baffled by the way Ally rejects the world of absolutes but also lives by them. The case brings out a sense of whimsy in Billy that Ally thought was dead. Ally says she misses him most at Christmas, but asks him not to respond to this as it would only hurt either Ally or Georgia. He misses the way Ally used to make him believe in things that weren't there, and Ally replies that getting attached to things that aren't there can be dangerous. Billy kisses Ally, holding mistletoe over her head as an excuse.

DA Renee: It's time for Renee to go through the emotional wringer again with the return of her married ex, Matt Griffin. He says he wants Renee, that his marriage is as good as over. It convinces Renee enough for her to go to bed with him. When Renee tells him they won't have a future until he leaves his wife, Matt admits that his wife is four months pregnant. She explains her vulnerability to Ally: 'He knew me before I was tough, Ally.' She finally dumps Matt when she realises that his wife has no idea he's seeing her. As she says: 'This might be a mistake, but it's the only one I'm willing to make.' She's left in tears.

Fishisms: You can tell Sheldon is a lonely man with only his work to keep him going – he counts Richard as one of his friends. Richard likes the fact Whipper is presiding over the unicorn case; as he says, 'She's probably seen a few unicorns herself.' He hears the bell when it's suggested he might do a number on stage.

Grrr!: Ling is in a happy, smiley, Christmassy mood, to the alarm of all concerned. She gives out candy canes and presents. As Elaine and Georgia say, it isn't that they don't appreciate Ling's good will – they just don't believe it. Ling doesn't like sweat – even her own.

Smile Therapy: John was once sent home from school when he thought he was Pinocchio.

We Got It Together, Didn't We?: John constantly tries to surprise Nelle under the mistletoe, but it never quite works. Yet again it ends up being her move, as she kisses him under the mistletoe.

Office Gossip: Elaine builds a stage for the office party, so that she can do one of her infamous 'numbers'. She says everyone wants to hear Richard sing again – there's an office poll going as to whether he'll hit a note. (A bit unfair after 'Silver Bells', we think.) She thinks her present from Ling is ticking.

Guy Talk: John talks to Richard about wanting to kiss Nelle and making his move. Richard, rather unkindly, points out that John's move is 'in the Yellow Pages under "Escort Services"'. Fish thinks John's problem with Nelle comes from her porcelain complexion: 'She reminds you of your toilet,' he suggests, sniffing the fragment of broken bowl in John's office.

Quotes: When Nixon asks Sheldon if he told his doctor about seeing unicorns, Sheldon replies, 'Yes. He diagnosed me as "lucky".'

Fantasy: In court, Ally fantasises about punching opposing counsel, Nixon. After inadvertently asking Billy if he is leaving Georgia, Ally imagines her head swelling like a balloon, popping and deflating its way around the room.

Song: Vonda sings 'Baby, Don't You Break My Heart Slow' from the second *Ally* soundtrack. John rehearses – badly – 'I Want a Hippopotamus for Christmas'.

. . . And Dance: Ally and Renee dance to 'Tell Him' around the Christmas tree. Elaine sings 'Run, Run, Rudolph' at the party, and her dancers include Richard and John in bondage reindeer outfits.

Fashion Victims: The goggles Elaine wears while drilling are as notable as her stage gear. John and Richard's reindeer gear beggars belief. Ally's matching scarlet hat, gloves and boots are quite nice.

Whip-Lash!: Whipper presides over the unicorn case and it is heavily suggested she relates to lonely people like Sheldon now she's lost both Richard and Happy. She thinks lonely people need hope: 'I think I'm going to let them keep their unicorns.'

The Case: Sheldon Maxwell, as a bond trader, is responsible for a lot of money. His company feel a man who sees unicorns cannot be trusted with such a lot of money; that it would be negligence on their part to allow him to continue working. Nixon, counsel for the company, gets Sheldon to admit to having a history of depression, questioning his mental stability. Billy cross-examines Sheldon's boss, Jackson Poile, and argues that there's no difference in believing the possibility of unicorns and believing it is possible to have visions of the Virgin Mary. Billy points out that the unicorn is a symbol of Christ: Sheldon might as well have seen Jesus.

Guilty?: Jackson Poile has a point: 'He's seeing mythical creatures. He's on the verge. Do I have to wait until he drops over?' They'd be negligent to allow Sheldon to keep working while suffering delusions and need to protect their shareholders. However, Whipper disagrees with us and rules for Sheldon, so what do we know?

Also Starring: John de Lancie played the villainous Q in various generations of *Star Trek*. Lara Flynn Boyle appears here as Helen Gamble, her character from *The Practice*, but before that role she appeared as Donna in *Twin Peaks* and opposite Matthew Broderick and Anthony Hopkins in *The Road to Wellville* (Alan Parker, 1994).

Trivia: David E. Kelley's executive producer credit appears in a Christmas typeface on this episode. It also launches a revised title sequence, with Lucy Liu and Portia de Rossi promoted to the lead cast, and a whole load of Season Two clips.

The Verdict: 'So you could never see a unicorn. Good for you. Or maybe not.' Crisis alert – the show hits a slight mid-season dip here, with this episode, 'In Dreams' and 'Angels And Blimps' all pushing way too far into an area of trite fantasy. The unicorn case involves such a vigorous application of Ally-logic over real-world-logic to work that suspension of disbelief almost collapses, and the decision to show the unicorn at the end is an ill-advised leap into pure fantasy. However, with hindsight there are undercurrents leading to better things at work here, with Billy's increasing nostalgia for his time with Ally leading towards trouble. The most notable performance here is from Lisa Nicole Carson, as Renee does the right thing in telling the self-centred and treacherous Matt where to get off, and suffers loneliness as a result.

211

In Dreams

#2M11
11 January 1999

Written by David E. Kelley
Directed by Alex Graves

Cast: Jesse L. Martin (Dr Greg Butters),
Dyan Cannon (Judge 'Whipper' Cone),
Eileen Ryan (Bria Tolsen),
James Greene (Father Robert MacNamara),
Joel Polis (Woodson), Sam Anderson (Mark Harrison)

Ally is woken by a phone call in the night; her favourite high-school teacher, Bria Tolsen, is terminally ill and wants to speak to her. Bria lives more of her life in her dreams than while awake, and wants to spend the rest of her short life unconscious. Ally goes to court to argue that Bria should be allowed to spend her last days in a better place, while trying to deal with the presence of Bria's doctor, Greg Butters, who left Ally – and Boston – to pursue his career in Chicago.

Meanwhile, Nelle is frustrated by the slowness of matters with John – will they ever get it together?

Everything Stops For Ally: Ally reassures Bria that she hasn't been institutionalised – yet. People are always telling her she should go on Prozac, but Ally thinks dreams are a better remedy. When Richard makes an exceptionally crass observation she asks, 'How do these things just spew out of your head like this? Can you at least try to use your brain as a filter?' He says the remark would hurt if he had feelings.

We Got It Together, Didn't We?: Nelle gets excited by public places and tries to get John to go for it in the unisex. He uses his remote to rattle the toilet seat in panic until she leaves him alone. Nelle is frustrated by John's failure to move things on and his evasiveness when she approaches the matter: 'I've given you the benefit of the doubt and assumed you're stuck in reverse because of your frog woes. But whatever world you live in, John, I'm not sure I get it.' When John tells her he doesn't want to accelerate the relationship for fear it will reach its inevitable end, Nelle is left speechless. Nelle replies that she's going to try John's inner world and closes her eyes. She imagines a dump truck: 'I see the end. We're done.' Later John returns to her, admits to his cowardice and says he is willing to go in search of her 'defrost button', to step into danger and take things as far as they will go. Nelle says that would be nice.

Sub Zero: Nelle doesn't like people talking about her behind her back.

Smile Therapy: Ally has her reasons for getting John to second-chair on Bria's case: 'So it's from Mars. Fine. John, would you second chair – it would help if I went in there with a native.'

Fishisms: 'You're not what you are, you're what other people think you are. Fishism.' When the hospital refuses to put Bria to sleep, Richard suggests they take her to a vet. He has a confusing conversation with Ling about sexuality (see **Grrr!**). He tells John he has to sleep with Nelle, just as Nelle walks in. He asks Nelle about how she hates people talking about her behind her back and adds, 'I can't do that when you're in the room.' Richard's cynicism about marriage comes out again: 'If a husband tells a friend he got lucky you can be sure he isn't talking about his wife.' When he says, 'Women think they have all the answers,' Richard hears the bells.

Grrr!: Ling tells Richard she thinks John is gay for not acting sexually with Nelle. She tells Fish that it's not the same with them – Ling doesn't want to have sex with him. (Richard hears his bell at this point.) Ling says she doesn't like sex because it's messy. Richard asks if that means that it's OK for a woman to not want sex, but if a man doesn't want sex he's gay. Ling says yes and that this is a medical fact. Ling doesn't like water with bubbles – it gives her gas.

DA Renee: When Ally has to leave in the middle of the night to go to see Bria, Renee makes sure to get the inflatable man from Ally as she goes.

Girl Talk: Ling and Nelle go to the steam room. Ling talks about thinking sex is overrated, while Nelle says she likes sex. Ling considers this to be because Nelle is 'emotionally inept', and mistakes sex for passion. 'Compared to you, the *Titanic* struck heat,' says Ling in reply to Nelle's protests. Ling thinks that she and Nelle like Richard and John because they'll never reach the women's emotional cores: 'They're fun, we laugh, they pick up the cheque.' Nelle thinks this is disgusting and accuses Ling of just being afraid she'll 'get a wrinkle from smiling'.

Doctor's Orders: The lovely Dr Greg Butters is back in Ally's life after running off to Chicago last year. Greg almost kills Bria with CPR due to a fault with her life support readings. He doesn't agree to the idea of inducing coma for the purpose of dreaming. Ally refers to Greg as being 'just a friend'. Bria's last wish before she goes into her induced coma is for Greg to ask Ally out to dinner – which he does.

Fantasy: When Bria tells Father Robert about Ally and Billy sniffing each other's bottoms, Ally turns red and steams. 'There was a context,' she insists. Ally flicks a long tongue at

Greg. We see a bizarre insight into Bria's dream where she dances with Henry in a derelict aircraft hangar. As Nelle is about to dump John she imagines him being thrown out of a dumptruck into a skip.

Song: Vonda sings the old standard 'Dream Lover' as well as the Roy Orbison numbers 'In Dreams' and 'Dream Baby'. We think there's a theme here somewhere.

Bria's Dreamworld

When young Bria wasn't invited to the prom, she imagined she was invited by a handsome young man, Henry. This fantasy figure became more real as time went on, and in her thirties she began to dream of him. Now Bria and Henry have three children and things can be chaotic in the morning as they get the kids ready for school. They're not wealthy, and that can lead to difficulties. Sometimes Bria has a dream within the dream world, a recurring nightmare of being old and dying from a terminal disease. She says: 'Sometimes I think this is the dream, and the other is the real world.'

. . . And Dance: The entire main cast perform a line dance at the end of the episode. While the authors of this book acknowledge the right of mature adults to engage in line dancing in their own homes if they so wish, we cannot approve of such a blatant and public display.

Fashion Victims: Ling's very sweet combination of fluffy coat and pigtails. Billy's co-ordinating purple suit, shirt and tie shows an eye for style.

The Case: Ally goes to court to force the hospital to put Bria into a coma, so that she can live out the rest of her life in her dreams. The hospital argue it's not their policy to induce coma and that the drugs used may stop her dreaming anyway. Ally is at her most zealous and aggressive in asserting Bria's right to disappear into her dreams. Essentially the hospital are arguing the big picture, the precedent this case would set, while Ally argues for the individual case as a unique example.

Guilty?: In Bria's case a coma is a kindness, but we can see how it sets a dangerous precedent. Whipper rules against the hospital, allowing Bria to be put under for a week as a trial.

The Verdict: 'So while your hospital has helped people to die, you have ethical problems helping them to sleep?' Another tedious venture into whimsy, 'In Dreams' is thematically sound as it deals with the different worlds that people live in through Bria's dreams and the barriers the regulars put between them, but the execution just doesn't carry the idea. Bria is a horribly trite and whiny character, and her dream world is painfully unimaginative and dull. Some brilliant directorial touches – such as John, Richard and Ally having a conversation while lying on the floor with their heads almost touching – help things along but don't rescue a painfully twee exercise from its own sentimentality. Nice to see Greg back, though.

212
Love Unlimited

#2M12
18 January 1999

Written by David E. Kelley
Directed by Dennie Gordon

Cast: Bruce Willis (Dr Nickle),
Jesse L. Martin (Dr Greg Butters),
Lisa Thornhill (Kimberly Goodman), Caroline Aaron (Laura),
Francesca P. Roberts (Judge Harris), Vyto Ruginis (Goodman)

Kimberley Goodman's husband wants to annul their marriage of many years because he's a sexually obsessive-compulsive – he claims this made him of unsound mind when he entered into the marriage. Richard's representing Kimberley with Ally in second chair.

With Greg back in her life, Ally has to face up to the threat of happiness. How can she cope, especially with Dr Tracy out of town?

Everything Stops For Ally: 'I think I need mental help. I feel happy. I'm just not equipped.' Ally fears she craves dependency and this makes her feel weak, and therefore a failure as a woman. She worries about falling for Greg, of trusting and depending on him. She hasn't loved anyone since Billy and fears loving anyone again – but she's working on it.

Fishisms: Richard doesn't think he and Ling are going anywhere as they have been dating for months and still haven't had sex.

More Fish wisdom: 'Ally, sex for men, when it's right it's right, when it's wrong it's still right. Fishism.'

Grrr!: Ling wants to sue the environment. She lets Richard brush up against her breasts in the elevator. 'Only when it's crowded,' he says. Ling says it's the time of the month when she feels like fun.

We Got It Together, Didn't We?: John discusses with Ally how he thinks Nelle has a spontaneity fetish, and how he intends to surprise and 'Don Juan' her. Nelle walks in and says she's very excited by this and is going to get ready. As John says, 'And now there's pressure.' Late at night he goes to Nelle in her office and she takes off her dress. 'I can't,' he says and runs away, leaving Nelle upset. The next day he explains that he's been living a fantasy with Nelle, and that was all he was ever doing: 'You don't really get me, and I don't really get you.' Nelle says John has met someone who shares his inner world, whether he knows it or not – Ally. 'But judging by the look I see on her face lately,' says Nelle, 'you may have waited too long.' Nelle runs off in tears, leaving John speechless.

Smile Therapy: John is suffering from a little 'Nelle anxiety', but offers to share his appointment with Dr Tracy with Ally, due to happiness being a far more urgent situation. John thinks he's close to a breakthrough with Nelle but later, when he runs away from their late-night assignation, his first port of call for help is Ally. He sucks on an ice lolly from her freezer.

Sub Zero: Nelle keeps suggesting she might chase after Billy: 'Kidding!'

Georgia On My Mind: Georgia is understandably annoyed with Nelle's games with Billy, and asks John what he sees in her.

DA Renee: When John arrives at the apartment after his problems with Nelle, Renee asks if it was performance anxiety, 'because that's big with lawyers'.

Girl Talk: Ling and Nelle meet at a café, and Ling asks if Nelle really wants to sleep with John. They discuss sex and Ling claims she can't even say the word because it drives men crazy . . . as well as some women. Indeed, when Ling does say 'sex' Nelle seems to get a little hot under the collar.

Men: Greg again, lifting Ally up and showing his credentials: 'I like marriage, but I only plan to do it once.' He tells Ally he didn't date anyone in Chicago.

Quotes: Ally: 'Don't trust passion, don't even trust trust, because even when you think you've found love, it's only temporary.'

Fantasy: When she's with Greg, Ally seems to walk on air, floating a foot off the ground – but Ling brings her crashing back to earth. As they stand on her doorstep, Ally and Greg seem to extend long tongues towards each other. Ally dreams of biting the nose off a journalist who wants to make her a better role model for professional women.

Fetishes: After the case is won, Richard touches Kimberly Goodman's wattle as she hugs Ally.

Song: Greg, Ally, Renee and Vonda all sing 'Ooh Child'. Ally sings 'Could I Have This Dance?' at the end of the episode, which fades into Vonda singing the same song.

... And Dance: Richard and John both perform the Barry White dance routine in the unisex. Elaine, then Ling, walk in and join in the routine. Nelle walks in and they all collapse – with Ling at the bottom of the pile. Greg and Ally slow-dance in the snow.

Also Starring: The big one – Bruce Willis as Dr Nickle, filling in for Tracy. Willis is best known for the *Die Hard* trilogy of action movies and probably received most acclaim for his role in Quentin Tarantino's *Pulp Fiction* (1994). His big break was the fantasy-tinged comedy *Moonlighting*, in many ways a precursor to *Ally McBeal*.

Shrink Wrapped: Dr Nickle, Tracy's temporary replacement, is relentlessly rude and aggressive towards Ally and John, who both refuse to sing their theme songs. Afterwards, John suggests they don't need Tracy anyway and should be each other's therapists.

The Case: Kimberly Goodman doesn't want her husband to annul their marriage by claiming he was under the influence of a sexual obsessive-compulsive disorder at the time. Richard argues Goodman just wants to avoid the alimony payments that will ensue if his wife divorces him. Goodman argues the sexual obsessive-compulsive disorder, which is rooted in childhood abuse and feelings of powerlessness, made him of unsound mind when he got married, and therefore the contract of marriage is not binding as he was in no fit state to enter into it. Even when Kimberly found out about her husband's compulsion-fuelled affairs, she tried to make the marriage work for the children. Kimberly's case is slightly weakened by her acknowledgement of her husband's condition, but the day is saved by Ally's impassioned closing, aimed at Mr Goodman: 'How dare you subject this woman to this embarrassment, how dare you subject your kids to it. How dare you live, you giant ass.' And the court applauds!

Judge Not: Judge Francesca Harris presides over the Goodman case.

Withdrawn: Counsel for Mr Goodman keeps objecting to Fish's comments, which he keeps withdrawing. A choice example is this objection: 'Move to strike, your honour, any man's crazy to get married. Withdrawn.'

Guilty?: Goodman doesn't deserve to pretend his marriage never happened because of his overactive dumbstick, and Judge Harris agrees, denying the Petition for Annulment.

Trivia: Ally says she had a dream where her face was on the cover of *Time* magazine – in the real world this really happened, with Ally suggested as the possible face of 90s' feminism.

The Verdict: 'As soon as you've found love, you've had it.' 'Love Unlimited' represents a massive return to form. The Goodman case is serious and cynical, but Ally's response to it, and her relationship with Greg, affirm that there is still love and honesty in the world. After a string of abstract cases, it's good to see the lawyers of Cage & Fish engaging in a case that really matters, jumping to the defence of someone who needs their help against a real villain like the odious Goodman. A strong moral debate is accompanied by some neat references to the media perception of the series, in the form of Ally railing against being a role model and dreaming of her face on the cover of *Time*. All this and a wacky cameo from, of all people, Bruce Willis – what more could you want? Well, to skip the next episode altogether perhaps . . .

213
Angels And Blimps

#2M13
8 February 1999

Written by David E. Kelley
Directed by Mel Damski

Cast: Jesse L. Martin (Dr Greg Butters),
Haley Joel Osment (Eric Stall), Mary Mara (Julie Stall),
Patrick Pankhurst (Dr Stewart), Keith MacKechnie (Gale),
Fred Sanders (Judge Stewart), Gary Graham (Rookey Wilcox),
Randy Oglesby (Harvey Kent)

Ally encounters a little boy who believes she's an angel and who, encouraged by Ling, wants to sue God for giving him cancer and killing his father with a lightning bolt. Meanwhile Richard and John defend a man charged with attempted murder.

Everything Stops For Ally: Ally considered becoming a doctor. She discounted the notion on the grounds that a) she doesn't like blood, b) she has a thing about death, but mostly c) because she looks terrible in hospital green.

Ally had a younger sister, who died aged five (when she was seven) of an unspecified illness. This destroyed Ally's faith in God for years, until her mother restored it to her by pointing out a Blimp and telling her that it was God, watching over them. Even young Eric can see that this was a pretty ridiculous story and that Ally must have been a particularly stupid child to fall for it.

The Boy Next Door: Nelle describes Billy as 'like a Ken doll' and is convinced that he likes her rather cute, though odd, panda-eyed facepaint. She's also convinced that this annoys Georgia a great deal.

Fishisms: Richard plans to defend a murder charge despite having no criminal law experience. Even Renee, who's prosecuting, advises him not to. Richard explains that 'if we lose the client goes to prison, we've lost his business anyway'. Richard's Withdrawn is so unorthodox that the judge explains to him that he is supposed to ask questions and 'should appear to be drug-free while doing so'.

Grrr!: Ling visits the hospital because she sent a sick friend of hers flowers, the friend subsequently died and Ling has returned to claim the flowers. She bumps into a guy in a wheelchair and harasses him about the disabled getting 'all the parking spaces'. She once again upbraids Ally for saying her name with a 'hard L'. She advises Eric to sue God. Billy and Ally are horrified to discover that Ling is a trained lawyer, having studied at Cornell alongside Nelle. Practice causes wrinkles. As Eric says, Ling is Cool.

Fantasy: 'One of my new year's resolutions – less fantasy, more reality,' says Ally, before snogging Dr Greg's face off.

Song: In this episode we're treated to 'This Old Heart Of Mine', sublimely performed by The Isley Brothers, and Vonda singing Don 'American Pie' McLean's tribute to Vincent van Gogh, 'Vincent' over the final scene. 'I'm Always Chasing Rainbows' (from the Broadway musical *Irene*) is sung by Eric's mother to her dying son.

Fashion Victims: Elaine and Georgia both look fabulous in grey. Ally sports a neat black trouser suit and grey V-neck T-shirt.

The Case: Harvey Kent, a man who tried to kill his wife and her lover – a man who was also his business partner of eleven years – after he discovered them in bed together. Renee is acting on behalf of the Commonwealth, and so John and Renee's cheery rivalry continues. 'I always beat you, I will do so here,' he tells her when she discovers that he, not Billy, will be defending the case. John uses an autobiographical story as part of his closing statement, explaining how on 4 April 1977 he asked Sharon Johnson, in his opinion the most beautiful girl at his school, to be his prom date. She agreed and he spent the next few weeks in a state of mind where 'humorous things seem more funny, joyous things more joyful'. Such is the price of love. He then argues that to commit like that to someone and to then not only discover that they are deceiving you and cheating on you, but are doing it with one of your best friends, would drive anyone into insanity. Renee attacks this defence: 'Sticks and stones may break my bones, but break my heart, I'll shoot you' which is rather an apposite summary, but the jury side with Cage.

Judge Not: Ling describes Whipper thus: 'Naked big hair blonde thing who believes in unicorns. She'll believe anything.' Harsh, but fair.

Also Starring: Gary Graham played Detective Matthew Sikes in the one full season and five TV movies that comprised FOX TV's *Alien Nation*. Haley Joel Osment starred in *The Sixth Sense* (M. Night Shyamalan, 1999).

The Verdict: This is a game of two halves. The Richard/John plotline is functional and works rather well, the Ally/Ling/Eric plotline is a different matter entirely. The legal gambit of obtaining money from the Church by naming God as the defendant in a legal challenge is a brilliant, deeply cynical move and exactly the sort of thing Ling would do; but the application of this plotline to a terminally ill boy unbalances the otherwise enjoyable legal chicanery. Eric's death scene is unpleasant to watch while lacking any real emotional impact, and the appearance of his 'soul' glowing like the spirit of Obi-Wan Kenobi is horrible. Possibly designed to negate Ally's bizarre legal victory, Eric's death just makes the episode even more grotesque, shapeless and ill-thought-out than it already is.

214
Pyramids On The Nile

#2M14
15 February 1999

Written by David E. Kelley
Directed by Elodie Keene

Cast: Jesse L. Martin (Dr Greg Butters),
Anna Nicole Smith (Myra Jacobs), Peter Birkenhead (Steve),
Lauren Bowles (Callie), Albert Hall (Judge Seymore Walsh),
Larry Brandenberg (Judge Raynsford Hopkins)

Nelle and John represent a couple who met at work and were sacked for not disclosing their relationship under the Cobb Company's 'Date and Tell' rules.

Back at the office, when Billy sees Ally kissing Greg, he begins to become jealous. Initially lashing out at Ally over a case she lost, Billy tells Ally he loves her, which leads to them kissing.

Ling joins the firm to the alarm of most of her new colleagues.

Everything Stops For Ally: When Billy confesses he still loves her, Ally thinks he should have kept quiet: 'That was a little too much truth.' Her reaction to Renee: 'I think I'd like to kill him.' However, when asked for instant reactions to both Billy and Greg, Ally replies that she loves them. She is insistent that she and Billy remember Georgia: 'Georgia, that's a very good word for us to keep saying, over and over.' Ally also claims to love Boz Scaggs – next to Ray Charles. Ally tells Billy she really likes Greg.

The Boy Next Door: Driven into a jealous rage after seeing Ally and Greg kissing, Billy accuses Ally of losing the Jacobs' case due to being unprepared and unprofessional, implying her mind is on Greg too much. He then redirects his anger into disgust at Richard hiring Ling and claims that he, Ally and Georgia are fighting for the soul of the firm. When Ally confronts him for overreacting, she thinks he might have bad news, that he might even be terminally ill. He admits what is really bothering him: 'I'll never love anybody like I loved and still love you.' He says he planned his resignation when Ling joined the firm, but found the idea of not seeing Ally every day difficult to take. Why should he cure himself of the best thing that ever happened to him?

Georgia On My Mind: Georgia demands to know how Richard can hire Ling to work at the firm. Although Georgia is completely clueless as to what is going on between Billy and Ally, they agree that they should keep her in mind at all times.

Fishisms: When Billy complains about Richard hiring Ling, Fish puts him in his place: 'Here's a flash, Billy – it's my firm.' He's not dumb – Ling is only paid for the work she brings in, mainly the legal aspects of her corporate ventures.

Bygones: On letting Ling join the firm: 'She licked my finger. I'm human. Asset. Firm. Bygones.'

Grrr!: Ling joins the firm, licking Richard's finger until he agrees. She doesn't laugh on weekdays, and tries on Elaine's face bra, which she is considering for her product line.

Smile Therapy: John defers to Richard on hiring matters. He is devastatingly dry in court and supremely confident when dealing with the battalion of lawyers sent against him. 'Sometimes I get overwhelmed by common sense,' he deadpans when faced with the absurdity of Cobb Company's rules.

We Got It Together, Didn't We?: While planning his closing, John tells Nelle she's a beautiful woman: 'I know it goes without saying, but the law shouldn't require it to go unsaid.' He brings their dating up in his closing – making Nelle slightly bashful – and tells the jury that although it didn't work out, the whole experience was worthwhile and people should not be prevented from finding someone at work.

Men: Ally is torn between Greg and Billy.

Quotes: Renee: 'If Billy's the guy, Billy's the guy.'

Fantasy: In court, when the judge asks Ally what her case is, she imagines her legs literally being sawn from under her. The colour drains out of Ally when she mistakenly thinks Georgia knows about Billy's confession.

Fetishes: Finger-licking. Ling gives Richard 'hair' – an operation she needs candles for – so that she can drip hot wax on him.

Guy Talk: Richard asks John about the hair tickle but John doesn't know what it is.

Song: Vonda sings '100 Tears Away' from the second *Ally* soundtrack album. 'Tell Him' (from the first soundtrack) speeds up and slows down according to Ally's mood. Vonda also sings 'You Belong To Me' from the first soundtrack; the lyrics gave this episode its title. Ally sings along tunelessly to 'Georgia' by Boz Scaggs.

. . . And Dance: John demonstrates a little Barry White hip-wiggle in court.

The Case (1): Ally and Billy represent Myra Jacobs, a woman who is not supposed to keep an inheritance if she remarries. Ally argues this is unfair, but loses. The viewer doesn't see enough of the case to make any solid judgement, but Billy seems certain they would have won if Ally had prepared properly.

The Case (2): The main event: John and Nelle represent a young couple sacked from Cobb Company for breaching a 'Date and Tell' rule. Cobb Company insist they need such rules to protect themselves against sexual harassment suits and employ an army of seven lawyers to make sure they win. John assures them they will lose. John and Nelle's clients testify they found the rule demeaning. They won't settle, even though John and Nelle aren't confident of winning. John's closing goes through the ups and downs of office romance, using him and Nelle as an example, and concludes that it's all worth it and ruling such things out is silly. Taking work out of the equation when it comes to finding love makes a difficult search even harder and people should be allowed to act like adults.

Judge Not: Judge Hopkins presides over Ally's case (1), while our old friend Judge Walsh takes the 'Date and Tell' case (2). When John gets the jury to repeat the word 'silly' during his closing, Judge Walsh isn't amused. John replies that considering his clients lost everything for keeping their private lives private, no one should be amused.

Guilty?: Cobb Company's 'Date and Tell' rule treats its staff like a potentially litigious nuisance and treats them with no respect at all. It's one rule that deserves to be broken. Thankfully the jury agree, and order Cobb Company to pay the plaintiffs $942,000 in damages for wrongful dismissal.

Toilet Humour: Billy accidentally hits Ally with a cubicle door in the unisex.

Kisses: The big one. Billy and Ally kiss in the office, only their mouths touching as they step around each other, bags and coats dropping to the floor. The kiss is shot as a full-blown love scene, treating the moment with all the intimacy the long-delayed reunion requires.

The Verdict: 'I just never figured you could meet the person of your dreams at age eight.' From the gutter to the stars in one bound, after the misery of 'Angels And Blimps', comes an episode that fires on all cylinders. With hindsight, Billy's increasing affection towards Ally and his hints at disenchantment with Georgia and his marriage, were all cleverly leading us towards his admission here. Billy and Ally could have been an on/off, will they/won't they type scenario for ever, but Kelley bravely decides to go for broke and push the series' founding romance towards a resolution, one way or another. In the presence of such scene stealers as Ling (who inevitably joins the firm in this episode) and the Nelle/John romance, it has been easy to lose sight of the show's star this season. 'Pyramids On The Nile' puts Ally and her love life centre stage once more, and by the end of the episode it's clear that hearts and friendships will be broken before this storyline is resolved.

215
Sideshow

#2M15
22 February 1999

Written by David E. Kelley
Directed by Alex Graves

Cast: Jesse L. Martin (Dr Greg Butters),
Tracey Ullman (Dr Tracy)

The unthinkable has happened: Ally kissed Billy. Should they betray Georgia and Greg so that they can be together? Does either of them have the nerve to go for it?

In an extended therapy with Tracy, Ally and Billy work out their feelings for one another, revealing more about themselves than ever before.

Everything Stops For Ally: Ally thinks there's no bigger betrayal than a kiss. While sex can be physical, even primal, a kiss is an act of pure intimacy. Her actions and conversation become increasingly erratic as she descends into confusion: 'Billy, I'll kiss you later' she tells him, then later, 'I think you should leave Georgia. Here. Leave here, dammit.' Ally thinks you can tell the way a guy makes love by the way he kisses.

The next day, when Elaine asks if she is free for a meeting with Billy she replies, 'He's not free for me so what difference does it make?' She tells Billy she's not going to allow him an easy get-out by being the one to hold up a stop sign, thereby allowing him to go back to Georgia thinking he followed his heart as far as he could. 'The road is open,' she tells him, 'let's go.' Billy replies that it's Ally who needs him to say 'not a chance', for exactly that reason. 'I've loved you my whole life,' she blurts. 'I've never loved anyone but you.' Billy suggests they meet at lunchtime at her place to make love.

Ally goes to see Tracy and tells her she believes Billy to be bluffing: 'He wants to be able to have his cake and not eat me. It. It.' She adds that if she has to second guess herself 'miserably ever after' then she wants him to too. She says she isn't going to have sex with Billy. Back at the office Greg is waiting for her and says that she shouldn't 'walk through life alone'. Ally replies, very drolly, that this isn't the problem at the moment. Greg agrees to give her time to sort out her 'crisis'. Ally meets Billy at her apartment during lunch and admits she's played this scenario through in her head many times. As they kiss Billy asks her how it ends. She replies that they kiss, and she cries. And she does. Ally goes to see Tracy, who wants to see Ally and Billy together. (See **Ally and Billy's Therapy Session**.)

The Boy Next Door: When Billy comes around to Ally's apartment and finds Greg there, he pretends to be arranging Ally's surprise birthday party with Renee – even though Ally is standing right in front of them. In his usual headstrong way he wants to immediately confront what happened and force a resolution, but he agrees to discuss matters the next day, by which time they should both know whether the kiss was a mistake or not.

Ally and Billy's Therapy Session

Not only does Ally and Billy's joint session with Dr Tracy take up the last third of 'Sideshow', it also brings to the boil all the issues bubbling between the two since the very first episode. Billy isn't happy to be there and when Tracy asks about Georgia he claims this has nothing to do with her. 'You kiss another woman and it has nothing to do with your wife?' asks Tracy incredulously. Tracy wants Billy to show her how he kissed Ally and promises not to touch herself. Billy gets angry and tries to leave when Tracy suggests he kissed Ally out of lust. When Tracy accuses him of running and Ally nods in agreement, Billy stays. When Billy asks Tracy what her 'human credentials' are, she says she isn't a happy person and gets frustrated when she sees people not taking a chance at happiness – she then sings a song. Tracy tells Billy his value system is the problem, as it won't let him accept he could act out of mere lust: 'Heaven forbid he could betray Georgia because he felt like it.' When Billy accuses her of trivialising the issue, Tracy replies that Billy's problem is he can't trivialise it, can't conceive that he could be unfaithful on a whim. Ally realises Tracy is right, that Billy believes in monogamy as much as her and has to believe there's a higher purpose to him betraying Georgia. Tracy points out that to sort out their feelings, Ally and Billy have to take guilt out of the equation. She gets them to hold hands and imagine themselves together at 60. When Billy says the older Ally has had 'a little work done', they get into an argument about Ally's vanity and whether she can ever be satisfied with anything. He refers to Ally as a narcissist and says he nevertheless fell in love with her because he was eight and too young to know better. He believes that although she believes in monogamy, she won't be monogamous: 'I think you have, and always will have, self-esteem issues, and if you don't get the necessary affirmation from your husband you might go some place else to look for it.' Ally says if Billy had shared that 'little insight' earlier he could have saved them both a lot of time and pain, as she would have got rid of him on the spot: 'Love, more than anything, is about respect,' she tells Billy. 'That wasn't respect.' She tells Billy he never loved her, and that's why he left her after one look at Georgia. Billy's reply is almost screamed: 'Love is wasted on you because you'll always be unhappy, that's why I left.' He couldn't have pulled her out of her world, she would have pulled him into hers. Ally replies that he's wrong, that she's gaining on happiness and will get there. Billy says he hopes to be there to see it. 'If you are,' Ally replies, 'it'll be from a distance. I love you. Goodbye.'

The next day he argues with Ally and tells her she's the only woman he can see himself growing old with. They end up shouting at each other, throwing accusations of weakness and deceit around. Billy suggests they meet at lunch: 'I can't go another day without making love to you.' After their assignation ends in her running away, he isn't keen on going to see Tracy with Ally, but goes nonetheless. (See **Ally and Billy's Therapy Session**.)

Shrink Wrapped: Much of the episode takes place in Dr Tracy's office, as Ally wrestles with her problems. Tracy's initial reaction is that Ally kissing Billy is 'fabulous'. She says that 'every patient that comes into this office thinks that he or she is the world's biggest loser. For the first time I agree.' She thinks Ally is a baby and throws her a rattle. When Ally says she hasn't slept with Greg, Tracy uses a remote to produce taped audience laughter. She tells Ally that she's a slut who finds sex meaningful. When Ally tries to leave, Tracy activates the sofa which sweeps Ally back off her feet. Tracy tells Ally she's falling for Greg but is afraid of falling in love again, so she is reaching for a guard rail to grab on to – Billy. Tracy tells Ally to sleep with Greg to find out if they're sexually compatible, then call her in the morning.

After her lunchtime encounter with Billy, Ally runs to Tracy for advice. Tracy tells her to dump Greg, as the whole situation is clearly about Ally and Billy. When Ally points out this directly contradicts her previous advice to sleep with Greg, Tracy replies that this is the problem when she doesn't take notes. Ally asks Tracy if she even knows what love is, but the anecdote Tracy replies with turns out to be filched from *Now Voyager* (Irving Rapper, 1942). Tracy decides she wants to see Ally and Billy together. (See **Ally and Billy's Therapy Session**.)

Doctor's Orders: Dr Greg Butters is put through the wringer by a wavering Ally. He waits an hour for her in a restaurant. Agreeing to give her time to sort out her problems, he sends Ally flowers with a card reading 'Thinking of you'.

DA Renee: Renee stops Ally from telling Greg about her kiss with Billy, taking the pragmatic line against Ally's idealism as usual. 'Every relationship starts with dishonesty, you dope,' she tells Ally. 'It sets the stage for marriage.' Renee is also practical about sexual compatibility and would never marry a man she hadn't slept with first.

Fantasy: When Renee says her new year's resolution is not to mess with other people's partners, Ally and Billy's eyebrows rise a good inch. Ally is pursued by cheesy saxophone music on the way to work, and sees a knife in Georgia's back. When Ally and Georgia are in the lift together the walls pulse with a claustrophobic heartbeat.

Office Gossip: When Billy and Ally shout at her, Elaine replies that they are 'Snap and Ish' respectively. Later, when Ally asks Elaine if Billy is in her office, she says no and smirks – Greg is in there instead. Elaine, like Tracy, is amazed Ally hasn't slept with Greg.

Fishisms: When asked if men judge relationships on the sex, Fish replies: 'Of course. True love means short refractory time. Fishism.'

Grrr!: Ling claims she is 'penile psychic', and can tell there's something up in the office.

Fetishes: Richard and Ling emerge from a cubicle in the unisex, him holding a just-licked finger.

Song: Vonda sings 'The Cheater' as Ally watches Billy in the office. Tracy sings the Soft Cell classic 'Tainted Love'.

Trivia: The music that stalks Ally to work was previously used in the UK as the theme to the gross-out sitcom *Bottom*. The way Ally runs home at lunch time suggests she lives *really* near the offices of Cage & Fish.

The Verdict: 'I'm gaining on happiness and I am going to get there one day.' No cases, no clients, no sub-plots, 'Sideshow' simply goes straight to the heart of Billy and Ally's relationship and works through all the issues between them. The result is the closure that Ally never got from her first break-up with Billy: she finds out that he doesn't really believe they can work out, that he can stray and disguise it as romance, and that ultimately they're not right for each other. All this in an explosive exchange of tears and laughs, confessions and insults. Lesser writers would have dragged the Billy/Ally flirtation begun in the previous episode out for weeks, but David E. Kelley just hits the viewer with it all at once. This emotional tidal wave represents a real change in the series, knocking the founding Ally/Billy romance out of the picture and beginning the loss of faith that will plague our heroine throughout the rest of the season. It really doesn't get any better than this.

216
Sex, Lies And Politics

#2M16
1 March 1999

Written by David E. Kelley
Directed by Arlene Sanford

Cast: Jesse L. Martin (Dr Greg Butters),
Harrison Page (Mark Newman),
Jennifer Holliday (Lisa Knowles),
Linda Gehringer (Shirley),
Albert Hall (Judge Seymore Walsh),
Peter White (Senator Watkins),
Zach Grenier (Benson)

John represents Peterson's, a bookstore on Beacon Hill which was put out of business by the political posturing of Senator Watkins. When the senator's counsel, Benson, backs out of a deal at the eleventh hour, John has to go into court without any preparation, to persuade the jury that the senator should pay for what he did. Having fired Richard from the case, John brings Ling in as second chair to help him out.

Meanwhile, Billy and Ally are busy not telling Georgia about recent events. But how long before guilt forces a confession from one of them?

Everything Stops For Ally: Guilt follows Ally everywhere. She confesses to Greg that for a couple of days there was someone else and Greg storms out, bumping into Billy on the way. That just leaves Georgia to deal with, and Billy and Ally both agree that not telling her is the right thing to do. Ally goes to church, but finds Mark's sermon to be too close to home with all its talk of adultery. Mark tells Ally afterwards that she didn't commit adultery and not to worry about betraying her friend – because if Georgia was her friend, she wouldn't have kissed her husband in the first place. Nevertheless, after Billy has let the cat out of the bag, Ally goes to see Georgia. 'I love your husband Georgia, I always have,' she says by way of explanation, but goes on to explain that she and Billy are not meant to be together, that Billy can't make her happy. Georgia asks her to leave.

Fantasy: Constant guilt-based delusions for Ally: Georgia's head pulsing, strangers criticising her, seeing the Pope in the street. Unfortunately, the dog urinating on her boots is real.

The Boy Next Door: All the counsellors Billy talks to tell him he shouldn't confess to Georgia, that it will only needlessly hurt her. He tells her anyway, unable to take the deceit any longer. Georgia suggests they split for a while. Billy later tells Ally that when Georgia told him she wanted to split, his life flashed before him. Ally replies that he should make sure he tells Georgia that. Later that night Billy finds Georgia in a bar alone, and although she looks away from him she doesn't resist when he puts his hand over hers.

Georgia On My Mind: We hear second-hand that Georgia thinks something is going on between Billy and Nelle. When Billy tells her he kissed Ally, her reply is predictable: 'I think maybe we should split for a while.' When Billy says he doesn't want that, Georgia replies that she does.

Smile Therapy: John resorts to Smile Therapy when Ling refers to him as 'the strange little man'.

Grrr!: In court Ling interrupts John's cross-examination of their client to complain that the witness is tedious and threatens the jury's attention span. This is just what John asked for. She is quite impressed by John after being in court with him: 'He's a funny little man. He cross-examined with *The Music Man*. I like it. He's fun.' Her closing argument is eloquent: 'He destroyed her and he's not even sorry.' She ends with an 'old Chinese saying', which is translated on screen as subtitles: 'It doesn't matter what I say here because none of you speak Chinese. But you can see from my sad face . . . I'm sympathetic. You hear from my tone it's appropriate to feel sorry for me. As I drop to a faint whisper you'll feel sadness yourself. I'm going to finish now, pretend to cry.'

Fishisms: Richard and Elaine are determined to get to the truth behind all the tension in the office. To that end Richard asks Billy if he and Ally are having sex: 'Put two and two together: sixty-nine.' Billy storms off without answering.

Office Gossip: Elaine thinks that Nelle is a tramp and, when she realises Nelle is behind her, claims she meant it in a good way. She stuffs tissues down her bra.

Doctor's Orders: Greg doesn't like being messed around, as being a doctor he doesn't get much time off.

Song: In court John sings 'You've Got Trouble' from *The Music Man* (Morton DaCosta, 1962). In church, Lisa sings 'Shake Your Tail Feather'.

. . . And Dance: Nelle catches Ally dancing to the guilty heartbeat.

The Case: Senator Watkins claimed in TV spots in the run-up to an election that Peterson's bookstore was selling prurient material. Shirley's store was put out of business, so she's suing the senator for damages.

Judge Not: Judge Seymore Walsh. When John repeats himself three times Judge Walsh points out that he is 'not impressed by trilogy'!

Withdrawn: Some interesting objections on display. Richard argues the jury should not be sequestered on the grounds that if they don't see the TV news they'll have to rely on what they hear in court. John throws him off the case and replaces him with Ling in second chair. Ling objects to her own witnesses and her own case in general, defending the senator's right to be a reprehensible scumbag. John sets a blowtorch off during the senator's testimony, claiming there must be gas in the room. John re-enacts sections of *The Music Man* when cross-examining the senator and gets the jury to sing along. Ling's closing is partially in Chinese, emphasising the emotion of her delivery over any actual content.

Guilty?: John and Ling deserve to win – the senator is a repulsive opportunist bigot – and the jury agrees with them, even after all the stunts in court, and gets the senator to pay $1.2 million in damages.

Toilet Humour: Ally follows Billy into the unisex and right into his stall. When they emerge to find Georgia standing there they realise it doesn't look good.

The Verdict: 'He's not even sorry.' The shockwave from Ally and Billy's kiss continues its impact as Georgia finds out and the tension spreads to the rest of the office. A lesson in the difficulties of knowing when to speak and when to keep silent, 'Sex, Lies And Politics' contrasts the impact of one politician's words with the possibly disastrous results of Billy confessing to Georgia. That there is no certain moral message here, only difficult decisions, makes the episode all the better. And, while the Ally/Billy/Georgia plotline is decidely downbeat, the tone is neatly lifted by John and Ling proving an unusually effective double act in court – their case against Senator Watkins is the kind of David and Goliath legal battle this show excels at, and this is no exception.

217
Civil War

#2M17
5 April 1999

Written by David E. Kelley
Directed by Billy Dickson

Cast: Jesse L. Martin (Dr Greg Butters),
Maria Pitillo (Paula Hunt), Anson Mount (Kevin Wah),
Carmen Argenziano (Harry Wah),
Robert Costanzo (George Chisholm),
Kurt Fuller (Bernard Marsh), Gibby Brand (Judge McGough)

Ally and John are representing Paula Hunt, who is making a civil date rape claim against one Kevin Wah on the grounds that he lied his way into her bed. To complicate matters, Kevin's father is Harry Wah, a big client of Richard's – so Richard and Georgia end up defending Kevin. It's war between the two partners of Cage & Fish.

Meanwhile another big client, George Chisholm, a big client who sweats profusely, is under investigation by the IRS. How can Nelle and Ling make him seem trustworthy when he perspires so much?

Everything Stops For Ally: Ally is still trying to get back with Greg, and when she gets a call from the phone company while waiting for Greg to call she calls the operator an 'annoying little bitch'. She claims she doesn't even want to speak to Greg: 'I just want him to call me so I can hang up.' Ally and Georgia clash in court as well as out of it, with Georgia deliberately bumping Ally. The second time Georgia barges past her, this time in the unisex, things deteriorate into actual fighting. At one point in the fight Ally climbs up onto a stall wall and jumps back in in true tag team wrestling fashion. Ally ends up in hospital with a cut on her head. When Greg comes to treat her wound, she tries to patch things up between them: 'People get back together in the strangest of ways,' she says. All she gets in return is a tetanus shot. Ally seems slightly sickened by Kevin and Paula being happy at the end – understandable perhaps, as she actually believed in Paula's case.

Georgia On My Mind: Georgia is understandably aggressive towards Ally and stops Ally having Billy as her second chair. When Georgia bumps into Ally for a second time, in the unisex no less, things rapidly descend into a full-blown scrap. Nelle tries to intervene and gets dragged in, while Ling jumps in to Nelle's defence. They all end up in a dirty great mêlée, and Billy and Richard have to break it up.

Smile Therapy: John once licked out his date's hearing aid while at college. He gives Ally the following sage advice: 'A relationship is rarely more passionate than it is during the beginning. If you're kissing somebody else during the beginning Greg would be a fool not to run.' John worries that the firm will not only lose a major client in Harry Wah, but that John and Richard will lose their friendship – all because John is better than Richard and will inevitably beat him in court. John and Richard hear military music as they face off. John considers the office hostile territory, so he paces barefoot at Ally's apartment to compose his closing argument. When Ally is injured, he takes her a stuffed parrot in hospital.

Fishisms: Richard prefers women with fat, juicy tongues to those with thin, lizard-like tongues. He considers Harry Wah a 'long-time meal ticket' and reassures him by telling Harry that Ally 'stinks'. Richard orchestrates the idea of the firm representing both sides in the trial: 'Fees on both sides, that's music.' Richard refutes John's suggestion that he's a better litigator than Richard and they're still bickering over their respective abilities when the case is settled. Richard gives Ally a 'Get Well Soon' balloon.

Bygones: 'Ally, what's with the big kiss. Case. Bygones.'

Sub Zero: Nelle claims not to sweat and dislikes those who do. She even claims to be allergic to sweat at one point. Nonetheless she lands George's case due to her tax expertise. To make George seem sincere they have to stop him sweating – so Ling and Nelle paint him with linament. Unfortunately, it doesn't work and a drop of sweat falls off George's nose – with spectacular cinematic effect – in his meeting with Marsh, the man from the IRS. Nelle thinks the meeting was a disaster and Ling tells her to go see Marsh with her hair down, as Ling thinks he likes Nelle. This works, which earns Nelle a hug from George – she squeals in discomfort.

Grrr!: To test George's ability to handle pressure, Nelle gets Ling to ask him a hard question: 'Is it hard going through life as a soggy hog?' she demands.

Office Gossip: When Ally asks Elaine if there have been any messages for her, she specifically replies that Greg hasn't called. Elaine videotapes the fight in the unisex.

DA Renee: Renee neatly sums up the developing conflicts at the firm: 'Your office is becoming a *hot* little place to work!' After Ally gets back from hospital, having been dumped by Greg, Renee passes her the inflatable man.

Guy Talk: Billy makes the mistake of telling Richard and John about kissing Ally. Richard is more interested in the mechanics of the kiss than anything else: 'She has one of those fat, wet, juicy tongues, doesn't she?' Richard does, however, think it was unconscionable – to tell Georgia, that is. Richard believes you should only tell if you know you're about to get caught.

Men: Ally thinks Kevin Wah is a 'spanky toy'.

Doctor's Orders: Greg comes to treat her in hospital and gives her the final brush-off: 'I don't know what you kissing Billy says about you and Billy, but it does say something about you and me. And I don't really need to tell you that, do I?'

Fantasy: When Ally tells John that she confessed to Greg about her kiss with Billy, she sees a little clock-cuckoo pop out of John's forehead. When Georgia and Ally face off in court, their heads turn into those of hissing cats. When Ally gets an intrusive call from the phone company while waiting for Greg to call, she imagines reaching down the line and pulling the caller's head out of the receiver.

Fetishes: When Richard tries to get Ally to dump her client or throw the case, she tickles his wattle while telling him where to get off.

Ouch!: Ally sustains a cut on the head during the fight in the unisex. Greg injects a tetanus shot into her buttock.

Fashion Victims: Nelle and Ling wear aprons and rubber gloves while painting George with linament.

The Case: A civil date rape claim made by Paula Hunt against Kevin Wah. Paula and Kevin met at a party and instantly felt a connection, they then spent two nights talking about all sorts of things, and on the third night they made love. A couple of days later Kevin revealed the truth – that he had learnt how to 'connect' with her by lurking in her internet chat room. Paula's claim is that although Kevin didn't force himself on her at all, he turned out to be someone other than the person she wished to sleep with. Georgia gets Paula to admit she laughed at Kevin's jokes and pretended to be interested in football – both deceptions and distortions of the truth about herself. Kevin testifies that he went into Paula's chatroom so that he could find her interests, as he had seen her before but was too shy to approach her. He knew that girls liked to feel special, so he took an interest. When Richard asks him why he felt the need to be honest, Kevin says that he genuinely believed all that 'sappy soul' stuff. Kevin insists that he never said anything he didn't mean. In his closing John argues for honesty and values: 'Attach a value to what he did.' Richard argues the difference between men and women and how they knowingly deceive each other. He also points out that Kevin was genuinely falling in love with Paula and didn't run off the next day: 'Kevin Wah was in this for real.'

Withdrawn: When Paula talks about 'souls interconnecting', Richard objects that such sentimentality shouldn't go unpunished, but the judge overrules him. John goes for a very low blow, using Georgia's marital problems to get at her in court. Cage bombards Fish with constant objections to throw him off course. Georgia and Fish constantly object to John's badgering of Kevin.

Guilty?: We're with Richard here. The idea that a man could be charged with rape after having had consensual sex with someone whom he has simply a) talked himself up to, and b) affected a greater interest in her hobbies than he really has is draconian. Worse, it insults people who genuinely have been raped, trivialising their trauma by putting it on the same level as this nonsense. On screen, the case is never resolved – Kevin and Paula patch things up and Harry Wah agrees to pay all expenses. However, the moral victory is Richard's, whose closing convinces Paula of Kevin's good intentions.

The Verdict: 'We all pretend to be what the other wants to see. It's part of the mating dance.' More lightweight than the previous couple of episodes, 'Civil War' is more concerned with the witty exchanges between the battling partners than any deeper issues, but that isn't necessarily a bad thing. Conflict is the engine of most humour, and the clashes between John and Richard, Ally and Georgia, and in particular the massive punch-up between the women in the unisex are all milked for the maximum comedy value. Such high entertainment is provided that we'll even forgive the stupid and offensive case John and Ally fight – and the fact that our heroes actually seem to agree with it.

218
Those Lips, That Hand

#2M18
19 April 1999

Written by David E. Kelley
Directed by Arlene Sanford

Cast: Barry White (Himself), Dr Joyce Brothers (Herself),
Dyan Cannon (Judge 'Whipper' Cone),
Albert Hall (Judge Seymore Walsh),
Tony Shalhoub (Shepley), Jody Wood (Kent),
Brad Blaisdell (Dr Moreno)

Albert Shepley claims he didn't murder his wife. In which case, why did he cut off her hand? John and Ally defend Shepley, while Renee is determined to see him go down.

Billy and Georgia have a difficult case of their own: insurance salesman Ross Fineman claims he was sacked out of ageism, but his employers claim no one can trust a salesman with an outrageous comb-over. Will a court order be issued to explore Ross's hair disaster, and can Georgia keep a straight face through the deposition?

Richard, frustrated by the fact he has yet to get Ling into bed, dumps her. Ling retaliates with temptation, but Richard has a few tricks of his own.

While others face murder charges, unemployment and loneliness, John and Ally face something far worse: their birthdays and the prospect of getting old. Can Nelle rescue John from the birthday blues? Only with some very special help . . .

Everything Stops For Ally: Ally finds a wrinkle and along with her twenty-ninth birthday this triggers a fit of obsession about ageing. She's worried about life passing her by: 'Do you realise all I got from my last relationship was a tetanus shot?' When Renee replies that her twenties have been a big disaster and she should be glad they're almost over, Ally resorts to smile therapy. When John is stuck in 'birthday blues', she realises she needs to do the closing rather than him. Her closing argument is as personal as ever, referring to Renee accusing her of being hopeless: 'Sometimes I wonder whether hope is the only thing I've got going.' She talks about her birthday, her fears of underachievement and her desire for emotional dependence, to be with someone she can't live without. Ally goes through a bitter struggle with Renee over the Shepley case, but afterwards tells Renee she loves her. Ally is moved to tears by Elaine doing 'a number' for her.

DA Renee: 'Ally, if you got a new wrinkle, I'm sure we would have seen something on the news.' When Ally is obsessing about her wrinkle, Renee reminds her that they both have a murder case tomorrow – the same murder case, in fact, on opposing sides. Renee doesn't want the Biscuit pulling any stunts or she'll have him in contempt. In fact, she begins to suspect that even Ally's usual self-obsession might, in this case, be a tactic to distract her from her preparations. Her conflict with Ally over the case, in and out of court, is bitter: 'Only you could interpret mutilation as love,' she tells Ally. She also tells Ally she is hopeless. Her summing-up in court is typical Renee pragmatism: 'Sometimes how it looks is exactly how it is.'

Smile Therapy: John doesn't make a fuss about his birthday, and it's only revealed to the rest of the office because Nelle brings it up. He doesn't want Elaine to organise a double celebration for him and Ally. John is uncomfortable that he's turning thirty-five and thinks he should be further along in life. He has difficulty summoning a defence for Albert, and when Shepley asks how anyone could think he would kill the love of his life, John replies that, to play devil's advocate, 'you took a power saw to her'. John tells Ally he has never been in love during his adult life and admits that Nelle said he was in love with Ally. He kisses Ally, for the joy of the moment. Later he bemoans being thirty-five, and wishes for some kind of omen. After winning the Shepley case, he reassures Renee that Shepley really is innocent – then kisses her too. 'Life is for the living,' he tells her, 'I like it.' At the bar he is reticent about Nelle's mystery gift, but dumbstruck and delighted by Barry White. He dances awestruck around White before the rest of the cast join him to do his Barry White dance routine.

Sub Zero: When John claims trials make him nervous, Nelle knows him well enough to tell that's a lie: trials actually relax him. When she tells John she ordered up 'a little something' for his birthday he replies he can't stand to be disparaged. When it turns out to be Barry White singing personally for him, Nelle's delight at John's amazed reaction is obvious.

We Got It Together, Didn't We?: When John confesses his concerns about ageing to Nelle, she replies that 'to get further along sometimes you have to go down that road not taken.' 'I'm not talking about me,' she hastily adds. For John's birthday Nelle manages to give him a personal appearance by Barry White – the omen he was looking for.

The Boy Next Door: Billy chooses Georgia to back him up on Ross's case because he wants a way, any way, to reconnect with her. He claims that he only knew Ross's hair was a comb-over because Georgia told him. After Georgia sweetly persuades Ross that his new haircut is good and it looks handsome, Billy tells her she is a good person and that it's good to see her smile. When she replies, 'Some things can't just be combed over,' Billy says he'd like to work on that.

Georgia On My Mind: Georgia finds it hard not to crack up laughing when she first meets Ross Fineman, who has an elaborate comb-over that spirals over his bald head. In the end Georgia has the nerve to tell Ross that *everyone* can tell his hair is a comb-over, and that it looks terrible. She tells Ross he is a handsome man and persuades him to accept a haircut in exchange for his job back. Georgia seems to accept Billy's offer to help work things out between them.

Fishisms: Fish checks the 'chemistry' is OK between Billy and Georgia. Fish tells Ling he wants to break up: 'I adore you, but for me a relationship has to include – how shall I put it – sex.' Ling points out the things they do engage in – hair, finger-licking – and Richard agrees that these are good, but asks, 'Whatever happened to good old-fashioned premarital intercourse?' Physically he can't take it any more. To prove his seriousness about breaking up he tries to withhold his finger from Ling but his resistance is brief. She licks his finger, lets him touch her wattle, and caresses him with her hair, then walks out of the office leaving him face down on the floor. Interestingly, the person Richard turns to for advice is Elaine, the one person in the office as sexually obsessed as he is. His frustration at the distanced relationship with Ling is obvious: 'I dumped her and things haven't really changed –

what does that tell you?' He tells Ling that he feels like a little yo-yo she plays with. After Ling confesses she is destructively great in bed, Richard isn't intimidated and says he isn't worried about satisfying her: 'It's not about pleasing you, the idea's making me happy.' He then goes on the offensive, demonstrating the knee-pit trick to her, and leaving her gasping for more. He even uses the promise of more knee-pit action to tempt Ling onto the dance floor after she claims to have stage fright.

Grrr!: When Richard talks about his human desires, Ling replies, 'It must be hard being human. I wouldn't know, because I've never tried it.' Ling thinks men want what they can't have, but seems to be persuaded otherwise by Elaine. She storms into Richard's office angry that he talked to Elaine about their sex life. 'Ling, we don't have a sex life,' he replies. She tells Richard that if she made love to him he'd go blind, that she's amazing in bed and 'cannot take another man saying there's nobody else after me'. No matter what she does, sex with her is apparently always the best the man has ever had. Her relationships therefore always end up ruined, with the man wanting to do nothing apart from have sex. She then storms back out of Richard's office, pausing only to cut Ross's hair in less than ten seconds. At the bar, when Richard demonstrates the knee-pit trick, she clearly enjoys it and wants more.

Office Gossip: Elaine has prepared a number for Ally's birthday, to be performed at the bar: she says Ally doesn't like the attention and Elaine is helping her by making herself the centre of attention. She criticises her backing singers, telling them to work harder. She offers to talk to Ling on Richard's behalf and does indeed give Ling a large dose of psychobabble about the ego and the id. Her message is simple: no matter how good all the tricks Ling employs to keep men wanting what they can't have are, 'eventually the little divining rod points them to what they can have'. While doing her number for Ally, Elaine sits on Ross's knee and kisses his bald head, a sweet little gesture to restore his self-esteem.

Fantasy: When Ally's birthday is mentioned, Ling asks, 'Would this be the big three five?' Ally imagines machine-gunning Ling to death for that little remark.

Fetishes: 'You're not the only one with erogenous tricks; I know a couple of ways to drive you crazy.' After being put in his place by Ling through the application of finger-licking, hair massages and so on, Richard fights back by blowing his fingers and touching Ling in a very delicate place – the knee pit. When Ling asks who taught him that, Richard replies, 'Oh, I'm the teacher on this one.'

Song: Elaine sings 'My Pledge of Love' at the bar for Ally's birthday. Ally hears Vonda singing about taking someone's hand – only for the song to be interrupted by the noise of a powersaw. Barry White, in person, sings, 'You're the First, the Last, My Everything' in the bar.

. . . And Dance: John steps up to dance around Barry White as he sings. The entire cast then join him to perform his dance routine, perfectly in sync. A fantastic moment and a pay-off to all the scenes where people mimic John's dancing through the season.

Also Starring: Tony Shalhoub, who plays amateur mortician Albert Shepley, is a notable character actor with prominent roles in films as diverse as *The Siege* and *Paulie*.

The Case (1): When Albert Shepley's wife died of a heart attack after years of vegetation, he wanted to keep a piece of her – so he hacked off her hand with a powersaw. He was taking the hand to his brother, a mortician, to have it preserved when he was pulled over by the police. Kent, the policeman who stopped him, says that Shepley was acting suspiciously when he was stopped for speeding and jumping a red light. When Kent searched the car he found the severed hand, and after obtaining a warrant they searched Shepley's house and found his wife's body. Shepley was then arrested for murder. When John presses him, Kent admits that Shepley volunteered all the information and told Kent about the hand and the body at the house without being pressed, and that Shepley was not necessarily suspicious –

he could also be described as emotional, stressed or many other words. John suggests the prosecution has rehearsed Kent to stitch up Shepley. Dr Moreno, the coroner, testifies that the likely cause of Mrs Shepley's death was trauma from her hand being amputated, but then has to admit that the evidence is inconclusive, and that death could have occurred before the limb was removed. Dr Brothers testifies that the loss of a loved one could drive a man to apparently irrational behaviour like the amputation. Renee offers a reduction to manslaughter, but Shepley refuses even though John is worried they might not win. Shepley testifies in court that he held his wife's hand all through her illness and when she died he just couldn't let go. Renee's closing emphasises the cost of home care, Shepley telling people he knew he hoped his wife wouldn't live long enough to suffer, and the nature of the crime: 'This isn't what loved ones do to one another.' Ally argues that Shepley didn't kill his wife, he loved her, and removing her hand was an act driven by being madly in love. Ally says: 'I pray that one day I'll know some of that madness,' and goes on to repeat that Shepley loved his wife so much he just found it hard to let go.

Whip-Lash!: Whipper is the judge in the Shepley case. She isn't impressed by the constant objections flying from both sides. Her failure to support John's objections disappoint him – he claims to have always considered her special.

Withdrawn: John objects to Kent giving psychological testimony. John insists the arrest was silly and tries to get the jury to say it with him. As John steps up to cross-examine Kent, Renee, getting paranoid, objects to John's shoes on the presumption they will squeak. The shoes stay silent. 'It's some trick,' Renee insists weakly. Renee objects to the idea that Kent's testimony has been slanted by the prosecution to put the worst possible spin on Albert Shepley's actions. Renee activates a powersaw in court.

Guilty? (1): Shepley is clearly nuts, but not a murderer. The jury agree and set him free. When Shepley asks Ally if he would be pushing his luck to ask for the hand back, Ally tells him firmly that this would be a bad idea.

The Case (2): Billy and Georgia represent Ross Fineman, who is suing for wrongful termination which he claims was due to ageism. In fact it's because of Ross's hideous, spiralling comb-over haircut. Why should a client trust the honesty of a man who isn't even honest about his own baldness? Opposing counsel goes to Judge Walsh for a court order to lift the offending hair and videotape it, in case Ross has the evidence cut off before trial. Reluctantly, Walsh agrees.

Guilty? (2): We wouldn't buy a newspaper from a man with hair like that. Ross's employer offers him his job back if he gets his hair cut, and after some persuasion from Georgia he agrees.

Hit The Bar: The bar is the venue for Ally and John's birthday, where Elaine sings a number for Ally and Barry White appears to sing a song for John.

The Verdict: 'He loved her more than life, and when she died he couldn't bring himself to let go.' It's been a while since Cage & Fish were involved in a murder trial, which always raises the stakes, and here we have a complex and morbid case to heighten the drama, especially with Ally and Renee defending and prosecuting respectively. There's a lot packed into 'Those Lips, That Hand', with all of the regulars getting a surprisingly large amount to do, all at the same time. The result is one of the most satisfying and important episodes of the season, with relationships shifting all around and everything up for grabs. When everyone converges at the bar in the final scene, resulting in the regular cast performing a dance routine in front of Barry White, the result is magical and leaves the viewer with a warm, fuzzy feeling for days afterwards.

219
Let's Dance

#2M19
26 April 1999

Written by David E. Kelley
Directed by Ben Lewin

Cast: Rosie O'Donnell (Dr Hooper),
Dyan Cannon (Judge 'Whipper' Cone),
Wendy Worthington (Margaret Camaro),
Latanya Richardson (Attorney Rose), David Dukes (Biblico),
Kate McNeil (Marianne Harper)

Having turned thirty-five, John's felt a change in himself. Unfortunately, Nelle doesn't seem to notice. However, Renee is aware of the change . . .

In court, John, Richard and Nelle are defending a law firm accused of discriminating against women. Is motherhood compatible with a high level career in the law?

Billy and Georgia are in therapy, but their therapist doesn't seem very helpful.

Last but not least, Elaine is preparing for a major dance contest when her partner drops out. Who can help her – surely not *Ling*?

Everything Stops For Ally: Ally doesn't like the fact that the firm is representing Biblico, Hutchings & Gold, a firm she thinks discriminates against women. She persuades Ling to continue as Elaine's dance partner for the swing contest with a very patronising speech about how Elaine doesn't get to do the important things that they, as lawyers, get to do, and that Elaine is somewhat pathetic. Ally is initially reluctant to go along to Billy and Georgia's therapy session, but eventually agrees – after running it by Tracy. At the therapy session she loses her temper and stamps on Hooper's foot so hard she breaks it. Ally patches things up with Elaine by telling her after the dance contest that she watched with envy.

Smile Therapy: John has undergone a change: he's more confident, especially with women, and seems to be able to tap into the power of Barry White at will. When Nelle doesn't notice the change in him and seems more interested in her case, he instead asks Renee out on a date. He asks if Renee is 'woman enough' to handle him, and when he gives her the knee-pit treatment he asks her to push his head between her breasts.

John is intuitive enough to realise that Nelle's parents divorced when she was young.

Sub Zero: Nelle says she got Barry White to appear at John's birthday by pulling strings, with help from Ling. Nelle doesn't want children and is irritated by the fact that John and Richard seem to presume that all women want kids. When Richard shows Nelle the knee-pit manoeuvre she's so curious about, her hair pops out of its bun. Nelle's parents split up when she was six. Although she talks about how lucky she was to have two of everything, she isn't very convincing. We later see Nelle at home, crying over her two teddy bears.

We Got It Together, Didn't We?: John tells Nelle he's changed his mind and might fall for her after all. He suggests they go out on a date, but Nelle says she's busy with a big trial – it seems she didn't notice the change. Nelle is notably jealous as John touches Renee's knee pit, and she shoves his head into her bosom. John's attempt to get Nelle to talk about the pain of her parents' divorce doesn't bring them any closer: 'John, if this is some weak attempt to try and get me to open up, I don't do that.'

Fishisms: Richard, ever the king of tact, lists the problems he thinks women bring to the workplace. He thinks Ally is such a good example of these that they should introduce her as an exhibit.

Office Gossip: Elaine has the final round of a big dance contest coming up, but her partner has torn his Achilles tendon. She is initially reluctant to dance with the only person available – Ling. Elaine is offended by the portrait of her life Ally uses to persuade Ling to stay in the contest, and her response is a neat riposte to the arrogance of lawyers and other professionals: 'Not everybody wants to be a lawyer, or a professional. I like my life, I like being a secretary. And I like that it gives me free time to do other things. To dance, to invent my stupid face bras. And I'm really sorry to disappoint you Ally, but I like my life.' You go, girl!

Grrr!: Ling can swing – she used to do it with her dad. When the others express surprise at her dancing abilities, Ling is exasperated: 'Don't you people know by now, I can do anything!' While practising with Elaine she backs out due to exhaustion, but is persuaded to continue by Ally. Unsurprisingly, Ling isn't interested in doing anything she can't win at.

The Boy Next Door: Billy is offended and alarmed by his and Georgia's marriage guidance counsellor. 'Am I going to get a fair trial with this person?' he asks. Billy describes his recent sex life with Georgia as 'indifferent'. When Ally initially refuses to come to one of his therapy sessions with Georgia, Billy loses his temper: 'You helped to ruin my marriage, you can't be bothered to help repair it?' As Ally says, 'That's a terrible thing to say.'

Georgia On My Mind: Georgia is clearly gratified to see Billy getting a hard time from their counsellor.

Shrink Wrapped: Billy and Georgia are seeing an aggressive, gum-chewing marriage guidance counsellor, Dr Hooper. 'If you were my husband, I'd kick your ass,' she tells Billy. When he complains, she replies, 'This is me neutral. Imagine me taking sides.' She thinks Billy is an awful person, not just to Georgia but to Ally. When Billy complains all she wants to talk about is sex, Hooper replies, 'Freud was a perv.' After Ally breaks Hooper's foot, Billy turns to Georgia: 'Without renouncing our need for therapy, she's terrible.' They agree to discuss their problems over lunch, and Georgia allows Billy to take her hand along the way.

DA Renee: Renee notices the change in John and accepts when he asks her out on a date. Her reaction to him touching her knee pit is extreme pleasure: 'Stop and I'll kill you.' She enjoys the date and asks John to call her some time.

Introducing: Margaret Camaro, the feminist expert who is here called in to speak about the long hours' culture and gender bias. She is insulted by Fish in court.

Fantasy: Ally turns grey when she realises Elaine has been listening to Ally's little speech about how empty Elaine's life is.

Fetishes: Richard gives Ling a little knee-pit action during the morning meeting. John asks Richard to demonstrate the knee-pit technique for his date with Renee. Richard describes Nelle as 'young blonde wattle'.

Song: Big Bad Voodoo Daddy play the music at the dance contest. John Cage hears a whole lot of Barry White in his head, now he's experienced 'the change'. Vonda sings 'Baby, Don't You Break My Heart Slow' from the second *Ally* soundtrack album.

. . . And Dance: John dances in the elevator to the Barry White music in his head. At the contest, Elaine and Ling swing! They manage well enough to qualify.

Fashion Victims: Another great co-ordinating outfit from Billy, this time in autumnal rusty browns. Ling wears a 30s-style man's suit, complete with hat, to dance in the swing contest.

The Case: Marianne Harper is a lawyer who went on maternity leave and returned to find she wasn't on the same track to partnership she was on before she had her baby. John, Richard and Nelle are defending the firm. Nelle argues that she didn't, indeed couldn't, put in the same amount of hours on the job once she had a baby.

Withdrawn: John's clockwork monkey goes off in court. When Camaro takes the stand, Richard asks her whether she is a lesbian, if she's married, and asks if Camaro is the name of a 'muscle car'. Opposing counsel understandably raise repeated objections to this line of question. Cage understandably insists on taking over the cross-examination.

Whip-Lash!: Whipper presides over the Camaro case and doesn't tolerate Fish's inappropriate line of questioning with Camaro: 'This court isn't even going to dignify that blatant bigotry.'

Guilty?: They deserve to win – to allow women who go home to their children to reap the same awards as people who spend those extra hours at work is discriminating against people who are genuinely dedicated to their jobs. Unfortunately, Biblico says on the stand that because of this women are a worse bet for hiring than men, which loses them the case.

Also Starring: Rosie O'Donnell, who plays Billy and Georgia's marriage guidance counsellor, has appeared in many films and TV shows. Her most notable roles include Betty Rubble in the big budget *The Flintstones* (Brian Levant, 1994) and hosting her own chat show.

Toilet Humour: Ally follows Ling into the unisex to argue how desperate Elaine is, not realising that Elaine is in one of the stalls with her feet up.

The Verdict: 'Hurt a lot, huh?' Anything would be a step down from the heights of last week, but thankfully this isn't too much of a drop from the previous episode. The change in John, his new-found confidence and gift with women, is both satisfying in character terms and the vehicle for some great comic moments. 'Let's Dance' is also, along with the next episode, a chance for Elaine to take the spotlight for a while. While relatively light on Ms McBeal herself, this is a worthwhile episode full of nice touches. Such a shame it's undermined by the idea that people who don't want children must be the product of a broken home, the kind of reactionary amateur psychology we could all do without.

220
Only The Lonely

#2M20
3 May 1999

Teleplay by David E. Kelley
Story by Andi Bushell, Jim Draytor and David E. Kelley
Directed by Vincent Misano

Cast: Jesse L. Martin (Dr Greg Butters),
Jennifer Rhodes (Gladys), Mary McDonough (Gloria),
Debra Christofferson (Vicki Sharp), Michael Gross (Volpe),
Bruce McCarty (Goodman), Gabrielle Ford (Martha),

Ashley Gardner (Casey),
Holland Taylor (Infomercial Actress)

Elaine's face bra infomercial is on air and success seems
assured. But Elaine learns a lesson in betrayal when her Aunt
Gladys sues her, claiming Elaine stole the idea of the face bra
from her dead daughter, Martha. Meanwhile Billy defends a
man accused of encouraging his employees to have fun, and
Nelle leads John into new territory . . .

Everything Stops For Ally: When John comes to Ally with
his problems, she manages to turn it into a conversation about
her problems in just eight seconds. Ally misses Greg. When
John asks if Greg is seeing somebody else, Ally replies, 'No,
he's just limited the field to not me.' When John asks Ally if
women like to be dominated, Ally says they don't. Ally spots
John and Nelle kissing, and it touches her. 'Couplehood is
good,' she says. She wants to follow in John's footsteps: 'It's
all about attitude, Renee, and I'm going to have my change
too.' The next morning Ally tries to have a change, acting sexy
and confident as she strides to work. She offers Elaine some
useful advice: 'You just learned the first negative thing about
success: people come out of the woodwork.' On John's suggestion Ally goes to see Greg, only to spot him from a distance, coming out of the hospital with another woman. Ally
goes home alone to Renee – and ice cream.

Office Gossip: Elaine watches her own face bra infomercial
with the rest of the cast in Ally's apartment. The next day she
wears the face bra as she tells her colleagues about the 800
overnight orders received – which is equal with the vegematic,
and slightly less than the spray-on hair. Elaine is shocked when
her Aunt Gladys sues her and doubly shocked when she finds
out her late cousin, Martha, claimed to have invented the face
bra. Elaine had always thought she and Martha were close. In
high school Elaine's friends didn't want to bring their boy-
friends around in case Elaine tried to steal them. They didn't
trust her and thought she always wanted to be the centre of
attention. Elaine is at least partially upset because she was

the only one who was ever kind to Martha. She remembers throwing a birthday party for Martha which no one else attended – and luckily she taped the party, including an on-camera conversation where Martha asked Elaine about her face bra idea. Once proven innocent, Elaine is left victorious but with her faith in friends and family shattered. When interviewed for cable TV, she hesitates when asked how her workmates reacted to her success, and overcompensates when asked about her family.

The Boy Next Door: Billy rants about how women, through constant harassment complaints and obsessing about their bodies, damage their own case for equality. Vicki Sharp is right when she says Billy 'doesn't get it' in relation to the bathing suit case. But why should he? The case is ludicrous.

We Got It Together, Didn't We?: John attempts to surprise Nelle with a little knee-pit action, but Nelle just shrieks, falls over him and they end up in a heap. In the unisex, John goes for broke: 'Let's just go out. End of the day we'll grab something to eat and just go. Like we read about these people with lives do.' Nelle accepts but insists they go out properly, not just to the bar. She chooses the place, a riotous hip-hop bar and John proves his mettle by dancing with Richard, to the delight of the crowd. Nelle admits to John afterwards that it was a test, and they kiss. The next day Nelle invites John over to her place for dinner. Ally and Fish both tell John that this means Nelle wants to sleep with him, and he's confident and calm about it. He thinks it's right, he likes Nelle. When he gets to her apartment that night, Nelle says that a lot of men think a woman inviting them over for dinner means she wants to have sex. John hesitates on the doorstep, and admits that maybe that's what he wanted. Nelle tells him that he will, at the very least, have to eat first. They kiss and later, at last, make love.

Smile Therapy: John tries to give the knee-pit treatment to Nelle, but ends up with a heel in the eye instead. He's impressed that Ally manages to turn his problems into a conversation about her so quickly – her record is six seconds. John tells Ally to take a second run with Greg, in the way that he's taking a second run at Nelle. John gets Richard and Ling to come along with him and Nelle as a double date because, for some reason, Richard brings him comfort.

Sub Zero: Nelle shows her consideration for the lesser members of staff by seeming totally unconcerned when Elaine walks past her, soaked and upset.

Fishisms: Richard has binoculars in his office. But what does he look at out of those windows? He reassures John about his date with Nelle: 'People are going to see the two of you together, presume she must be paid for, but she isn't. You did it, John. You got a beautiful woman to go out with you for free. Enjoy the milestone, it's a life moment.' John's smile therapy increases throughout this speech. When Nelle and Ling take them to a hip-hop club, Richard leads the way, obtaining shades so that John looks less like Nelle's father and getting John to follow his dance moves: 'Just do what I do. We need to think survival!'

Grrr!: Ling sums up the Cage & Fish price promise: 'We never lose, that's why we charge a lot.'

Georgia On My Mind: While Ally has total faith that Elaine is telling the truth, Georgia clearly has doubts, something Elaine realises. Georgia wants to settle, as otherwise it's Elaine's word against a dead woman with seven witnesses. When Elaine is proven innocent, Georgia says she never said Elaine was lying. 'But you believed it,' replies Elaine. 'Right down to your brown roots.'

DA Renee: When Ally talks about her decision to stop waiting for the right guy and to go out with the wrong ones because it beats loneliness, Renee sets her straight: 'There's nothing lonelier than being with the wrong guy.' Renee suggests Ally pretend she's seeing Greg – as he's a doctor she'd hardly see him anyway. Besides, as Renee points out, 'We've got ice cream, who needs a guy?'

Guy Talk: John and Richard discuss John's change, Nelle's failure to notice and the possible strategic use of the knee-pit manoeuvre. Richard counsels caution over the knee pit, but acknowledges it will certainly get Nelle's attention.

Girl Talk: Renee and Ally discuss harassment cases and the 'weaker sex' over lunch. Ally admits to having called Greg eleven times, and says that she read an article that claimed there are only two good men per state.

Fantasy: When John points out how quickly Ally can turn a conversation around to the subject of herself, she imagines slapping him around the face with her tongue. When John says he likes Nelle, Ally imagines snapshots of his expression, a record of the look on a man's face when he meets a woman he really likes.

Fetishes: Fish touches Ally's wattle.

Song: On the video of Martha's birthday, Elaine 'does a number'. Rappers bark over big beats at the club Nelle takes John to. 'Big Girls Don't Cry' seems to be Ally's new theme tune as she tries to have a 'change' of her own. Vonda sings 'Tears On My Pillow' at the end of the episode.

. . . And Dance: Richard and John lay down some hip-hop moves at the club. Fly!

Fashion Victims: Nelle's blonde dreadlocks.

Also Starring: Bruce McCarty was one of the regular cast in *Spy Game*, a short-lived 90s' American equivalent of *The Avengers*.

The Case (1): Elaine's Aunt Gladys was told by her daughter, Martha, that *she* invented the face bra. Martha has been dead for two years, leaving Gladys to sue Elaine on the basis of a dead woman's testimony. Gladys produces seemingly damning evidence – a patent application and sketches for the face bra by Martha from March 1996. Gladys has a stack of Elaine and Martha's mutual friends to back her up.

Guilty? (1): Elaine is innocent, as proven by a video of Martha's birthday party where Elaine explains the face bra to the dead woman. Gladys gives up the case and is left in shock: 'My own daughter, she lied to me.'

The Case (2): Mr Volpe runs a computer firm. Mr Volpe wanted to make his office fun, so he ran beach days where people came to work in swimsuits. But Vicki Sharp, who was never forced to wear a swimsuit or ostracised in any way for not doing so, decided to sue Mr Volpe for being discriminatory. How nice. Billy vigorously represents Mr Volpe, arguing that there was no compulsion to go along with the Beach Day, and all Mr Volpe ever tried to do was make his staff happy and more productive.

Judge Not: The bathing-suit case is presided over by Judge Rudy Fox, a severe-looking woman in spectacles.

Withdrawn: Opposing counsel pulls a stunt – filling the court with people in bathing suits.

Guilty? (2): Billy deserves to win the case on Volpe's behalf, and he does. Good for him.

Kisses: John and Nelle at her apartment – leading to much more later.

Toilet Humour: Just as things can't seem to get any worse for Elaine, John somersaults out of a cubicle and kicks her head-first down the toilet.

The Verdict: 'I guess this is victory.' Paralleling success and failure, 'Only The Lonely' shows how the greatest moment of Elaine's life, the success of her invention, is undermined by the lack of faith shown by her family and colleagues. And, while Ally, Renee and Elaine are alone in their own ways, John and Nelle at last make a connection as they finally get it together. Both the consummation of John and Nelle's relationship, and Richard and John's hip-hop dance routine, are crowd pleasers of the highest order, so it's a good job there are more sober plotlines on hand to balance things out with a little downbeat seriousness. To be both utterly romantic and slightly cynical is quite a juggle, but somehow this episode manages it.

221
The Green Monster

#2M21
10 May 1999

Written by David E. Kelley
Directed by Michael Schultz

Cast: Jesse L. Martin (Dr Greg Butters),
Antonio Sabato Jr (Kevin Wyatt), Enya Flack (Kimba),
Albert Hall (Judge Seymore Walsh),
Christine Estabrook (Bonnie Mannix),
Denis Arndt (Michael Mannix), Sara Botsford (Valerie Post)

John and Richard represent Bonnie Mannix, who dropped her cheating husband's antique piano on his Porsche, while Ally hires a male escort, Kevin Wyatt, to make Greg jealous.

Everything Stops For Ally: Ally is in a post-Greg rut, singing along to Boz Scaggs in her office. She claims to Elaine and Ling that this is just because she really likes Boz Scaggs, but neither seems to believe her. When Ling suggests Ally hire a male escort from her agency – purely to make Greg jealous – Ally initially resists, but gives in to the idea. When Ling introduces Ally to her escort, Kevin Wyatt, Ally gains enthusiasm. Kevin is 'incredible', she tells Renee: 'Figures I'd have to rent him.' Ally admits to stalking Greg to find out that the woman he was with at the end of the last episode was 'just a date'. Renee and Ally decide to throw a belated thirty-fifth birthday party for John as a pretext to get Greg to come to the bar. She practises nose-nuzzling with Kevin. By the end of the episode Greg has agreed to meet up with Ally, but Ally would rather date Kevin, who can't date her out of professionalism. She admits to being hopeless.

Grrr!: Ling isn't pleased to see Nelle and John so happy around the office: 'This is a place of work, people shouldn't be happy.' She says loud, bad music gives her a headache. Ling owns a male escort agency and one of the escorts is Kevin Wyatt, whom Ally hires. Ling signals to Kevin over Ally's head at one point, as if directing him in some way.

Smile Therapy: Ling asks Nelle what she sees in John – apart from the top of his head. Once Ling and Nelle have gone, John replies: 'What does she see in me? I'm a love machine, baby, that's L-O-V-E machine.' Ally creeps up to him: 'John . . . or is it Mr Machine?' John uses smile therapy back at her. Later, when Renee tells John the birthday bash they want to throw for him is just a pretext to make Greg jealous, he resorts to smile therapy again. As Nelle walks in, Renee thrusts John's head into her bosom. She uses Nelle's furious reaction as an example of what they want to achieve with Greg: 'See that, John, that's jealousy. That's what we need from Greg.' John babbles his way out of the room, unable to explain anything when trapped between Renee and Nelle.

Fishisms: Fish says he promises victory to every new client: that's how he gets the business. He tries to touch Bonnie's wattle but is slapped back.

Bygones: Fish sums up what Bonnie did to her husband succinctly: 'You crushed his Porsche. Next best thing to his penis. Bygones.'

Georgia On My Mind: Georgia goes through a bizarre period of rebellion in this episode. She dresses in a provocative manner and tells Billy she's realised that she's 'hot', and threatens to take her backless dress off in the middle of the office when Billy disapproves. Later she engages in some very bad singing at the bar. We would go into this character development further, but as it is never mentioned again in subsequent episodes it hardly seems worth the bother. Chalk this one down as a comedy sub-plot.

The Boy Next Door: Billy is alarmed to find Georgia at the office wearing a slinky, revealing black dress designed by Ling. When Georgia is demonstrating her complete lack of singing ability in the bar, Billy seems to disappear into his drink.

Office Gossip: When Elaine meets Kevin, the first thing she says to him is 'sex'. She hides under a desk to listen to Renee and Ally. When Greg and Ally are facing off with their respective dates, Elaine smells 'a great evening ahead'.

DA Renee: To persuade John to allow them to throw a fake birthday for him, Renee sits on his knee. She shoves John's head into her chest to use Nelle as a demonstration of jealousy in action.

Doctor's Orders: Greg seems alarmed that Ally has met someone. He's initially reluctant to attend John's fake birthday, and when he does he brings a date, Kimba. He and Kimba seem to have a great time together, and Greg says he trimmed his moustache because Kimba said it tickled. Greg seems uncomfortable when Ally and Kevin are singing to each other, and his response is for Kimba and him to get up and do a number too. Although Greg and Ally argue at the bar, the next day he comes to see her at the office and they agree to meet for coffee.

Girl Talk: Although ostensibly busy lawyers, Ally and Renee still get time to meet for another heart-to-heart over lunch. Renee thinks the escort idea is nuts. Ally replies that Renee should stop looking at everything through logic: 'That is your problem, too much logic.' 'You shouldn't criticise something you never try,' replies Renee.

Men: Kevin Wyatt, the smart and handsome escort Ally hires from Ling's escort service. Kevin pretends to be an actor, as he knows a career man like Greg is more likely to feel threatened by someone working in the arts. He asks Ally if she wants to kiss him in public and fake other signs of sexual attraction.

Fantasy: When Kevin asks Ally if she wants to 'fake' a sexual attraction between them, she imagines swallowing him up whole, head first.

Song: In her office Ally sings along, loudly and badly, to 'It's Over' by Boz Scaggs and later plays 'Bye Bye Love' very loudly. At the bar Ally and Kevin sing 'All I Have To Do Is Dream', while Greg and Kimba reply with a duet of 'Your Precious Love'. Even Georgia has a go, murdering 'You Don't

Have To Say You Love Me' and 'Son of a Preacher Man', with Vonda encouraging the audience to sing along – loud enough to drown out Georgia's tortured warbling. Vonda sings 'This Is Crazy Now', from the second *Ally* soundtrack album. Ally and Renee sing 'Bye Bye Love', which fades into Vonda's version of the song.

Fashion Victims: Richard wears a horrible red plaid shirt.

The Case: Bonnie Mannix, infuriated by her cheating husband, destroys his prize possessions. Because Boston is in a no fault state, he can sue her for criminal damage but he can't be held responsible for destroying their marriage. John recommends Bonnie settles, but she refuses. She denies diminished responsibility: 'Committing eleven years of my life to him was diminished capacity. Flicking that button was an act of acute sanity. The only thing saner would have been to drop it on his head.' Mrs Mannix feels humiliated, her husband having appeared quite publicly with his mistress. John's closing outlines how love isn't mature and rational, how people can engage in childish games like trying to make each other jealous. While he acknowledges what Mrs Mannix did was wrong, he points out that what Mr Mannix did was worse, even though he couldn't be prosecuted for it: 'Maybe we can't hold this lying, cheating philanderer liable in a court of law, but we would be damn fools to reward him.'

Judge Not: Judge Seymore Walsh presides over the case of Mannix vs Mannix. When he dismisses John's attempt to file a counter-claim for emotional damage, John expresses disappointment – John claims to have always considered Judge Walsh special, the same line he pulled on Whipper in 'Those Lips, That Hand'. Walsh is close to the limit. 'Don't be pulling your stunts in my court,' he tells Cage.

Guilty?: It would be vindictive for the court to find against Mrs Mannix, whose husband betrayed her so badly. The court agrees, ordering her to pay damages – to the tune of 35 cents. John makes sure to get the keys to the crane she used to cause the destruction from Bonnie before they part, and tells her she needs to move on.

Kisses: When Ally is told by Kevin that he can't date her, that it would be unprofessional, Ally understands. But as he leaves, she grabs Kevin and kisses him: 'I was just testing the merchandise,' she explains.

Hit The Bar: Renee and Ally hold their fake birthday celebration for John in the bar, and many songs are sung that night – some are even sung well.

Trivia: Calista Flockhart clearly has a cold in this episode.

The Verdict: 'Sooner or later we have to grow up, even emotionally.' A minor episode, saved by some notable scenes. Richard and John's case is great, with Bonnie Mannix a rightfully furious woman, and John's 'love machine' speech is a joy. But the other plotlines are sloppy and unfocused: the Georgia rebellion phase goes nowhere, and at the end we're uncertain what the situation is with Ally. Kevin puts himself out of the frame, so why is so much significance placed upon him? Greg is painstakingly drawn back into Ally's life, but we don't see him again. Overall the episode is fun, but a bit of a mess, and an indication that Kelley isn't quite sure in which direction to take his heroine at this point in the series.

222
Love's Illusions

#2M22
17 May 1999

Written by David E. Kelley
Directed by Alan Arkush

Cast: Al Green (Himself),
Albert Hall (Judge Seymore Walsh),
Wendy Worthington (Margaret Camaro),
Robert Picardo (Barry), Barbara Alyn Woods (Kelly),
Amy Castle (Ally aged 8), Jill Noel (Ally aged 15)

Ally represents Kelly, a woman who couldn't find the man of her dreams and so settled for the next best thing. In arguing against the idea of only marrying your true love, Ally finds herself questioning her own beliefs. Is that one special guy really out there?

Meanwhile, Richard gets Ling into bed at last, but has trouble rising to the occasion . . .

Everything Stops For Ally: Ally's romantic ideals get a battering in this episode. To defend Kelly she has to argue for pragmatism in matters of the heart and compromising when deciding who to spend your life with. John tells her that her dream man isn't out there and that the world in her head is the only world she'll ever really be happy with. When she asks Nelle, Ling and Elaine if they ever expect to meet 'the one', the man of their dreams, none of them says yes. When Ally asks as a follow-up if finding your one true love ever actually happens, the women remain silent. In court, as Camaro gives evidence and tells the court about marriage for pragmatic reasons, Ally becomes increasingly twitchy. That night Ally explains to Renee how her mother never loved her father and how she once caught her mother with another man. That was the day she started pretending – she got an early start at romanticising love. Renee tells Ally to let it go, to let herself cry, but Ally refuses. Barry asks Ally in court whether he's crazy and Ally replies that he isn't, but it might be their little secret. Ally cries as she gets lost in childhood memories at the end of the episode.

Fishisms: Richard wants Ling to have sex with him. He describes dating Ling as a 'six-month, twelve-step semen retention plan'. When Ling reminds Richard how long it took him to recover from their first kiss, he tells her he has sick leave coming. When they finally get to bed, Richard has problems rising to the occasion and Ling ends up watching *Chicago Hope* instead. The next day Fish tells John that things like this don't happen to him. At times of crisis, Richard takes inspiration from Bob Dole. He goes to his doctor to get a drug to restore his potency, in spite of the worrying potential side effects, and gets Ling to agree to a rematch by threatening to withdraw knee-pit privileges.

Bygones: Richard explains how easily he's sexually stimulated: 'You know, cute poodle and . . . bygones.'

Grrr!: Ling charges into Richard's office demanding knee-pit action. Fish refuses because he wants sex: 'Ling, I've heard a lot of talk, it's time to put your mouth where the money is.' Ling insists that no man has ever been able to make love to her twice in one day. Ling usually hates sweat, except during sex, when she *drips*. In bed, she tells Richard there is a 'minimum size requirement to ride'. She gets Richard to sign a waiver and confidentiality agreement. After Richard fails to manage it, she tells him it's a blessing: 'I really don't crave sex and you're no good at it. We could be a perfect match.' However, when they do get it together she's impressed by his performance and persistence – unaware that it's drug induced.

The Boy Next Door: Billy is very cynical about Georgia's sex drive: 'The only time I see you truly, deeply lit up it means you bought a new piece of furniture.' Billy gets a black eye when he falls out of a stall with Georgia.

Georgia On My Mind: Georgia denies not being interested in sex and claims the problem is that she's tired at the end of the day and Billy isn't a morning person. Billy suggests the middle of the day, and after some flirting with the idea she drags him into the toilet cubicle for sex. Georgia thinks Billy looks sexy with a black eye and follows up their adventure in the unisex by another in his office.

We Got It Together, Didn't We?: Nelle, wearing another great air stewardess uniform, asks John if he wants to 'fly the friendly skies'. John hears a snatch of Barry White before being dragged off by Richard.

Smile Therapy: John is uber-cool in this episode, his 'change' having made him confident in both word and action. While in the jail cell to which Judge Walsh sentenced him to for contempt, John tells Ally some things she doesn't really want to hear. 'Men lie to get women into bed, women lie to get men into matrimony.' He believes women compromise so as to get married before their biological clocks kick in. John says Ally's fear of being alone is her biggest fantasy of all and that she would probably be happier alone: 'At some unconscious level I think you know that the only world that ultimately won't end up disappointing you is the one you make up.' Ally denies this and says she's just nuts, she really loves the world. John suggests that if she loves the world that much, perhaps one day she'll choose to live in it with everyone else.

Sub Zero: Nelle seems genuinely delighted that Ling has decided to go for it with Richard.

Office Gossip: Elaine displays an uncanny ability to home in on the use of the word 'sex' from a great distance. 'Like a little homing pigeon,' says Ling. She's great in bed, but then admits that she *is* a slut. When Ally asks if the women expect to meet the man of their dreams, Elaine replies, 'Over and over again.' Elaine stalks around the unisex with her camera, while Georgia and Billy try to stay silent in one of the stalls. Elaine thinks Ally is really cracking up this time.

DA Renee: Renee is understandably concerned by Ally's mental state and knows about Billy's 'bootie call' with Georgia in the unisex.

Also Starring: Robert Picardo (Barry) is best known as the holographic doctor, the only interesting character (we think) in *Star Trek: Voyager*.

Fantasy: Ally keeps seeing scenes from her own childhood. She sees Judge Walsh turn into Al Green in court. Kelly asks a valid question in relation to Ally: 'Is she mental?' When Kelly suggests on the stand that love is probably an illusion, an emotional Ally shouts, 'Objection, objection, objection,' and begins to see Al Green instead of Judge Walsh again. She comes out of her delusion to find herself dancing in court. Ally flashes back to her parents arguing when she was young.

Song: Young Ally and her friends sing along to Robert Palmer's 'Addicted to Love'. 'Play That Funky Music' plays when Billy and Georgia are tearing each other's clothes off in the unisex. 'Love Machine' plays as Richard prepares to make a second pass at Ling. The episode's title is taken from the lyrics to 'Both Sides Now' which Vonda sings as Ally remembers her childhood.

. . . And Dance: Richard dances to 'Born to be Wild' in the unisex.

Fashion Victims: Ling's negligée – hot!

The Case: Barry married Kelly and truly loved her. When he found out that he wasn't the one true love she wanted, that she was settling for second-best, he decided to sue her for fraud. Ally and John defend Kelly. In court Kelly explains how she had an imaginary love affair with her dream man, writing letters to him in her diary: the man may not have existed but the love affair certainly did. Barry wanted more from her than just love – he wanted passion. He tells the court, 'She loves me like you love a pet.' This episode sees the return of Margaret Camaro from *Let's Dance*, who here appears as a witness for John and Ally, who have to promise not to vilify her in the way Richard did. Camaro tells the court that the idea of a soulmate is a 'dangerous myth', and that Kelly did the smart and practical thing, finding a partner who was suitable and would last.

Judge Not: It's Seymore Walsh, who is increasingly annoyed with John Cage's objections: 'Please sit – unless you would like to object to the hardness of the chair.' John finally pushes Walsh too far by asking him how much alimony he pays – implying a personal agenda behind Walsh allowing the fraud case to go ahead – and accusing the judge of holding him in contempt. Walsh responds by having John thrown into a cell.

Guilty?: Barry's attorney argues the case isn't about love, it's about fraud. Ally argues, going against her own nature, that the real fraud is that people can get the person of their dreams. 'The men or women in our dreams live in our dreams,' argues Ally. 'And, in the real world, we should be allowed to settle for the ones who come close.' We're with what Ally says rather than what she believes, and the jury agrees by finding Kelly not guilty.

Toilet Humour: Billy and Georgia try to spice up married life by making love in one of the cubicles. After evading Elaine's attempts to catch them, they end up falling out of the stall half dressed when John and Ally bang on the door frames so hard the door falls open, depositing them on the floor. Billy ends up with a black eye. Ally contemptuously figures that 'the one marriage to have passion would be theirs' while John suggests they have to work on their dismount.

The Verdict: 'Everything I ever believed in . . .' A change of direction for Ms McBeal, as Ally finds her illusions about love and life systematically shattered and begins to retreat further and further into her own fantasy world. The division between Ally and the other characters is highlighted by the tone of their respective plotlines – while the sexual misadventures of Billy and Georgia, as well as Richard and Ling, are pure comedy, Ally is isolated in a world of sad memories and a case dominated by betrayal and hard compromises. The one big let-down here is the use of Al Green as a guest star – he doesn't really work as Ally's internal voice and deserves better than to be relegated to some ill-conceived fantasy sequences. Thoughtful and interesting, 'Love's Illusions' unfortunately doesn't know quite what it wants to say for itself.

223

I Know Him By Heart

#2M23
24 May 1999

Written by David E. Kelley
Directed by Jonathan Pontell

Cast: Wendy Worthington (Margaret Camaro),
Michael Badalucco (Ally's date), Gerry Becker (Stone),
Al Green (Himself)

Ally refuses to come out of her bedroom, while John and Nelle hit a rocky patch.

Everything Stops For Ally: 'How many people get haunted by Al Green?' Ally is stuck in her own delusions, staying in her bedroom and refusing to come out to go to work. She says her heart is broken, 'one giant stress fracture', and that Al Green, 'sings her heart' – his words reflecting her feelings. She isn't too pleased when Richard comes to visit her: 'Richard, I want you to leave. It's easier for me to pretend you don't exist if you are out of my eyeline.' Ally tries to growl like Ling, but the result is just a slight hum – Richard thinks it's cute. After Richard has gone Ally tells Renee she's just beginning to face up to the fact that the guy she *knew* was out there really isn't out there after all. Renee says that Richard was right about one thing, that they shouldn't wait, they should go out and grab the guys. The next day, Ally is suspicious when everyone is smiling and sympathetic with her. After Ling tries to 'out' her, Ally screams, 'I am not a lesbian!' and walks straight into Camaro. Ally claims not to hate lesbians – she wrote to ABC when they cancelled *Ellen*, and wishes there were more lesbians so as to free up more men. Ally goes on some awful dates and accepts Ling's offer to bring her some men, believing it won't really happen. She tries to let the spirit of Barry White fill her, as it does with John, but it doesn't work. Ally tells John that she spends her time in her bedroom imagining the man of her dreams, being with him. She often seems to imagine them being together on a merry-go-round. At lunch the next day a huge crowd of men arrive, gathered by Ling that morning. Ally talks to them, takes cards and numbers, but decides not to touch any of them: 'The guy I want to meet isn't going to respond to a cattle call.' When Camaro tells Ally she rejects the idea that a woman's life is empty without a man, Ally replies that it's only half empty. Ally begins to crack up in front of Camaro, singing to herself and staring into the middle distance. The season ends with Ally alone, sitting on a merry-go-round full of couples. As the picture fades, Ally smiles.

DA Renee: Renee, concerned about Ally, goes to Cage & Fish to ask for help. She tells John he should go to talk to Ally because he's so weird, at which he engages in extensive smile therapy. Renee thinks Ally is getting lost in her own dream world.

Fishisms: When Fish finds out Ally is staying in her bedroom he asks, 'Is she naked?' Even though she isn't, he still wants to be the one to go and talk to Ally: 'Everybody else at one time or another has tried to connect to this loon; it's time she heard a little common sense.' Richard impersonates John dancing to Barry White, to illustrate why he should go instead of John: 'If we want to connect with her on a cracker level, you'd get the assignment, but for common sense I'm the one who should go. I'd send Billy, but he might kiss her.' In spite of resistance he insists on going, saying, 'Enough is enough.' When he gets there, Ally points out that he wasn't invited and Richard replies that if he waited to be invited to go into a girl's bedroom he'd never see the inside of one. Ally's bedroom disappoints him. He gives Ally one bit of advice worth having: 'If you want a guy, you've got to go out and grab him. Just grab; it's why God gave man the handle for woman to latch on to. Fishism.' He forgets that bedrooms are private because his has 'all the cameras'. He gets into bed with Ally and tells her she's not strange for being weak, because all women are weak: 'I am woman, hear me whimper.' He then tries to give her a little knee-pit treatment before she throws him out. Richard represents Margaret Camaro, whose insurance company won't cover fertility treatment after she failed to get pregnant through artificial insemination. When, in a deposition, counsel for the insurance company suggests Camaro try getting pregnant 'the old-fashioned way', Richard objects: 'I object to opposing counsel hitting on my client. Move for costs. Where's the judge?'

Bygones: 'Bygones,' says Richard. 'Bygones for what?' asks Ally. 'Whatever,' replies Richard. When Camaro asks if she should put out a call for men to fertilise her eggs, Fish says: 'Think of the lines. Bygones.'

Grrr!: When Ally tells Ling to 'cut out the nice', Ling reverts to normal with a growl. Ally asks if Ling does make-up as well as hair and Ling replies: 'Look at me – is my face not flawless?'

Ling tries to out Ally as a lesbian, asking her to stick out her finger. When Ally does so, Ling freaks out, shouting 'Gross!' and running away. 'I tricked her to see if she's a lesbian,' she tells Richard. 'I think she is one.' Later Ling tells Ally the good men are out there, but they don't go to bars. She rounds up some cute men for Ally the next day on her way to work, so that Ally can take her pick. Ally refuses all the men and attacks Ling's attitude to men and relationships, asking what kind of man Ling is going to end up with if she has that kind of attitude – at which point Richard walks in. Ling tells Ally she doesn't really want to meet anybody as 'no one can measure up to this mythic dreamboat you've concocted for yourself; it's easier to be alone and pretend you just haven't met him yet'.

Smile Therapy: John wants to go to see Ally, but is prevented by Nelle. Later, he somersaults over her head in the unisex and ends up sprawled over a cubicle door. He tells Ally her eyes have seemed dead to him recently, that the hope seems to have drained right out of her. Ally accuses John of draining the hope out of her with what he said in the previous episode (see 222 'Love's Illusions'). John tells Ally about the change: 'Once I let myself feel the change, it emanates through me. And women – they love me.' He demonstrates by drawing Elaine to him, but stops when Nelle walks in. Later he tells Ally Nelle is jealous because 'I connect with your imaginary life'. When Ally asks John if he thinks she's crazy to retreat to her room, to her imaginary world, John replies by telling her how he was dropped from Little League when he was nine and imagined a little league of his own in his room over that summer. 'In my room or not, the memory is as real as any from childhood. And it was wonderful. Nothing crazy about it.' Ally thanks him. After arguing with Nelle, John splutters and snaps at everyone in the office, and ends up in the unisex doing isometrics, looping madly around and around the cubicle frame.

Sub Zero: Nelle suggests if Ally wants to act like a ten-year-old they should leave her there: why should they bother? When Renee says this is what friends do, Nelle points out that she isn't Ally's friend. Renee tells Nelle to beat it and Nelle pretends to be intimidated: 'I'm shaking so much I probably look like your vibrator, don't I?' Nelle stops John from going to talk to Ally. She isn't pleased when Elaine drops into her cubicle in the unisex to pry into her life, and digs a heel into Elaine's shin to get rid of her. Nelle screams for people to let her go to the bathroom in peace.

We Got It Together, Didn't We?: Nelle and John argue over Ally's influence on him. Nelle thinks Ally uses John for support, and it's only ever about her and never works both ways. John points out that 'with Ally, everything's about her'. When Nelle asks why Ally can't settle like everyone else, John asks whether Nelle is settling for less with him. Ally demonstrates what Nelle meant by running in with a problem and Nelle walks off. Later she tells John that the next time Ally comes running for support, she wants John to tell her to leave – through the window. Nelle doesn't like Ally's legitimation of living in a fantasy world, her influence on John. John asks Nelle if she never believed in holding out for perfection and Nelle says she did, but stopped when she turned nine. Nelle admits she's jealous of Ally and tells John to get out. He says this anger isn't attractive and Nelle makes fun of his stutter and smile therapy. Nelle finds John angrily spinning in the unisex: 'Well, anger may not be any more attractive on you, John,' she says, 'but it's certainly more exciting.' John tells Nelle she's a mean woman for making fun of his stuttering and smile therapy. She replies that she is an angry woman and a threatened one, that she is threatened by the odd and fundamental connection between John and Ally. Nelle is afraid of John adopting Ally's notion of looking for the perfect person, because she won't be that person. John asks why they're even bothering if they're so different, and Nelle replies that she wants to be with someone different: 'Why can't two people grow together, meet somewhere in the middle?' When John tells Nelle he needs her to love Barry White, she snaps: 'I'm beginning to love you, don't you get that? And every time she comes running to you it just makes me insecure that you'll run to her.' John replies that he's not running anywhere: 'I'm not going anywhere. And I'm beginning to love you too.' They kiss and hug, with Nelle slightly tearful.

Office Gossip: Elaine tapes the arguments over how to deal with Ally with her camcorder. She drops into Nelle's cubicle in the unisex to offer her support and gets a heel in the shin as the price of her intrusion.

Girl Talk: Renee and Ally sit in her office, massaging each other's feet. When Ally asks where all the good men are, Renee replies, 'At home with their wives.'

Men: Ally and Renee meet a number of men at the bar, all of whom seem like losers. One tells Ally a riveting anecdote about passing a kidney stone, while another would appear to be Jimmy from *The Practice*.

Fantasy: Ally is still seeing Al Green in her bedroom and dances with him. When Ally tells Richard she isn't interested in a man at the moment, her nose grows like Pinocchio's. After bumping into Camaro, Ally turns grey and runs off across the floor, tiny.

Song: Vonda sings 'Did You Ever Have To Make Up Your Mind?' as Ally tries to pick from the men Ling brings her.

Kisses: After all their arguing, Nelle and John kiss and make up in the unisex.

The Verdict: 'Enough is enough.' The second season ends on a slightly uncertain note. John and Nelle, as for much of this season, are the focus here, while the title character seems to wander aimlessly between set pieces. There's no real conclusion to the thread of Ally losing her belief in love: one minute she's retired to her room, the next she's going out on wacky dates with a bunch of eccentric men, and by the end she's alone again. While there are some classic scenes in here – Richard in Ally's bedroom springs to mind – the episode as a whole doesn't give a satisfactory conclusion to the season, leading to an odd feeling of anticlimax.

Season Three

Regular Cast

Calista Flockhart (Ally McBeal)
Courtney Thorne-Smith (Georgia Thomas)
Greg Germann (Richard Fish)
Lisa Nicole Carson (Renee Raddick)
Jane Krakowski (Elaine Vassal)
Vonda Shepard (Vonda Shepard)*
Portia de Rossi (Nelle Porter)
Lucy Liu (Ling Woo)
with
Peter MacNicol (John Cage)
and
Gil Bellows (Billy Alan Thomas)**

Created by David E. Kelley

* Vonda Shepard is featured in the title sequence again this season, but does not appear physically in every episode. However, as her voice is featured in every instalment we choose not to note her absence from particular episodes as we do with other cast members.

** Gil Bellows is credited on episodes 301–320, but not 321.

The Episodes

301
Car Wash

#3M01
25 October 1999

Written by David E. Kelley
Directed by Billy Dickson

Cast: Jason Gedrick (Joel),
Dyan Cannon (Judge 'Whipper' Cone),
Albert Hall (Judge Seymore Walsh),
Tracy Middendorf (Risa Helms), Alec Murdock (Mr Helms),
Ray Walston (Minister)

Risa wants her local minister to perform her wedding at her local church, even though said minister caught Risa having sex with a man other than her fiancé. Ally persuades the minister to go ahead with the wedding, only to realise she knows the groom; in fact, Ally had casual, wild sex with the groom in a car wash only days before . . .

Renee is setting up her own practice and is pleasantly surprised when Whipper decides to join her. And back at Cage & Fish, John has lost contact with the power of Barry White . . .

Everything Stops For Ally: Including, in this case, a wedding. Ally seems to be over her depression from last season's finale, judging by the *joie de vivre* act of having rampant sex with a stranger in a car wash. She's even not ashamed to tell John that it wasn't 'making love', but was 'that vulgar verb', and that all she wants to do is go back and do it all again. When Richard asks if she's having sex, Ally denies it. She claims to John that sex with a man you don't love can be 'OK', although it's clear from her car-wash experience that it can be rather more than that. Ally is a bridesmaid at Risa's wedding and realises that Joel, Risa's husband-to-be, is the man from the car wash. Ally screams but regains her composure, allowing the wedding to go on. However, when the minister asks if any person present has a reason for the wedding not to go ahead, Ally interrupts. She tells the minister about the car wash and her voice is broadcast to the congregation by the minister's lapel mike. Because she knows Joel is an amazing lover but that Risa thinks he's terrible, Ally thinks Joel has no passion for Risa and that she is just marrying him for his money. She tells Richard it was difficult to interrupt the wedding, as everyone in the church now thinks she's a 'cheap slut'. When Risa and Joel patch things up and the wedding goes ahead, Ally is booed as she takes her seat with the congregation, having been unsurprisingly dismissed from bridesmaid duty. Ally then interrupts again and tells Risa that Joel is incredible, 'the most amazing lover I've ever been with', and if Risa thinks he's terrible there's something wrong. The wedding is cancelled. Ally tells Joel that Risa deserved honesty from him. Ally then has to tolerate the abuse of the congregation as she leaves the church.

Smile Therapy: After hearing Ally's story about the car wash, John's nose whistles. John is troubled by 'a rash of oversexed women': not only with Ally and with Risa but also Nelle, who wanted to have phone sex with him when he was in Detroit. He couldn't, and he's lost his sexual ability. When Ally asks if he's talked to Nelle, John quotes Richard: 'Communication is the death knell of any relationship.' 'I have been unable to access him,' John says. Ally asks if he means God, but John doesn't – he means Barry White, whose lurve power he can no longer channel. John has always thought the key to making love to a woman was the 'emotional connection', but Risa and Ally's experiences have shown him that women can want sex for sex's sake too. John's frustration with women's sexuality climaxes with him ranting to Nelle about the effect of ovulation on women's sexual urges, that they search for stable providers most of the time and 'virile, masculine' men when they're ovulating. He thinks women can't have a purely physical sexual fantasy, because it's always about emotion with them. He wants Nelle to regulate her thoughts and not think about other men. His connection with Barry White is re-established by Elaine and he goes to Nelle reinvigorated, energetically ripping his vest off.

Sub Zero: Nelle is bugged by John clicking his tongue at her, thinking it's akin to him talking to his horse. Nelle, quite rightly, thinks John's rant about sexual fantasies is insane.

Office Gossip: Elaine listens to John and Nelle's argument about sexual fantasies and laughs when John says women's fantasies are always partly emotional. She goes to John later and tells him that he's in the fantasies of the women in the office, that he's the hottest man there. She calls him a 'hot little Biscuit'. 'If you ever became a predator,' she tells John, 'you'd ruin lives.' She tells John to go to Nelle, and if Nelle sends him away to come straight back to her. The question is, what does Elaine do with her hand during this scene?

Grrr!: Ling is having a small dinner party. She tells Ally, 'I wasn't planning to invite you, but if your feelings are going to be hurt I suppose I could make room.' She thinks Risa's wedding is the best she's ever been to. She thinks Ally felt upstaged by the bride and that her outburst was to make herself the centre of attention. Ling thinks Ally is very brave to have a fantasy and pursue it, then points out that in Ancient China Ally's head would have been cut off for what she did.

Fishisms: Richard thinks that if a judge could order a minister to perform a wedding, Elaine would be married. He thinks most women don't have affairs in the week before their wedding, they wait until after. Richard thinks the Church shouldn't be criticising people for being immoral; the Church makes its money from guilty parishioners seeking absolution. He turns up at Risa's wedding, telling Ling he's there because the father of the bride is a big client. He's therefore very upset when Ally's outburst and confession destroy the wedding, especially after Ally defended Risa's right to have one last fling. He thinks Ally should have kept quiet and left it as their problem. Richard asks Ally a valid question: 'Are you sticking up for Risa or are you punishing him?' Richard likes women fighting over him and lets Whipper and Ling struggle for his attention at the bar.

Ex-DA Renee: Renee leaves the DA's office to set up her own firm. She is delighted to accept Whipper as a partner, as a judge would be an asset any firm would be glad of. Together they audition potential male staff by getting them to take off their shirts.

Whip-Lash!: Whipper joins Renee at her new firm as she wants to practise law again. She picked Renee's firm out of all the firms in Boston and only wants to do limited hours. She says 'Ling' with a hard 'L'.

Men: Jason Gedrick as Joel, the man with the oddly inconsistent sex life: he's amazing with Ally, but his fiancée thinks he's a boring lover.

The Case: Risa is the daughter of one of Richard's big clients, and is about to be married. The minister is refusing to perform the ceremony, or let them use the church, on the grounds that he caught her having sex with a man other than her fiancé. Ally doesn't think there's a legal recourse but she has to try. After Judge Walsh throws out their case, Ally has to go to the minister himself, and Risa explains that Joel is a terrible lover and she wanted one last moment of pleasure before she took her vows. He agrees.

Judge Not: Unsurprisingly, Judge Walsh refuses to order the wedding to go ahead. He tells Risa to get a refund. Richard accuses Walsh of being a 'gender bigot'.

Fantasy: When John drops a hint about Ally's sex life, she imagines daggers hitting him. John sees Barry White in the bedroom with him instead of Nelle, but doesn't let it stop him.

Fashion Victim: Ally claims being soaking wet is 'the new look'. Ling wears a vast hat to the wedding.

Toilet Humour: Elaine tells John how hot he is in the unisex, dancing with him and re-establishing his connection with Barry White.

Song: 'Sweet Inspiration' from the second *Ally* soundtrack album as Ally walks into the office wet from her car-wash encounter. 'Walking on the Sun' is performed by Smash Mouth as Whipper and Renee audition shirtless men for their firm. Vonda sings Bananarama classic 'Venus' as Ally leaves the church.

The Verdict: 'Women love sex. They love to think it, dream and talk about it, so long as they retain the right to sue you after.' Hot sex, sharp comedy and Ally becoming a pariah for taking a moral stance – the third season takes off like a rocket, with all manner of scandal and weirdness. The church scenes are pure farce, but there are serious points about the sexuality of men and women made here. What's more, Ally herself is centre stage after being rendered aimless at the end of the previous season, and Calista Flockhart is in her element bringing a sexier, more dangerous side to the character. With Renee and Whipper going into practice, it's clear that this episode marks the beginning of a season full of big changes for the show.

302
Buried Pleasures

#3M02
1 November 1999

Written by David E. Kelley
Directed by Mel Damski

Cast: Heidi Mark (Alice Gaylor),
Dee Wallace Stone (Gail Clarkson),
Paula Newsome (Phyllis Butters),
Michael Kagan (Robert Perry),
Nancy Stephens (Judge Washington)

Alice Gaylor and her employer, Corbin Technology, are both being sued by disgruntled female employees who consider Gaylor's provocative dress sense is sexual harassment. While Billy represents the firm, Renee represents Gaylor herself.

Meanwhile, sexual tensions run rife through the office. Ally and Ling experiment with their sexuality, while John wonders whether Nelle's hairbrush is for more than grooming purposes . . .

Everything Stops For Ally: When Ling approaches Ally asking if she's ever kissed a woman, Ally thinks it's another trick (see 223 'I Know Him By Heart') but it turns out Ling has been dreaming of kissing another woman. Ling wants them to be friends so Ally accepts her dinner invitation, albeit nervously after the previous line of questioning. Ally tells Renee that Ling was hitting on her and that gay women are often attracted to her. Ally thinks her dinner with Ling is a date, so Renee asks why she said yes. Ally admits that although as a general rule she is grossed out by kissing another woman – 'ick' – sometimes the idea of kissing certain women seems OK, and Ling, possibly because of her 'perfect, perfect face', doesn't gross her out. She claims not to be attracted to Ling – but is worried about what she's going to wear. At dinner, she and Ling nervously talk about how excellent the food is, until Ling finally admits it was Ally she dreamed about kissing. Ally is then relieved when Ling says she isn't interested after all. After that, dancing with Ling to wind up a group of men seems like harmless fun. They have a great time: 'Who ever would have guessed I could have fun with you?' Ally tells Ling. There's an obvious tension between them on Ally's doorstep, but when Ally suggests Ling come in for coffee and to 'make prank phone calls', Ling excuses herself. Ling kisses Ally on the cheek before she goes. The next day Ally is flustered because she wanted to kiss Ling goodnight on her doorstep. Ally isn't ashamed to admit she doesn't want to be gay – she isn't gay. But she had an 'urge' to kiss Ling. So they do, just to 'see what it's like'. Ally tells Renee that Ling 'can kiss. You know Ling, there's nothing she's not good at.' Ally is so self-obsessed that when Billy turns up at her apartment, she presumes he's heard about the kiss – even though he's obviously there to see Renee, his co-counsel. The next day Ally and Ling agree that they both like men, but that it was a worthwhile experiment. They shake hands, saying that neither of them will kiss another woman. Ally still has time for Renee – toasting her first civil court victory.

Grrr!: Ling has a dream about kissing a woman and is drawn to Ally. When Richard makes his little speech about sexuality, she isn't impressed: 'I consider myself pretty homophobic, but what you just said is disgusting.' She tells Richard that if she becomes a lesbian, it'll be his loss. After confessing to Ally that it was her she dreamed of, Ling tells Ally that dinner with her has confirmed that what she really wants from a relationship is . . . 'a penis'. She asks if she and Ally can resume disliking each other, but when some Neanderthals seem likely to make advances Ling suggests she and Ally dance together to get rid of them. The next day when Ally tells her she had an urge to kiss Ling, Ling locks the office door and advances on Ally, suggesting the urges might go away if they do kiss. After they've kissed, we're told Ling has a dream where she tells Richard that after Ally she can't go back to kissing him – but it's just a dream. She concedes that Ally is almost as good a kisser as she is, but that they both like men. As she dances with Richard at the end of the episode, Ling tells him she's 'pretty much' heterosexual.

Boy Next Door: Billy isn't surprised by the absurdity of the Gaylor case: 'We're talking about sexual harassment law, Ally; let's not expect it to make sense.' The law makes him seem genuinely angry. He covers the firm's side of the case while Renee takes Gaylor's side. Billy tells Alice she can't come across as a 'sexual predator'. Midway through the case, he tells Renee that she and Alice should dress down to gain jury sympathy. Billy doesn't doubt that Alice's dress sense is 'inappropriate', and the case comes down to a simple contest of sympathy. He says Renee is beautiful and her look is great – 'on cable'. Later he attacks Renee's strategy, saying it has 'all the integrity of a lap dance'. He accuses her of 'throwing her breasts out like they're two condos she's trying to sub-let'.

Ex-DA Renee: While Billy represents Corbin Technology, Renee is brought in as co-counsel to defend Gaylor. When Ally confides in her about Ling, Renee calls her 'a perfectly normal dyke'. Renee thinks that if Alice dresses down for giving testimony it will seem like an admission of guilt. Renee thinks the issue is about a woman's right to individuality, and that Billy is threatened by women being sexy. She calls Billy a 'male chauvinist King Kong pig', and says he rejected a strong woman like Ally in favour of his 'Barbie doll' wife – Georgia. She then tells Billy that Georgia is too good for him anyway. When Billy comes around to the apartment that night to co-ordinate closing arguments, Renee tells him to go home and concentrate on his – she'll do her own closing.

Fishisms: When told that one of his clients is being sued for sexual harassment, Fish asks, 'What did he do, breathe?' When Ling asks if he's ever thought about kissing another man, Richard is disgusted, although he dreams of women kissing all the time. He justifies this by explaining how two women kissing arouses men and therefore helps the procreation of the species, while two 'butt pirates' going at it will have the opposite effect. (Richard clearly doesn't realise the arousing effect two men kissing can have on *women*, but there are some things even a show like this isn't ready for!) When Ling says she feels she may end up with a woman, Richard says he'll be there for her, 'watching; touching myself'. Richard says people don't turn gay, they just are, and those who decide they are gay late in life are sexually ambiguous or confused, things which he couldn't say about Ling. Later, Richard gets suspicious when Ling talks to Ally then runs off without speaking to him. When John tells him about Nelle's spanking fantasy, Richard's first question is whether *Ling* wants to be spanked. He tells John the first thing he has to do is not panic, just sit down with Nelle . . . and spank her. As far as Richard is concerned, neither he nor John are pleasing their women in bed, what with Ling's dreams and Nelle's desires. He advises John not to talk to Nelle, but go straight for the spank – surprise being part of the appeal. Fish says the knee-pit treatment doesn't work on Ling any more: 'She's built up a small callus.' 'What's happened to us, John? We're not our usual sex machines.' By the end of the episode he's telling Ling he's been on the internet – and picked up some new tricks.

Sub Zero: Nelle isn't surprised or shocked by Ling's dreams of kissing another woman. Nelle says she's had stranger fantasies than that herself, and when pressed admits that she has fantasies about being spanked on her 'white little bottom until it turns pink', but that she would never do it in real life, that she has no desire to be 'victimised or dominated'. But there's something a little 'Victorian' about spanking that Nelle likes. Nevertheless, she absolutely freaks when John takes a hairbrush to her, throwing him out and threatening to have him arrested.

Smile Therapy: John overhears Nelle talking about her spanking fantasies. Unfortunately, he doesn't overhear her saying she would never want to act out this fantasy in real life, and so labours under the misinterpretation that she genuinely wants to be spanked. He tells Richard it's an emergency, that he isn't a 'sexually adventurous person'. Deriving pleasure from pain makes John uncomfortable. He thinks spanking is 'violence'. When Richard tells John that women sometimes leave their hairbrushes by the bedside in the hope their men will use it to spank them, John recalls that Nelle often brushes her hair in bed; is she waiting for him to make that move? Just as John had thought he'd got his sexual esteem back, this happened. When Nelle talks about 'whipping up' something exotic that night, John's anxiety gets worse. He then needs Elaine to tell him what a 'hot, hot Biscuit' he is to restore his self-assurance. Nevertheless, that night after dinner he feels he has to leave – especially when Nelle starts brushing her hair with a 'brush the size of a tennis racket'. After discussing the problem with Richard, he decides to turn over a new leaf: 'If I can't be the old John Cage, I'll be the new one.' He's changed before and he can change again. 'I'm a new man,' he tells Richard. 'Again.' This 'new' John Cage tries to give Nelle a spanking with her hairbrush – and gets thrown out of her apartment for his pains. John also makes one of his more outrageous claims in this episode: 'I flex my pupils sometimes, to strengthen my eyesight.'

Office Gossip: Elaine is happy to act as John's 'fluffer', boosting his ego by telling him how 'hot' he is.

Song: Ally and Ling dance to Roy Orbison's 'Pretty Woman'.

. . . And Dance: Ling and Ally dance sexily with each other to get rid of a 'hockey team' group of men. Ally is surprised they didn't get thrown out. Ling and Richard dance in the bar at the end of the episode.

Kisses: Ling kisses Ally on the cheek after their 'date'. Ally says she expects kissing Ling to be 'soft', and when they kiss in the office the next day it seems to be just that. As Ling says, 'That didn't suck.'

The Case: Alice Gaynor and her employers are being sued over Ms Gaynor's provocative dress sense, because her sexually aggressive dress promotes a sexually charged working atmosphere. She admits to using sex as power, to manipulate the men around her; she considers this power an 'equaliser'. Opposing counsel argues it isn't too much to expect Alice to dress more modestly. Billy argues 'there is no harassment going on here', that the jury can't punish the company for hiring an attractive woman. Renee defends a woman's right to be sexy and attractive, and to use that to manipulate men, that sex appeal is a 'gift' women can use.

Guilty?: Although it's hard to sympathise with a woman who uses sexuality to push herself ahead at work, it's harder still to see this as the basis for a harassment suit, so Gaylor and her company deserve to win – and they do.

Shrink Wrapped: Richard says that Freud said pain was arousing. John replies, 'Everything aroused Freud: he was a little pervert.'

The Verdict: 'Ally, look, he's got your girl!' Pure exploitation, but with some serious points about drawing the line between sexual fantasies and reality, 'Buried Pleasures' is an obvious ratings booster with substance. The central case is pretty dumb, but offers some interesting tensions between the increasingly chauvinistic Billy and the ever-strident Renee. Meanwhile, on the blatantly headline-seeking side of the plot, Ally and Ling engage in some rather sweet and tentative explorations of their sexuality, while John gets matters horribly, horribly wrong. Prepare to hide behind your fingers as Cage reaches for the fatal hairbrush . . .

303
Seeing Green

#3M03
8 November 1999

Written by David E. Kelley
Directed by Peter MacNicol

Cast: Gladys Knight (Herself), Al Green (Himself),
Brad Wilson (Harold), Gerry Becker (Stone),
Keegan De Lancie (Kirby Gallin),
Marnie Mosiman (Marcia Gallin),
William Stanford Davis (Jim), Ashlee Turner (Kim),
Brian Eyers (Mr Puckett), Wylie Small (Mrs Puckett)

While Ally's new therapist recommends Prozac, Billy opts for group therapy.

Everything Stops For Ally: Ally is having hallucinations about Al Green again, and with Dr Tracy away she confides in Tracy's current substitute, the pro-medication Dr Flott. Flott wants to put Ally on Prozac. Ally tells John and Richard this, claiming that she's a 'very happy person'. She claims to Renee that she likes seeing Al Green, that she finds the delusions 'magical'. Ally thinks Prozac is a mind-altering substance and that taking it is somehow 'wrong'. However, after a major production-number hallucination at work Ally accepts a prescription from Dr Flott. She does feel that taking the Prozac will be like killing Al Green, though. After getting the Prozac and prevaricating for a while, Ally makes her decision and flushes the medication away, much to Flott's displeasure. Ally makes a bad joke about Nelle wanting a spanking, giving away the fact that John told her about that incident. At the end of the episode she's left dancing down Green Street with Al.

Boy Next Door: Billy starts attending group therapy sessions (led, oddly enough, by regular opposing counsel Attorney Stone) which help men deal with their chauvinistic feelings towards women. In true AA fashion he introduces himself: 'My name is Billy, and I'm a male chauvinist pig.' He tells the group that although generally he's pro-women, when it comes to his own home he wants his wife waiting for him when he comes home and that he wants to feel 'worshipped'. The next time Billy goes to a session, he takes Richard, who turns the therapy group into a gang of rabid chauvinists chanting to be allowed their penises back. Afterwards Billy tells Georgia what he told the therapy group, and what Renee said to him (see 302 'Buried Pleasures'). He tells Georgia he considers her a possession of his, and that if they have children he expects her to quit work. He doesn't want her putting on weight, either. He doesn't want Georgia to be a bimbo, but neither does he want her to be a 'fat, raging, feminist'. Their argument ends with Billy getting a sound beating from his rapidly estranged wife, leaving Elaine to try to rouse him in her usual manner.

Georgia On My Mind: Georgia initially accepts that Billy should not apologise for his 'Cro-Magnon' attitudes if that is how he genuinely feels. However, when they get into an argument about why he married her and what he expects, Billy ends up angrily telling Georgia to 'go do your hair'. Georgia's response is to slap then kick Billy, knocking him to the ground. 'Feminine enough?' she asks.

Fishisms: Richard takes Creatin for his pectorals and Propecia for his hair. Fish tells Billy's discussion group that they, essentially, have no dicks. He goes on to rant about how women like being sex objects, how it is their place to stay at home and look after the kids. 'We're not the same,' he says, 'it's why God made different sexes.' His analysis of the differing desires of men and women is, er, interesting: 'What we want is sex, what they want is money.' He calls the group 'whipped things' and tells them to go home and demand their penises back. The men start to chant 'I want my penis', whipped into a frenzy by Richard's rousing, if absurd, speech. Richard thinks the group is a cult but likes it. He tells Georgia that he'd be surprised if Billy had been 'any good in bed lately'.

Office Gossip: Elaine finds Billy lying on the unisex floor after being beaten up by Georgia. She tries to give him some air by the radical method of sticking her tongue down his throat.

Smile Therapy: John thinks Dr Flott is good and isn't surprised that she suggested putting Ally on medication, considering Ally hasn't been happy in all the time he's known her. He asks Nelle when they're going to talk about him spanking her by mistake (see 302 'Buried Pleasures'). His musical monkey keeps going off through their conversation. John doesn't think Nelle is showing much compassion. John tells a sweet story about a date he had as a teenager, about the humiliation he felt when he failed to kiss her due to his nose whistling and her giggling.

Sub Zero: Schoolgirls consider Nelle 'cool' and like the clothes Ling designed for her. She doesn't feel she has anything to talk about with John, that the spanking he gave her was 'criminal' and that it was a mistake to try to realise a sexual fantasy he had overheard. However, while working on a case of a shy boy who kissed a girl at school and was slapped back, Nelle realises how much humiliation a mistake like that can lead to. She fixes things at the school by kissing the boy, Kirby, in public, and through that realises how embarrassed John must be by his hairbrush mistake.

Shrink Wrapped: Dr Tracy gets an equally annoying replacement, the medication-obsessed Dr Flott. Flott takes Prozac in suppository form, and it gives her a 'wriggle'. She keeps a pill dispenser on her belt, and suggests Zoloft, or Thorazine mixed 'with a little Lithium', as alternatives. She thinks Ally is both a 'little tramp' and, after Ally flushes the pills away, a 'pissy little thing'. She's through with trying to help Ally by the end of the episode. Unbelievably, John thinks Dr Flott is actually quite good.

Fantasy: Ally sees Al Green everywhere: in the consulting room, on a computer screen, in Renee's office, singing to her in the unisex, in the mirror, fixing the electrics and outside a bookstore in Green Street. Ally also sees Gladys Knight and a choir, as well as all her colleagues performing a song and dance routine. In the pharmacist she imagines herself tiny as she asks for her Prozac prescription. When she flushes the Prozac away she imagines being flushed with it.

The Case: At school young Kirby tried to kiss l'il Kim. Now Kirby is being kicked out of school because Kim's parents complained. Nelle and John represent Kirby and his parents, with Nelle arguing that the case is a misunderstanding and that everyone should put their hurt aside and move on.

Kisses: At the school Nelle gently kisses Kirby, raising his self-esteem and reputation no end.

The Verdict: 'You won't find happiness through love or by turning to God; it comes in a pill.' Silly episode, stupid case, daft characters. The use of medication for mental problems is treated both with excessive melodrama – in Ally's soul-searching as to whether to take Prozac – and with undue flippancy in the form of the pill-popping Dr Flott. Ally's solution – throwing the pills away – is a reactionary and unhelpful answer to the questions posed, showing that a programme steeped in fantasy isn't really equipped to deal with the serious issues surrounding mental health. The school case is both twee and silly, although it does give Nelle a chance to show her sweeter side. Thank God for the Billy sub-plot, throwing some desperately needed drama and tension into the mix.

304
Heat Wave

#3M04
15 November 1999

Written by David E. Kelley
Directed by Alex Graves

Cast: Dyan Cannon (Judge 'Whipper' Cone),
James Naughton (George), Jason Gedrick (Joel),
Tracy Middendorf (Risa), Aaron Lustig (Bowe),

Gina Philips (Sandy), Gerry Becker (Stone),
William Sanford Davis (Jim), Brad Wilson (Harold)

Risa Helms, the woman whose wedding was destroyed by Ally
(in 301 'Car Wash') returns to sue Ally for intentional infliction of emotional distress.

Meanwhile, Billy becomes a whole new man, Richard faces
some difficult truths and Georgia finds a shoulder to cry on . . .

Everything Stops For Ally: Ally remembers Risa Helms, of
course; how could she forget the woman whose wedding she so
publicly disrupted? When Risa sues she is determined not to pay
out, to the extent that she goes to Joel to try to get him to be a
witness for her. She goes to see Joel at the car wash, where Joel
tells Ally she ruined his life. Ally's defence is that as 'her bridesmaid and her lawyer' she had a duty to Risa. Ally admits that
Joel was as good as she told Risa, and tells Joel that Risa said he
touched her like he didn't know what he was doing. Ally
thought this meant Joel had no passion for her. Joel is surprised
about what Risa said. 'I was about to be married to the woman I
love,' he says. 'You destroyed that. I won't get over it.' After
their conversation Ally thinks maybe Joel isn't such a woman-
iser after all, and maybe he only seemed so phenomenal because
he 'kept up' with Ally's own 'incredible' love-making. At
Renee's suggestion Ally goes back to Joel to arrange a meeting
with Risa. Once he's agreed to the meeting, Ally asks why Joel
was different with her than with Risa. Joel says, 'The truth is that
was the first time I didn't feel a little inhibited when making
love.' He says it was 'incredible', and will never happen again.
Nevertheless, when Joel arrives at the office early for his
meeting with Risa, he and Ally talk briefly – he says he wouldn't
have had her down as a lawyer and thought she was an artist or
something similarly 'soulful' – and end up making love, even
after arguing that neither was sending signals to the other. Afterwards Joel puts it down to 'animal attraction'. Ally gets nervous
when everyone else arrives, stuttering and stumbling over her
words. She advises Joel not to tell Risa about their 'indiscretion'
and asks if there's any chance of a relationship between Joel and
Ally. 'Ally, you're a lawyer, I'm the manager of a car wash,'

Joel replies, and says they're physically compatible but that he loves Risa.

Introducing: Sandy Hingle, Billy's new young secretary. Her first line is 'I'll have to get used to this whole unisex thing'. We also meet George, an older man whom Georgia meets in a bar, and who turns out to have greater significance.

The Boy Next Door: Billy defends selecting Sandy as his secretary, saying she was 'the best candidate for the job'. He says that if Georgia is going to make home 'hell' over Sandy, he'll spend more time at work. 'You going to hit me again?' he asks Georgia. At Billy's group therapy he rejects the group's aim to 'develop a greater sensitivity to women'. He says that the men there actually feel emasculated because of their wives, who make them feel like failures. 'We're really here because we're not having *our* needs met.' Billy gets the group wound up into a frenzy: 'They don't like being dominated, well why the hell should we?' When Georgia says she wants them to work through this problem together, Billy replies that he's angry at himself for allowing himself to be a modern man when he doesn't want to be one, denying his old-fashioned nature. He wants children, with the mother at home, and he wants his needs to come first. 'I'm sick of playing the sensitive male thing, I'm just sick of it.' Billy goes out and emphasises the new Billy by getting his hair bleached blond. 'There's a new man in town,' he tells Georgia, and as he slaps his fist into his palm we hear Billy's 'sting' for the first time. Later, Billy comforts John: 'Women talk. They don't like it when men talk.' To Billy, the fact that Nelle is trying to pick John's friends for him shows she's serious. He tells John that Georgia 'objects to everything'. Unfortunately, Georgia is standing behind him at the time.

Georgia On My Mind: Georgia doesn't approve of Sandy: 'What is she, nineteen?' She wants him to get rid of her and is disgusted when he rejects this on the grounds that it's a work decision, not 'home'. She doesn't know what's going on, but she wants them to work through his problems together. In a bar Georgia meets George, an older man who doesn't drink, but still buys the drinks so he can have the comforting sensation of sitting with a drink and imagining the sensation. George realises this sounds strange. He compares it to taking off a wedding ring, because it makes you feel closer to not being married. Georgia thinks Billy's new hair makes him look like Billy Idol: 'Clearly you're losing your mind.' When Billy tells her he's a new man and walks out, Georgia mutters to herself that she *hates* the new man. When she catches Billy telling John that she objects to everything, Georgia says he wants her to leave him, and that when Billy goes for therapy the therapist will eventually tell him that everything Billy is doing is a mechanism to get Georgia to leave him, because Billy's too nice a guy to break it off himself. Georgia returns to the other bar and sits with George. 'I came to sit next to something I know I can't really have,' she tells him. She has her wedding ring on and points it out to him. 'I'm old enough to be your father,' says George, 'so if I were to make a move on you it would take the form of a lecture.' They dance.

Fishisms: Richard has his home and office wired with alarms which react to certain words being spoken: 'can we talk' activates alarms, as does the word 'marriage'. He pretends it's a smoke alarm, using the distraction as an avoidance technique – Ling of course sees through all of this easily enough. He considers Sandy 'young enough to spank', says the firm should get her to sign a sexual harassment waiver and watches her through binoculars. He's shocked when Ling admits to faking orgasms and that she is bored with his sustained sexual performance – she wants him to just go for his own climax and let her satisfy herself. This disturbs Richard: 'To give is to receive, and if she's not getting there's a danger she may stop giving.' Richard goes to Whipper for reassurance about his prowess. She mentions her wattle, but Richard is good with necks so that doesn't really count. When Richard overhears Nelle asking John how he'd like it if she mimicked the noise he made in bed, Richard says he'd like to hear. Later he goes to Whipper's office alone and ends up touching her wattle. 'You're a great lady, Whipper,' he says, 'I'm sorry I never said that enough.' Whipper calls him a 'bad, bad boy'.

Grrr!: Ling wants to talk with Richard. When he fails to give her his time, she tells him what the problem is in front of John: 'I've been faking my orgasms.' That gets his attention and they continue the conversation in private. She tells him she fakes orgasms so he will 'roll off and go to sleep'. She's very sexually satisfied – just not necessarily when Richard is there. She doesn't like sex to go on for more than ten minutes and wants Richard to stop taking the Viagra. 'We live in New England. Be a Minuteman again, it's colonial. I'll take care of myself.' When Ling overhears Richard and John talking about female orgasms, she wishes she'd never raised the issue: 'We're talking about five seconds here, that's how long the big "O" lasts.' She thinks there are far more important things than orgasms in a relationship. Ling doesn't like faking it because she hates to end her day on a lie, and thinks the polyp on her throat might be from screaming.

Whip-Lash!: Renee and Whipper take Ally's case, but the case isn't helped by Whipper getting emotional at Risa's account of the failed wedding day. When Richard comes to Whipper to ask if she experienced orgasms when they were together, Whipper says, 'You really don't have anything to be insecure about.' When she meets Joel immediately after he's had sex with Ally, Whipper notes that his expression is that of a man who has just had sex. When Richard comes to her office, gutted by Ling's sexual disinterest, Whipper says Ling has 'no idea'.

Sub Zero: According to John, during sex Nelle makes little 'ooh' noises and that he isn't even sure a control freak like Nelle would approve of orgasms. Nelle thinks it's better to deceive a man than tell him he doesn't please a woman in bed, and is furious when she finds out John has been impersonating her 'oohs' – especially when Ling repeats a comment by John about Nelle being 'drowned out by a lone cricket'. Even though John says he told Richard, and Richard is John's best friend, Nelle still doesn't like it; she doesn't want Richard to be John's best friend, and she certainly doesn't want them to discuss that kind of thing.

Toilet Humour: The staff of Cage & Fish recap the plot of 301 'Car Wash' by accosting Ally with accusations in the unisex.

Song: Snatches of 'Lady Marmalade' play in relation to Ally's car-wash experience. When Billy emerges with his new hair, we hear 'There's A New Man In Town' by Mighty Sam McCain.

Kisses: Ally has one last kiss with Joel – and still wants more of that car-wash action.

The Case: Risa Helms presents Ally with a summons and complaint, suing Ally for intentional infliction of emotional distress. Risa's description of what Ally did, that it was 'the height of cruelty', is very persuasive. Renee acts for Ally's defence and argues Ally was looking out for Risa's best interests. Renee suggests the only way to avoid serious damages is to prove marrying Joel would have been more damaging, and the only way to do that is to get him to testify. After Joel refuses but appears to be devoted to Risa, Renee suggests brokering a reconciliation between Joel and Risa. In spite of Ally having sex with Joel for a second time, Joel and Risa manage a reconciliation and Ally dodges the expensive lawsuit.

Fantasy: When Risa approaches Ally with the summons, Ally imagines her still wearing her wedding dress. When Joel is talking about Ally not being the mother of his children, Ally imagines firing out his babies in a maternity room.

The Verdict: 'I swallowed the wrong thing.' A fractured episode about fractured relationships, *Heat Wave* answers the questions left hanging from 301 'Car Wash' over Joel's motivations, while bashing holes in the relationships of the regulars. A couple of significant new characters and one significant new haircut add up to a steady development of the ongoing themes and plotlines, as things begin to fall apart and temptations are gradually succumbed to.

305
Troubled Water

#3M05
22 November 1999

Written by David E. Kelley
Directed by Joanna Kerns

Cast: Tracey Ullman (Dr Tracy Clark),
Dyan Cannon (Judge 'Whipper' Cone), Gina Philips (Sandy),
Amy Castle (Young Ally), Jill Clayburgh (Jeannie McBeal),
James Naughton (George McBeal)

It's Thanksgiving, but with surprises all round Ally and her friends have little to be thankful for.

Everything Stops For Ally: Ally gathers her friends and family around her for Thanksgiving, but it soon turns out to be one big free-for-all argument. Matters hardly improve when Ally finds out that Georgia kissed her father, resulting in Ally throwing everyone else out so she can have a long talk with her parents. Thus we go back to the root of Ally's delusions, as described last season: that she retreated into her fantasy world after seeing her mother have sex with a man other than her father. As Ally and her parents argue, Jeannie McBeal says that her affair was only a retaliation against George's infidelities, and that if Ally can't handle the reality of her parents' complex relationship perhaps she should stay in her dream world. Ally responds by finally telling her mother what she saw as a child: 'Reality is walking into your parents' room as a three-year-old child and seeing you in bed with another man.' Ally's mother is shocked, as is her father. After this, Ally sits alone remembering her childhood with her father, and when her mother comes to justify her affair Ally doesn't want to listen. Her attention is pricked by what Jeannie then tells her: that George wants a divorce. After Jeannie admits she loved the man she had an affair with, Ally drags her parents to Dr Tracy to try to sort things out. Ally's father talks about how his relationship with Ally's mother is based on 'a history', a history undermined by the fact that she had an affair long ago. Jeannie snaps back that George was unfaithful first, by feeling so much more for his daughter than his wife. George as much as admits this by saying he didn't start having affairs until Ally had left home, which Ally sees as hardly a defence. After the therapy session George and Jeannie go home, their marriage surviving again, as it has for all these years. Jeannie apologises for Ally having to see what she did, all those years ago.

Georgia On My Mind: Georgia meets George, the mysterious older man, at the same bar they previously met. When she suggests meeting up the next day, George reminds her the next day is Thanksgiving, and they kiss before Georgia rushes back to the bar beneath the office, desperately wondering where to get a turkey this late in the day. That's one concern that is dismissed when Ally invites her friends over for Thanksgiving, but Georgia has even bigger trouble when she realises her George is George McBeal – Ally's father. Ally overhears them talking about their kiss, and throws Georgia and the rest of her friends out so she can talk to her parents alone. Later Georgia tells Billy that she can't handle being labelled a 'Barbie doll' any more, and that Billy can have his way out. She stops only to ask Renee and Whipper if there's a place for her at their firm.

The Boy Next Door: Billy challenges Nelle's childish flirting with him, accusing her of acting like a schoolgirl – he gets a knee in the groin for his trouble. When Georgia walks out on him, Billy gets what Georgia predicted he wanted all along (in 303 'Seeing Green') – a chance to get out without seeming like the villain. At the end of the episode Billy meets up with Sandy and goes for coffee with her.

Sub Zero: Nelle thinks Billy is going through some kind of crisis, and when he becomes tired of her teasing and the way she treats him Nelle just pretends to be titillating him. When Billy points out just how juvenile these sexual power games are, Nelle assaults him – how charming of her.

Fishisms: Richard is still torn between Whipper and Ling. He's surprised that Georgia forgot Thanksgiving, it being the biggest cooking day of the year: 'How often does a woman get the chance to shine outside the bed?' Ally's mother remembers Richard as 'the one who kept touching my neck' from when she visited Ally at university. When Ally throws everyone out on Thanksgiving, Richard asks if he can take the turkey. Later, when challenged by Whipper, Richard tells her that she is his 'soul mate', but because of that there would be no time for what Richard considers important to him in a relationship – sex. At the end of the episode he goes to Whipper, babbling incoherently about how he doesn't see proper relationships being successful: 'The relationships don't work, they seem like work.'

Grrr!: Ling thinks Billy has all the personality of a nail – 'minus the sharp end'. Ling constantly insults Whipper, to the point where Whipper feels she has to leave the room.

Whip-Lash!: Whipper can't understand why Ling is so vile to her: 'What did I ever do to you?' She wants to know what's going on with Richard and isn't impressed by the same old stories about prioritising sex and not believing in long-term relationships. She closes her door on Richard when he proves himself still unable to give her the commitment she wants from him.

Shrink Wrapped: Dr Tracy insults Ally's father, then stops him from leaving with her remote-activated chair. She insists that it's not history that matters, it's the current state of the relationship. Tracy thinks Ally's parents' marriage is not beyond repair, but that George needs to either commit himself to his marriage or go back to trying to pick up girls half his age.

Song: Elaine and Billy sing 'Swinging On A Star', which is also essayed by Vonda and the legendary Levi Stubbs towards the end of the episode. Billy can't sing.

The Verdict: 'Don't make fun of my fantasy life, Mom; you inspired it.' No cases or courtrooms in this very personal episode, as the troubled marriage of Ally's parents is dissected, revealing the traumas that made Ally the person she is. Other dysfunctional relationships abound: Billy and Georgia slide further into the abyss, while Richard is torn between his sexy young girlfriend and his older 'soul mate'. There are some disturbing implications here: a young girl traumatised by an encounter with her mother's sexuality, a father looking for a daughter-substitute in bars. Not bad for a supposedly lightweight show, and a brave step out of the usual formula for a series in its third year.

306
Changes

#3M06
29 November 1999

Written by David E. Kelley
Directed by Arlene Stanford

Cast: Farrah Fawcett (Robin Jones), Dan Butler (Bender),
Andy Umberger (Fordham),
Jack Shearer (Judge Alan Rancor), Drew Snyder (Hughes),
Gina Philips (Sandy Hingle), D. C. Jefferson (Reporter#1),
Nancy O'Dell (Reporter#2),
Jerry Lander (Reporter#3/Anchor),
John Harnagel (Jury Foreman)

Another sexual harassment case looms, and John begins cracking up. Richard and Ling split, and Billy makes the biggest mistake of his life . . .

The Boy Next Door: Billy to Georgia: 'I was a wussified piece of wet toast woman's guy. Well, there's a new man in town.' In a scene unthinkable in season one, Billy is accused of being a male chauvinist pig and replies, 'Card carrying and proud of it.'

Fishisms: In a flash of humanity Richard shows genuine concern for the increasingly erratic John. 'My fellow senior partner, who's also my best friend . . . may be cracking up.'

Smile Therapy: Both cameras and reporters make John nervous: when interviewed for television his stutter gets so bad he sounds like Porky Pig. This leads to a clip of him being used on every television news programme on every single channel. Richard claims to be worried that Warner Bros will sue for copyright violation. All this sends John into an insecure rage: 'I'm tired of people thinking I'm this funny little man,' he says, explaining to Ally how the courtroom has always been his 'haven from ridicule', the one place where people treat him with respect. As of today he feels he's lost even that. 'I've made a big mistake,' he tells her. 'Before you came to this firm, I never went down to the bar after work; I never talked to anyone except Richard. I was content to be this litigant savant, because there was safety in it. And you brought me out and I'm grateful for it. Don't get me wrong – but you also made me believe that I was mainstream and I totally bought into that.' Pondering his eccentricities John comments, 'I'm also fascinated with frogs, I draft my closing arguments in bare feet, remnants in toilet bowls actually traumatise me. I can only make love to a woman if I pretend I'm Barry White, and just when I think I'm normal . . . my nose whistles.' Ally tells John that she regards him as a soul mate, and the most extraordinary person she has ever met. She asks him to 'embrace how wonderful all your little eccentricities are'.

Georgia On My Mind: In order to get more 'space' from a now insufferable Billy, Georgia quits Cage & Fish and goes to work with Renee and Whipper. Rene tells her, 'The pay's pretty lousy but you keep a piece of any action the firm brings in.' Georgia tells Richard she's going to quit and he begs her to take one more day to reconsider. She agrees and after she goes home he changes the locks on her office door and steals the files on her personal clients. Fish explains that one of the reasons he hired Georgia in the first place was because he knew she'd steal files from her old office (see 108 'Drawing The Lines'). He points out that she knows this and can hardly pretend to be shocked at his actions. He then gives her the plaque with her name on, which he's unscrewed from her office door, telling her it's a keepsake for her. He makes clear that if the new job doesn't work out, as senior partner he would 'take you back in a second'. Which makes her cry.

Grrr!: Ling apparently wants 'somebody quiet and rich who can please me in bed without chemicals'. Richard talks to her about their relationship and concludes, 'If there's anything to learn out there, I doubt we'll learn it together.' 'I'm bored with my character,' she exclaims at one point. Good job we're not.

Guy Talk: Richard and John witter on about selfhood for quite a long time. John feels that 'we are who we are, don't you find that devastating?' Richard's response is simply, 'If you don't like who you are, if you're truly unhappy with your life, it only means you're ready to have children.' Which isn't really very helpful.

Fetishes: Richard runs his finger along Robin Jones's wattle when she comes to see Billy.

Song: Billy's shift in character and increasingly outrageous behaviour are accompanied by 'New Man in Town' (performed here by Mighty Sam McCain). Billy Paul's 'Me and Mrs Jones' plays as Billy and Robin begin to make out in his office.

Fashion Victims: Billy wears a combination of a red shirt and greyscale tie that inexplicably works. Richard looks positively presidential in a black suit, dark shirt and black tie. Ling appears to have taken to wearing something resembling combat gear. Sandy looks fantastic.

The Case: Robin Jones, the lover of a deceased newspaper editor-in-chief, was appointed as his replacement upon his death. Staff at the paper conspired to fraudulently ring in sick, causing the magazine to miss its deadline, and she was subsequently fired. She feels, and Billy argues, that this was sexual harassment, so she is suing for damages. They hated her because she was an attractive woman who had been put in a position senior to them. They contend that she didn't get the job on merit but through her connection with the previous editor. Despite representing her, Billy initially agrees with the opposition, telling Robin, 'I think you're a bit of a gold-digger looking to capitalise on a stupid law that works as an equaliser for weak women, and if ever a jury found the right case to say "take sexual harassment law and shove it", this would be the ideal opportunity.' He tells her to settle, firstly when she's offered $75,000 and later when the offer is raised to $100,000.

Although it doesn't work on the jury, Billy's summing-up in court is brilliant, so brilliant in fact that Robin tells him it was 'so impassioned I thought for a second you actually believed what you were saying'. Billy admits that he did, although he *may* just be saying this to try to get Mrs Jones into bed.

Also Starring: Dan Butler is best known as shock jock 'Bull-dog' Briscoe from NBC's massively popular *Cheers* spin-off *Frasier*.

Toilet Humour: There's a huge scene in the unisex where just about everyone drops in and out over a five-minute period. The bulk of it is devoted to Ally and Georgia discussing the state of Billy and Georgia's marriage. Ally feels that Georgia quitting her job is not the solution and says of Billy, 'He changed, he'll change back.' The final scene, of course, renders all this discussion academic.

Kisses: Billy stupidly kisses Robin Jones, seemingly as part of his attempts to act as unlike himself as possible. Georgia walks in, and seeing this as the final straw, gives Billy back her wedding ring saying, 'I quit my job . . . and now I quit you.'

The Verdict: Ally's involvement in this episode is minimal as most of it is given over to Billy's behaviour, John's crisis, and Richard and Ling's split. The final scene is shocking and leaves you feeling kind of numb.

307
Saving Santa

#3M07
13 December 1999

Written by David E. Kelley
Directed by Rachel Talalay

Cast: Gina Philips (Sandy),
Albert Hall (Judge Seymore Walsh),
Amy Castle (Young Ally), Nicholas Pappone (Young Billy),
Vicki Lawrence (Dana), Lenny Wolpe (James Russell),
John Short (Larry), Jim O'Heir (Steven Mallory)

John represents a sacked Santa, Billy and Georgia fail to reconcile and Ally gets in touch with her inner child.

Everything Stops For Ally: Ally starts seeing a young girl; not the most disturbing of her delusions until she realises it's her younger self. Young Ally tells the adult Ally to help Billy, to 'save him'. To this end Ally spends the episode talking to Billy and Georgia, trying to get to the root of their problems and help them to reconcile. Her methods are pure Ally, using aggression to find the truth; she calls Billy a 'pig' and tells him that his behaviour gave Georgia some justification for kissing Ally's father, while he didn't even ask for an explanation of her actions but went out and kissed Robin Jones instead. Billy retaliates by arguing that Ally is just upset because she isn't the only woman Billy's willing to betray Georgia for. In the unisex, Ally sees visions of Billy and herself as children, talking about what they wished to be in later life: a fireman and an artist. When the real Billy comes in, Ally tells him that her visions are telling her to 'save him'. When Ally talks about their childhood ambitions and how they both became lawyers instead, Billy suggests that they might need saving. Ally has to force Georgia into listening to her, but eventually manages to tell her that both she and Billy kissed other people out of anger, anger that came from love. Ally explains Billy's patriarchal childhood and gets Georgia to agree to talk to Billy. Finally, she gets them to talk – but Georgia won't take Billy back. Billy tells Ally that she doesn't need saving, that even though she isn't an artist she still tries to paint the world 'in beautiful colours'.

The Boy Next Door: Billy thinks that when Georgia takes a case which involves going into court against Cage & Fish, it must be about trying to get at him, which Georgia vehemently denies. Billy is upset by Ally's attitude to him kissing Robin Jones, and notes that this is rather hypocritical since last year it was *her* kissing him. Billy prefers to dance the night away with the girls from the office rather than let Ally 'save' him, which he doesn't take too seriously. Through Ally, we learn about Billy's childhood and how it led him to aspire to the chauvinism he now espouses; his father ruled the house while his mother ruled the kitchen, and at school Billy was a quarterback while the girls were cheerleaders shouting for him. When asked if he hates his life, Billy answers, 'Maybe.' What he wants most of all is for Georgia to put her wedding ring back on – something she refuses to do.

Georgia On My Mind: When Georgia witnesses a sacked department store Santa arguing with the management, saying that his lawyer is John Cage and the management won't get away with firing him, Georgia wades in to represent the store – she tells them that she knows how to beat Cage. When Billy accuses her of taking the case just to beat him, Georgia replies that he's being stupid: 'I've heard that can happen when a person soaks his head in bleach for too long.' She tells Ally she's been on a diet, and lost '170 lbs of dead weight'. She tells Ally she's welcome to Billy, to which Ally replies that she doesn't want him. When Ally tries to talk to her, Georgia snaps that she doesn't have to put up with Ally any more, but apologises and listens to what Ally has to say. Georgia infers that Ally is acting out of guilt, which is none of Georgia's concern. Her closing in court is about dreams and disappointment, and she is almost in tears by the end of it. Georgia agrees to meet Billy but can't bring herself to take him back. After winning her case, Georgia sits alone instead of celebrating.

Smile Therapy: John is described as 'probably the best lawyer in town' by his client, Steven the sacked Santa. When he loses his case, John gets fined for calling the judge a 'Grinch', in reference to Dr Seuss's *How the Grinch Stole Christmas*.

Sub Zero: In a sweet character touch, Nelle testifies in court as to how important going to see Santa was when she was young, on how sitting on his lap could make Christmas real in a way that her parents, who constantly argued through the holiday, could not.

Grrr!: 'I'm not going to kiss you,' Ling tells a dazed Ally (see 302 'Buried Pleasures').

Fishisms: When John's client seems likely to lose, Richard wishes the client in question could be something more sympathetic and PC than a fat white man: gay, perhaps, or Indian. Richard tells Billy that whatever kind of dyed-blond schmuck he may be, at least he isn't boring like he used to be.

Fantasy: Ally is haunted by visions of herself and Billy as children. At the end of the episode, we see Young Billy walking next to our Billy without Ally as a viewpoint – suggesting these apparitions somehow exist independently of Ally's imagination.

The Case: Steven Mallory, a Santa Claus impersonator, is fired from Newman's department store for being too fat; John Cage is his attorney. Georgia represents the store and argues that there was no written contract, while John replies that there was an oral contract. There is much argument over the necessity of plump Santas and the veracity of verbal agreements. In court Mr Russell, head of Newman's, argues their thinner Santas appeal to a better demographic of shopper.

Guilty?: John doesn't deserve to win as he really doesn't have a case, and for once he does indeed lose to Georgia. However, on the basis of Steven's devotion to his job in court Newman's decide to re-hire him as their Santa. So that's all right then.

The Verdict: 'At the end of the day, life is just this big wall of reality that we all crash into.' Ally takes a proactive and selfless stance in this episode, driven by the child she once was to try to save Billy's marriage. That she fails is a testament to how, sometimes, dreams just aren't enough. The reinstatement of a department store Santa can't really stop the ending of this episode being fundamentally depressing; the old certainties of the show are still collapsing as relationships break down and characters experience radical change, but as yet there's nothing new and exciting to be hopeful for.

308
Blue Christmas

#3M08
20 December 1999

Written by David E. Kelley
Directed by Jonathan Pontell

Cast: Wendy Worthington (Camaro), Gina Philips (Sandy),
Robert Curtis Brown (McCabe), Linda Pine (Lynn),
Brad Wilson (Harold), Aloma Wright (Judge Harris),
Gerry Becker (Attorney Stone),
Joanna Sanchez (Janine Waller)

It's Ally's third Christmas at Cage & Fish and she and Elaine find an abandoned child. Meanwhile the traditional Christmas party is being planned as usual . . .

Office Gossip: Ally and Elaine are looking at a nativity scene in a store, when they realise that the Jesus mannequin is a real baby. 'Oogachaka,' says Ally, looking doe-eyed at the little infant. Elaine and Ally take the baby to the office where Elaine decides to apply to adopt the baby, whom she calls Elliot. The effect on the rest of the office is profound, with everybody taking an interest and being affected by the new arrival in some way. Eventually baby Elliot's mother turns up and demands him back even though she abandoned him. After considering letting the firm fight the mother on her behalf over custody of Elliot, Elaine returns the baby to his mother.

The Boy Next Door: Billy goes to his therapy group, and tells them that he went to Georgia and asked her to go on a date with him. She blew him out. The group leader asks Billy why he kissed Robin Jones, and he retorts that whatever he did Georgia would disapprove. He says she is the sort of person who always sees the glass as half empty, and she makes him feel as though it was him that drained it. After some prompting Billy tells the group that Georgia is a bitch. 'Bitch,' chant the rest of the group. Ouch! After Georgia has turned him down, Billy asks Sandy, his secretary, to go to the party with him. She turns him down, partly because she works for him, and partly because she thinks he needs to wait longer before he starts dating again.

Fishisms: Richard asks Billy to talk Ally out of singing at the Christmas party. 'She plans on singing something sexy,' Richard says. 'Next we'll have Mary Tyler Moore doing porn.'

Everything Stops For Ally: Billy goes to see Ally in her office and finds her with baby Elliot. 'Seven years ago, I would have thought this would be us,' she tells him. 'What did happen to us?' he asks. Ally sadly tells him that she doesn't know.

Georgia On My Mind: Asked for an opinion on whether Elaine will make a good mother, Georgia provides the court with a life history of our Ms Vassal, stressing both positive and negative aspects of her character. When challenged about this, Georgia points out that fundamentally what's best for the child is more important than what Elaine wants.

Grrr!: Baby Elliot repeatedly pisses in Ling's face. Harsh. Despite this she goes all gooey around the infant, reconsidering her decision to never have kids – especially in the light of the fact that they can now laser off stretch marks.

Song: In the unisex Billy and baby Elliot dance to Billy's theme song, 'New Man in Town' (as performed by Mighty Sam McCain). John arrives, takes the baby off Billy and then he and Elliot dance to 'You're the First, the Last, My Every-thing', John's theme song, performed, of course, by Barry White. Billy and John feel that Elliot enjoyed himself, but Richard insists that he's just smiling because he has gas. Elaine once again campaigns to get Ally to sing at the office Christmas party; amazingly this time she succeeds, and so Ally performs 'Santa Baby' whilst dressed in a sexy Santa outfit, complete with micro-mini skirt and red velvet hat. Vonda Shepard sings 'No One Is Alone' (from the Stephen Sondheim musical *Into the Woods*) and Lieber/Stoller's 'Saved'. We also get to hear the Village People classic 'Macho Man'.

Fashion Victims: Nelle's hair. Er, why? How? What?

The Verdict: 'I have very little reason to doubt that Ms Vassal will make an exceptional mother.' Baby Elliot's plotline gives Jane Krakowski a chance to shine, but is ultimately a little too twee for our tastes. The subplots that result from this plotline are great, however, particularly Richard pretending to throw the baby across the office, and the effect baby Elliot has on Ling. But one of the weakest of the season.

309
Out In The Cold

#3M09
10 January 2000

Story by Josh Caplin and David E. Kelley
Teleplay by David E. Kelley
Directed by Dennie Gordon

Cast: Ted Marcoux (Louis), Fred Koehler (Marcus),
Rikki Dale (Leslie), Albert Hall (Judge Seymore Walsh),
Austin Tichenor (ADA Warren Tisbury),
Harry Danner (Hallen)

Ally meets Louis, a homeless man who can seemingly see into her soul. When Louis turns out to be an insurance agent pretending to be homeless as research for a book, Ally thinks she might have met her man. Unfortunately, Ally's first impression was correct: Louis is really homeless and he has a paranoid personality disorder. Even though he's begun taking medication and wishes to get treatment just to be with Ally, she nevertheless rejects him, and Louis returns to life on the streets.

Meanwhile, Ling is arrested when it turns out girls from her escort agency have been sleeping with teenage clients. Are the girls prostituting themselves or did they really like the boys in question? The issue is highlighted when Nelle finds out about John's past use of hookers . . .

Everything Stops For Ally: Ally is walking to work when a homeless man criticises her for pretending he doesn't exist. He calls her a 'rich bitch single lonely-heart lawyer'. He calls Ally a dreamer and tells Ally hers aren't coming true. In the office Ally tells Elaine that her life is a fraud, and that the homeless guy knew it. When Ally goes back the homeless guy calls her a narcissist, and he correctly identifies her as someone afraid of becoming her own mother. Ally takes him for coffee and asks if it is too much recognition for him. The homeless man is called Louis, and says Ally had the look of someone whose life has not gone the way she expected. She asks if Louis chooses to be homeless, to live outside society, but he tells her it was due to bad financial decisions. When Louis says he was once haunted by The Pips, Ally admits she was once haunted by Al Green – she says she almost went on Prozac to get rid of him but eventually did it on her own (see 303 'Seeing Green'). Both Ally and Louis have music in their lives but, as Louis says, Ally doesn't have time in her life to let that music live. When she meets Louis in the building wearing a suit and he tells her he was pretending to be homeless to research a book, Ally is a little put off that he had deceived her. But Louis says he really did see all those things in her, and when he says he never really saw The Pips, Ally replies that she really did see Al Green. Louis tells Ally this means there's still hope for her and Ally invites him for another coffee. When Louis stands her up, Ally worries he's not interested, but he turns up at the

office saying he was nearly run down. She tries to teach him
how to hear the music in his head, but they have difficulties.
When Louis walks her home like the perfect gentleman, Ally
tells Elaine he's too perfect, that there must be some secret.
She's right: when she tries to visit him at his office, she finds
he hasn't worked there for a while and that Louis has a paranoid personality disorder and genuinely lives on the streets. In
spite of all they have in common and his desire to get better,
Ally dumps him.

The Boy Next Door: Introducing the Billy girls, six slinkily
clad beauties Billy hires from Ling's service to impress an
important new client, Hallen. He goes into the meeting with
Hallen with the girls around him, and gives an impassioned
speech about how the CEO of a hip advertising agency should
be represented by hip young lawyers. Hallen asks who the girls
are and Billy replies that they're his assistants: 'I do my best
work operating on a heightened sense of acuity, mine is best
derived from sexual energy. Pretty women make me a better
lawyer. It's a fact, I won't apologise for it. I like the way they
look, the way they smell. The testosterone they generate makes
me a bigger ass and I've discovered the more of an ass I am,
the better I litigate: putting modesty aside, you won't find a
more gigantic ass than me.' Billy describes the girls as a
'look'. When Ally asks him what the point is, he says, 'It
becomes me.'

Smile Therapy: In a wonderfully post-modern moment, Nelle
asks John if he really went with a call girl, and he says it was
before he knew his 'character', a neat reference to how odd
that first Cage plotline now seems. John tells Nelle that by
going to a call girl he was being honest, not picking up women
and pretending he was interested in anything but sex. As a
busy man, he just bypassed the singles scene and went straight
to the escort services. He now regrets it and says he's 'a different person now'. It happened in the past and he gets frustrated
when Nelle pursues the issue: 'Bite me,' he tells her. He
doesn't want to sit next to Nelle in court after this. In the bar,
he seems to call her a bitch – but he's just quoting Louis shouting at Ally. John calls Ling an 'ungrateful little pimp'. He isn't

pleased that Nelle judges him on his past, especially considering Nelle believes in legalising prostitution when he doesn't. When she explains her reasons, her hurt, John tells Nelle he never meant to hurt his children, or her, through what he did.

Sub Zero: Nelle is upset when she finds out John used to use prostitutes. She thinks John's self-justification is an evasion of responsibility for his actions, and that even though it was in the past it still matters. 'People are made up of what they do in the past.' She calls John a 'poughke-poughke-poughke-peckerhead!' 'Hated your stupid frog, too!' she shouts at him later. Nelle admits she is hurt by John's use of prostitutes in his past, she doesn't want 'the man I marry, the father of my children' to have been with a prostitute. (This little speech seems a bit odd, considering Nelle has previously shown active disinterest in having children.) She feels John has a duty to the children he will one day have, who would be devastated to find out their father had been with a hooker.

Grrr!: Ling is arrested in the office for running an escort service for under-age boys. She makes eighty to ninety thousand dollars a year from running the service, but insists sex isn't part of the deal. In court Ling argues that the escort service allows boys to get real girls later – girls see a young guy with a good-looking date, they want him for themselves. She says there's an implied offer of sex on any date: 'That's how we get you to buy dinner.' Women, she says, are 'vain, appearance-driven animals ruled by envy'. Ling knows Judge Walsh hates her.

Office Gossip: Elaine comforts Ally after she dumps Louis: 'There was no other choice,' she tells Ally.

Ex-DA Renee: Cage & Fish bring Renee in on Ling's case to advise – she advises that Ling testify at the Probable Cause hearing. Renee lets slip that John used to go with call girls – in Nelle's presence.

Fishisms: Richard throws a coin to Louis in the street, showing he isn't entirely without kindness, albeit of a very off-hand variety. Richard tells Renee he only got her in for

Soul Searching

Ling's case because she's an ex-DA, and they hoped she'd have dirt on the DA on Ling's case, almost causing Renee to walk out. In court, Richard says that almost all women are bought, and it's good that kids learn that at a young age.

Bygones: When Renee reveals that John went with call girls, Richard thinks this is 'such a major bygone'. Richard uses 'bygones' to stop an argument between his colleagues.

Men: Louis, the homeless guy with the paranoid personality disorder, who tries to win Ally over by claiming to be just an insurance agent pretending to be homeless while writing a book. Confused? Us too. His ability to hit a nerve in Ally by getting to the heart of her is a plus point, but in the end Ally just can't cope with his mental problems. At the end of the episode Louis is back on the streets.

Girl Talk: Ally and Renee discuss Louis and how long it is since Ally has met a genuine 'maybe', someone who might actually work out.

The Case: Ling, as previously established in 221 'The Green Monster', runs an escort service. This service provides teenage boys who can't get a date with attractive girls to take out, but it isn't a prostitution operation. When the mother of one of the boys catches her son having sex with his escort, Ling is arrested. At the Probable Cause hearing the boys in question testify about how they hired escorts because they couldn't get a date. Marcus, one of the boys, is so insecure he can't imagine the girl could want to sleep with him, although John gets him to admit he didn't pay directly for sex, and that the girl involved, Lesley, said she really wanted to. The girl confirms this.

Judge Not: 'Mr Fish, I don't even want to see your lips move.' It's Judge Seymore Walsh, unimpressed by Ling and her escort service. He doesn't like Ling making speeches and wants her to stick to answering the questions.

Guilty?: As John says, no crime has been committed. It's an escort service, and although boys hiring dates may be a little off, it isn't illegal. Judge Walsh agrees and dismisses the charges, allowing Ling to go with 'the moral condemnation of the court'.

Song: After her first encounter with Louis, Ally hears 'Neighborhood' sung by Vonda, from the first soundtrack album.

Fashion Victims: It's Ling's chance to wear those prison togs as she gets her day in jail.

The Verdict: 'So now we both know each other: I'm a proud loser and you're a desperate lonely lawyer.' Keep that Prozac on standby, have a video of *Pokemon* ready to lift your spirits, because this is a really, really depressing episode. Ally discovers just how low delusions can take somebody, meeting a man who shares so much in common with her but has descended all the way into madness and homelessness. Ally's decision to not date Louis is understandable, but a bravely unsympathetic and real decision for a lead character to take. The John and Nelle plot is equally miserable, as even though their argument is resolved we know that, in some sense, John will always be stained by what he did, in Nelle's eyes and his own if no one else's. Amongst all this doom and gloom thank God for Billy and his retinue of girls, a much needed thread of amusing lunacy in an otherwise crushingly heavy story.

310
Just Friends

#3M10
17 January 2000

Written by David E. Kelley
Directed by Michael Schultz

Cast: Carlos Jacott (Bob Russell),
Gina Philips (Sandy Hingle)

Has 'The One' been under Ally's nose all this time? And if so, what can she do about it? Georgia returns to the office with devastating news.

Fantasy: Ally and John wait for the elevator after working late. He asks her how they both manage to spend every day in the same office and not see that they belong together. They grab each other, kissing frantically, and then Ally wakes up. Ally tells Renee about this dream and ponders as to whether John Cage, her best friend, could be 'The One'. Later, Ally and Renee stand in front of the same elevator. Renee tells Ally that she'll have to take bold steps in order to get what she deserves. Ally concurs and steps into the elevator. Which isn't there. She falls down the empty lift shaft, plummeting to her death. Then she wakes up, of course.

Georgia On My Mind: Georgia returns to her old office and hands Billy an envelope. She's divorcing him. Renee will be representing her and she tells Billy to get himself a lawyer. Broken, he asks Georgia if she really had to serve the papers herself. She says yes and leaves a stunned Billy alone in his office.

The Boy Next Door: Ally attacks Billy for walking around with the 'Billy Girls', only to be informed that he's brought them with him because he has an important meeting to go to and the girls will impress his client, who makes $500 million a year.

Later, Sandy tells Billy she can't work for him any longer. She thinks the 'Billy Girls' are silly and is worried that people won't take her seriously if she works for him. Billy apologises and says that if she stays he'll get rid of his entourage.

Smile Therapy: Following her moment of revelation, Ally fails dismally to act casual around John. He immediately realises that there is a problem and asks her if she's sick or dying. Later she tells John about her epiphany, spinning for him the 'hypothetical' story of someone who suddenly realised that someone might be 'The One' but who was inhibited by the fact that that person was involved with someone else. John replies by telling her that he knew a woman who, he was convinced, was 'The One'. She had issues with a significant ex-boyfriend, who was a friend of his; a complex predicament. Ally asks what he did and John tells her that he asked her out. He had to, he wouldn't have been able to live with himself afterwards if he hadn't. The date was hopeless, but he's glad he tried, and he and the woman are still friends. Ally asks him if she knows this woman (duh!) and John surprises no one by saying that it's her he's talking about.

Office Gossip: Elaine has a very important date with a man who sounded 'dreamy' on the phone. She's wearing trousers that have been specially marinated in pheromones for the occasion. She later discovers that her date only went out with her because he thought sex was a sure thing. This gives Elaine a crisis about how she is perceived.

Grrr!: Ling tells Ally that the best men are always taken and that the only way to get one is to steal him from someone else.

Sub Zero: John has either made, or had made, a pair of shoes with retractable heels. His hope is that Nelle will wear them. When she retracts the heels he'll be able to kiss her on the lips in a way he's never been able to before. Nelle seems somewhat troubled by this. When they're alone together, Nelle asks John why he's been so troubled recently. He tells her that it's nothing she needs to concern herself with. She retorts that couples don't keep secrets from each other. 'You want to know the big secret?' he asks. 'I love you', and he kisses her.

Song: Ally hears snatches of 'Tommy' Pete Townshend's phenomenal rock opera, as recorded by his band, 60s' mod heroes, The Who. Both Billy and John's theme songs are heard again (we surely don't need to tell you what they are, do we?) and Vonda sings instantly recognisable easy-listening classic 'It's So Easy'.

Hit The Bar: After Georgia has given him the divorce papers Billy sits alone in the bar, drowning his sorrows. Sandy sees him and points out that doing such a thing is very clichéd. He asks her if he should be out there on the dance floor instead and she admits that this would be even more clichéd. She asks him if there's anything she can do to help and Billy offers to walk her home. 'And that's all you'll do,' she tells him. 'That's all I'm offering,' he replies sadly.

The Verdict: Everyone is put through the wringer this week. Elaine, Georgia and Billy get the bulk of the sympathy, but John and Ally are hardly having a picnic either. John's decision not to risk his friendship with Ally for the sake of a potential relationship seems to fly in the face of everything the series has ever said about romance, and only time will tell if they've made the right decision. Special mention must go to Gil Bellows for his performance in this episode. 'Just Friends' makes extraordinary demands on him and he rises to the occasion with aplomb.

311
Over The Rainbow

#3M11
7 February 2000

Written by David E. Kelley
Directed by Alan Myerson

Cast: Amy Castle (Young Ally),
Curtis Armstrong (Attorney 'Tiny' Tim Fallow),
Roy Brocksmith (Judge Norway),
Jim Davidson (The Process Server)

Once again, Cage & Fish is sued. Once again, it's an interminable, untenable case with sexual harassment overtones. This time there's a difference. Georgia is suing the firm for destroying her marriage – and might just tear the office apart in the process.

The Case: Georgia's case essentially consists of claiming that Cage & Fish is a sexually charged office, and that such an atmosphere contributed to the collapse of her marriage. As Ling points out, this is too bogus even for her.

Everything Stops For Ally: At the beginning of the episode Ally is sitting alone in her office after hours, waiting for the rain to let up so that she can walk home. Billy comes in and they have an interesting discussion which takes in both Billy's recent behaviour – Ally thinks he is clearly heading for a breakdown – and the fact that Ally is always 'waiting' for something. Billy shows her the empty main office and tells her that it's a room full of people with 'lives which they all go home to'. Later, Billy and Ally discuss their lives. Billy, with startling clarity, demonstrates that he does understand the problems of everyone at the firm. 'We are grown up, that's the problem. We've gone from being people with bright futures to people who should be living those futures now . . . I'm an attorney with a failed marriage and a bleached head.'

The Boy Next Door: Billy claims to regard Georgia's suit as 'a frustrated, angry, weak woman looking to exact a pound of flesh like typical angry male-hating, frustrated, embittered weak women like to do'. As it turns out he couldn't be more wrong, of course. No surprise there then. Nelle puts him on the stand to testify as to the lack of merit in Georgia's case. He begins well, not defending kissing Ally and explaining how he and Georgia have grown 'angry' with one another in recent years. However, after a while he lets rip, telling the court about his rediscovery of his 'deep-seated values', saying that mothers should stay at home, and that he has no objection to women having careers as long as they don't want children. He describes the 'Billy Girls' as 'a look'. Success begets success, apparently, and if you show up dripping with beautiful models it makes a statement. Billy argues that women as a gender are vindictive – they live to belittle men. It's no wonder that Richard objects to Billy's testimony on the grounds that he's ruining the firm's case.

Fishisms: Once Georgia has filed her suit Richard is understandably aggrieved. 'How can she sue us for breaking up her marriage?' he asks. 'Did the firm kiss Robin Jones? Did the firm soak its head in Clorax and pledge allegiance to schmuckhood?' On the stand Richard does himself and the firm no favours. Asked if women are sex objects he returns,

'Yes.' Asked if he would extend this to all women he replies, 'Not the ugly ones. Fat, that depends on individual taste.' John objects to this and Richard attempts to withdraw his testimony. Unorthodox to say the least.

Georgia On My Mind: Ally traps Georgia in the lift and tackles her about her case. 'I was standing in my office, staring out of the window and actually it made me think; suppose somebody hated the way their life turned out. Who would they sue? And then I thought, "Well, that's pretty silly." You can't file a lawsuit just because you hate your life. But that's exactly what you're doing, aren't you, Georgia?' Georgia has supplied Fallow with all sorts of personal material on the employees of Cage & Fish including John's use of a call girl (See 102 'Compromising Positions') and his spanking of Nelle (see 302 'Buried Pleasures').

Grrr!: 'Maybe we should call Ling to the stand,' suggests a desperate Richard. 'She could verify that women live to belittle men.'

Ex-DA Renee: Renee tries to tackle Georgia about the case, telling her that these people are her friends and that she consequently shouldn't treat them like this.

Smile Therapy: 'Put Georgia on the stand. I want to get her,' says John. In preparation we see him pour enough glasses of water to fill his office and then he lets rip. He takes Georgia's case to pieces in what may be the best, the most vicious cross-examination the Biscuit has ever performed. He wins every point but his ire is so obvious that Billy stands up and says, 'That's enough!' 'You're not being sued here, Billy, I am,' John responds.

Fantasy: This episode makes great use of child versions of the regular case. Billy and Ally have a discussion where they switch from their normal selves to children and back again, as do John and Richard. At the end of the episode we see the entire cast as children, walking together away from the courthouse.

Fetishes: While on the stand Richard is forced to explain what 'wattle' is. Shudder.

Song: Many *Ally McBeal* episodes take their names from song titles and lyrics, and this is no exception, the title coming, of course, from 'Over the Rainbow' (written by Harold Arlen and Yip Harburg), a song from *The Wizard of Oz* (Victor Fleming, 1939). It's performed here by the musical voice of this show, Vonda Shepard, who also gets to sing Gene Pitney's 'He's A Rebel'. We hear the Biscuit's bells as he prepares to take on Georgia.

Toilet Humour: The role of the unisex is attacked here. Richard claims that the reason it exists is so that 'we can all go together when we go'.

Guy Talk: Richard asks John if he remembers when he came up with the great idea of starting a law firm. He had four reasons: 1) money, 2) money, 3) fun and 4) money. Richard wonders what happened to number three. Richard doesn't think being sued by Georgia is fun. He doesn't think that John bullying Georgia on the stand is fun. 'When I was little I just hated the grown-ups. I would vow that when I grew old, I didn't want to become an adult. I harboured this fantasy that we'd all get to be kids at this place. We'd work together, play together . . . fun! Look how it's turning out. It's war! What happened?' Richard decides that his dream is over and that Cage & Fish should be run 'like a law firm instead of a warm-up act for happy hour'. 'This informality is stupid. The associates don't know their place. They overstep.' 'Let's run this place like a damn law firm, that way nobody gets hurt and we don't bust up any lousy marriages.' He acknowledges he can't do this of course. 'We do have something here, don't we?' he asks John. 'The people, the friends. We have built something special. Right?' John shakes Richard's hand, smiles and says, 'Indeed.'

Guilty?: Of course Georgia doesn't win. Her case is absurd and she's up against John Cage! You can't but help feel sorry for her after all she's been through, but her case is about anger, not justice, and about making them feel some of the pain that she's been through.

The Verdict: 'The point is Richard Fish shouldn't apologise for this place that he's built.' Painful and funny. 'Over The Rainbow' is a brilliant statement of the series' heart: that Cage & Fish is different from other law firms and that is its greatest strength. John's epic defence of the firm's soul is wonderfully written and brilliantly played. The episode ends with the entire regular cast, including Georgia, going to dinner together, with all wrongs forgotten. Beautiful.

312
In Search Of Pygmies

#3M12
14 February 2000

Story by David E. Kelley and Josh Caplin
Teleplay by David E. Kelley
Directed by Arvin Brown

Cast: Albert Hall (Judge Seymore Walsh),
Orson Bean (Marty Brigg),
Craig Bierko (Dennis),
Annie Abbott (Taylor),
Daniel Nathan Spector (Donald),
Lillian Adams (Marion),
Richard Penn (Yellen)

Ally crashes a car to get a date, only to find her new man has a laugh from hell.

Ling reveals her softer side when an ageing friend gets threatened with eviction.

Everything Stops For Ally: Ally spots a decent-looking guy while driving and tries to get his attention. In the end all she can do is crash into the back of his car. 'Why would I want to go out with a woman who runs her car into me?' asks the man,

Dennis. But he does, inviting her out for dinner later. Dennis turns out to be an oncologist, but over dinner he reveals another trait – a horrid laugh. She dumps him on the grounds of his laugh and later Dennis returns with a neck brace and a lawyer. He threatens to sue over the accident, and Ally has to pay $25,000 to get Dennis and his laugh out of her life for good.

Grrr!: Ling uses a white cane and sunglasses to pretend she's blind, allowing her to jaywalk with impunity. Her best friend turns out to be Marty, an old man in a nursing home, who's being thrown out of his home for being too disruptive. Ling goes to court to fight for Marty, but they lose the case. Nevertheless, Ling is willing to let Marty live with her rather than alone. Unfortunately, Marty gets hit by a car and left comatose on life support. Ling's façade cracks and she is devastated. Ling is left trustee of Marty's affairs and has to make the decision of whether to turn the life support off. After some resistance she follows Marty's long-held wish by letting him die.

Fishisms: Richard ineptly follows Ling, suspecting she has a new lover. When she turns out to be going to an old people's home, Richard has a great time, caressing the wattles of various old women.

Smile Therapy: John is baffled by Marty's battles with imaginary pygmies in the nursing home. 'Pygmies are a peaceful people,' he insists.

Men: Dennis the oncologist, who Ally is so attracted to she crashes her car into his just to find an excuse to introduce herself. Unfortunately, Dennis has the worst laugh on earth and when Ally dumps him over it he resentfully seeks damages for the accident.

The Case: Marty Brigg is the life of the nursing home he lives in, telling tall tales and leading his fellow residents on exciting adventures. Unfortunately, the effect of all this is rather disruptive, and Lucy Taylor, who runs the home, gives him two weeks to leave. When Ling goes to court to try to force the home to keep Marty, Taylor recounts some of Marty's exploits:

convincing residents that pygmies prowl the home, scaring them with tales of a 'long-faced ghost', racing down the corridors, fighting monsters. She argues Marty is delusional and is badly affecting patients with dementia, sinking the home into chaos. Ling retaliates by arguing that Marty did a lot for the spirit of the home, while John gets one resident to testify that Marty's stories made the home a better place. The case collapses when Marty takes the stand and testifies that the pygmies are real, and when he actually sees the pygmies there in the courtroom his credibility sinks even further.

Guilty?: The judge decides that it's Taylor's right to run the home how she sees fit, thereby allowing Marty's expulsion. We can only agree – how annoying must that man have been?

Fantasy: Marty sees pygmies in the courtroom, and is pursued by them in the street – resulting in him running under a car.

The Verdict: 'Twenty-five thousand, is that how much you get for break-ups? You must be rich.' Like last year's 213 'Angels And Blimps', this episode attempts to give Ling a softer, more caring side and throws all sense of drama or subtlety out of the window in the process. While the pygmies are a wonderfully bizarre image, the case itself is twee and Marty's death just seems like a desperate way to end a flailing plot. Dennis is an impressive addition to the list of unsuitably awful men Ally has dated and dumped, though, so things aren't a total write-off.

313
Pursuit Of Loneliness

#3M13
21 February 2000

Written by David E. Kelley
Directed by Jonathan Pontell

Cast: Mark Feuerstein (Raymond Dearing),
Gina Philips (Sandy),
Richard Topol (Evan Stevens),

Pamela Warren (Lisa Treadway),
Rosemary Forsyth (Judge Graves),
Eric Christmas (Judge Morrison),
Eric and Steven Cohen (The Twins)

Note: Although credited Lisa Nicole Carson
doesn't feature in this episode.

Ally fights Georgia on either side of an unusual divorce case, whilst John and Nelle fight each other. Billy's divorce papers come through, although he's too busy trying to seduce his secretary to comment in depth. Lots of coffee gets spilled . . .

The Boy Next Door: Billy's attempt to chat up Sandy is more than a little sleazy, especially considering what he's been up to this season, but you still want him to succeed, partly because he's become such a pathetic figure, and partly because Sandy might actually help him find the real Billy again. He tells her that he goes 'home every night to an empty place and instead of missing Georgia I miss you'. See . . . sleazy. As they kiss for the first time we can see that Billy still wears his wedding band. (Georgia doesn't: see 306 'Changes'.) Ally makes clear she thinks Billy is out of his mind and still considers herself a friend of Georgia's.

We Got It Together, Didn't We?: Nelle's observation that 'there's nothing worse than being hit on by one of the little people' leads to a massive argument between John and Nelle. Nelle unfairly interprets John's willingness to date someone of any social status as chauvinism, reasoning he'd date anyone beautiful regardless of what they were like on the inside. It's clear, of course, that John simply means that he wouldn't pre-judge someone based upon his or her profession. This disturbs John, leading him to conclude that Nelle is an elitist, and he tells her that it bothers him that she draws class distinctions. Nelle responds by unfairly labelling John a hypocrite. He calls her a 'stuck-up, intolerant snob'. She then drives a freight train through his world by cruelly saying, 'Have you any clue as to just how weird you are?'

Fishisms: Richard and John see Billy and Sandy kissing, and recalling both the first season and the events of 311 'Over The Rainbow', Richard comments, 'Excellent, she'll sue, excellent,' with a kind of perky resignation.

Georgia On My Mind: Billy's soon-to-be-ex represents soon-to-be-divorced Lisa Treadway and wins without having to say a word.

Office Gossip: Elaine practically begs Ally to let her stay and watch her conversation with Dearing. Ally of course refuses.

Grrr!: Ling only appears briefly but is given the episode's best line. She looks at the Twins and comments, 'Such a cruel joke, God making two of them.' Mia-ooow!

Girl Talk: Ally giving romantic advice to Sandy is lovely. Ally feels that beneath his bleached head Billy is one of the greatest guys she's ever known; and that if Sandy feels there is even the smallest chance of her and Billy making it work she should try.

Guy Talk: Richard and John's discussion about the latter's relationship with Nelle disturbs John greatly. Richard's enthusiasm for money aligns him with Nelle in the argument; and he seemingly fails to notice that he effectively suggests to the already insecure John that Nelle simply wants him for his power, position and status.

Men: Judge Raymond Dearing, the bisexual owner of four coffee shops whom Ally first meets when he's serving behind the counter at one of his shops. He asks her out and then kisses her. Ally covers his head in coffee. It later transpires that he's also a judge, and what's more that he's sitting over the case Ally is preparing to present. He throws Ally in jail for contempt of court, and when he asks her to apologise she responds, 'I am deeply sorry that you're such an ass.' Raymond sentences her to community service and puts her to work in his coffee shop. Dearing, perhaps bizarrely, functions as the voice of sanity throughout much of this episode.

Fetishes: Richard freely admits to having a fetish about lesbians. Completely different from all other straight men, then. Ally's coffee obsession is referred to. She drinks a 'tall, semi-dry, non-fat cap'. Well, actually she pours it over Dearing's head. But she'd normally drink it.

Song: Vonda gets to sing The Beach Boys' 'I Get Around', plus the old stand-by 'Tell Him' rears its head, in both fast and slow versions. 'The Java Jive' by Manhattan Transfer pops up, whilst Dearing's bisexuality is emphasised by choice lyrics from 'Love on a Two-Way Street' and the Joni Mitchell classic 'Both Sides Now'. Subtle.

. . . And Dance: John does his angry dance to 'Gimme Dat Ding' by The Pipkins. This, he explains to Richard, is because he is 'ANGRY!!' Figures.

Fashion Victims: Nelle's hideous purple and pink figure-hugger, although Elaine looks very nice in a simple skirt and sweater combo.

The Case: Lisa Treadway, a recently outed woman seeking a divorce. She wants the alimony to which she is legally entitled. Her husband, Evan Stevens, asks for annulment rather than divorce, which would leave him unobliged to pay her any money at all. Ally contends that a marriage contract contains the implicit promise of heterosexuality, and that for Treadway to marry Stevens knowing she was a lesbian constituted fraud – effectively the marriage isn't legal because her sexuality constitutes a breach of the marriage contract.

Withdrawn: Ally loses the plot completely, with the judge getting angry and running rings around her. She loses because there's no legal basis to her claim. Which makes a change from her winning despite there being no basis to her case.

Judge Not: Aside from the aforementioned Raymond Dearing, we have Martha Graves, a standoffish matron, and Edward Morrison, a silent, seemingly senile old fool.

Kisses: Ally imagines kissing Raymond, but swiftly replaces the image with the sight of him kissing another man. The image clearly shakes her and she wimps out of dating him.

The Verdict: 'I let my fear take me over and now a good man is gone.' Hit and miss, but there's much bravery here from writer David E. Kelley. For Ally to admit to a prejudice, confront it, and still not be able to get around it is a remarkable step for Kelley to take. Television leads are rarely allowed to be so deeply flawed, especially in such a socially illiberal way. John and Nelle's argument leaves a nasty taste in the mouth; but you can't help siding with John. Some of Nelle's argument is solid, but much of it is both obnoxious and untenable. The final scene where Ally has her head in her hands having failed to follow her own advice, is worth the price of admission on its own.

314
The Oddball Parade

#3M14
28 February 2000

Written by David E. Kelley
Directed by Bryan Gordon

Cast: Tina Turner (Tina Turner),
Anthony Anderson (Matthew Vault),
Cheryl Hawker (Mindy Platt), Eddie Kehler (Paul Potts),
Robert Clendenin (Benjamin Winter),
Davenia McFadden (Gloria), Steven Culp (Dixon),
Gina Philips (Sandy), Mark L. Taylor (Judge Hawk),
Peter Choi (Foreman)

Note: Although credited, Courtney Thorne-Smith and
Lisa Nicole Carson do not appear in this episode.

John and Richard act on behalf of a group of people who have been unfairly laid off by their employer. Billy tries to patch up his friendship with Ally. Meanwhile Elaine and Ally become rivals as they both enter a competition to become backing singer/dancer for a pop icon.

The Boy Next Door: Billy and Ally have a huge conversation which motivates Billy to confess, 'I've been acting crazy, acting out. I admit it,' and apologise for his recent behaviour. They row over Ally's entry into the competition and then both apologise minutes later. 'I am so over you,' Ally tells Billy, but confesses that 'every time you're with somebody else I feel a pinch.' Billy tells Ally that if she wants to dance then she should dance, but that the competition strikes him as a little silly. 'I've become a big fan of silly,' she retorts. Billy refers to 109 'The Dirty Joke', pointing out that a few years ago Ally was terrified to get up on stage and tell a joke, and *now* she wants to become a back up singer/dancer. 'A few years ago I didn't have the need,' she explains. 'I'd put on these suits every day, go to work with my briefcase, living my life as a working professional. Now it'd be nice to . . .' 'Escape your life?' interrupts Billy. Their conversation is disarmingly frank, with Billy saying 'Every once in a while I get a hit, I look at you and . . .' before Ally stops him from going somewhere neither of them really want to go. When criticising his recent behaviour and trying to explain why they are no longer close she says, 'You went off and became the new Billy,' someone she describes as 'a massive dope'. 'How could I be your friend?' she asks. Considering how he's been acting, it's a totally reasonable question. At the end of the enormous heart-to-heart, Ally tells him, 'I so want your friendship back, I so miss it.' Billy replies that his friendship with Ally is 'everything. I'm sorry I've gone off the way I have. I'm back.'

Fishisms: John feels that given the aberrant nature of some of the firm's clients, Richard's habit of compounding their problems by coming out with Fishisms in court is inappropriate. Richard is interviewed on television about their case and tells the viewing public, 'This is an assault against all of us, really. Massachusetts is an ugly state. All of New England, hello . . . Boston Terriers named after the people who live here. Bow Wow city, you can't just sit here and let the funny-looking people get trampled on.' After the interview goes on air, he gives John his considered opinion of his performance: 'I was great.' The next day at the court dozens of people turn up to attend the hearing and support their clients, just as Richard knew they would. Talking to one of his defendants Richard informs them, 'You came off as a wackadoo – a nice one.'

Bygones: During an argument John begs Richard not to speak: 'Can you do that? Can you not talk?' Fish replies, 'I can try. Ooops. Seems I can't. Kidding. Bygones.'

Smile Therapy: John responds to Richard's suggestion of a group hug with the only reasonable response to such a suggestion: 'Oh balls! Group hug!' By his own admission this case makes John 'fraught', even leading to him getting so angry in court he's labelled a 'rabid little bulldog'.

Office Gossip: Elaine is devastated when Ally beats her to win the 'become a Not-Ikette'. The next day, still visibly upset, she tells Ally, 'They picked you. Like always – it was you.' She needs to believe that there are some things she's better at than Ally, just to get through the day.

Grrr!: Ling trips another contestant for the hell of it, and as Ally goes onstage calls out, 'Break your legs.' In a seemingly out of character act of kindness Ling convinces one of Ms Turner's assistants to lie to Elaine, telling her that she was the best dancer in the competition, and that Ally was picked because Tina was jealous. 'Lady don't like to get shown up,' she pretends to explain.

Fantasy: Whilst dancing, Ally visualises a room literally full of Billys. 'The whole room was you,' she tells him and goes on to say that he is the last thing she wants to be fantasising about. She's so angry she brutalises a cubicle in the unisex with John's gloves, and when Nelle interrupts she lays her out with one punch.

Fetishes: One of Richard and John's defendants is a huge African-American guy with a neat beard, who's wearing both a floral dress and blond wig. 'I'm a woman trapped in a man's body,' he tells John. 'This here is a medical thing.'

Richard takes one look at Ms Turner and says, 'Sixty years old. What do you think, wattlectomy?'

Song: Guest star Tina Turner sings three of her numbers: 'A Fool in Love', 'Proud Mary' and 'When the Heartache Is Over'. A marching band performs Barry White's 'You're the First, the Last, My Everything' as John leads the titular parade through the streets.

. . . And Dance: Richard and John boogie shamelessly together to Tina's opening number. Once the dance contest begins we get to see Ally shake some serious booty and Elaine leap around like a mad thing. In a line included in the trailer but cut from the finished episode Richard responds to Ally's dancing simply and directly – 'Ally, I want sex.'

Fashion Victims: Elaine, firstly in a skin-tight orange top and later in a vile Paisley patterned number. Ling's Technicolor dreamcoat defies the senses in its colour-clashing horror.

The Case: A group of graphic designers, all with at least one spectacular . . . quirk, who have been dismissed from the firm they worked so hard to build. The argument put by their ex-employer is that their quirks made it impossible to build up a client base. One of John's clients, Paul Potts, is a small, thin man who repeats the last word of some of his sentences three times, jerks his head, and claps rhythmically four times at various intervals. It's claimed that this 'never affected the job'.

Judge Not: Judge Walsh who, at least according to John, doesn't like Richard at all. Apparently it upsets him when Richard's lips move, but he gets especially angry when words come out of them.

Also Starring: Tina Turner is a music legend with a forty-year career as a singer/dancer behind her. She has also occasionally acted, most notably in *Mad Max Beyond Thunderdome* (George Miller and George Ogilvie, 1985) alongside Mel Gibson.

The Verdict: A perfect example of the kind of episode that made us fans of the series – a deliciously absurd case, fantastic lines from Richard, and an attempt to get to the heart of the Billy/Ally relationship. Billy and Ally walking home together and laughing after everything they've been through is touchingly and beautifully done.

315
Prime Suspect

#3M15
20 March 2000

Written by David E. Kelley
Directed by Richard Talalay

Cast: Eddie Kehler (Paul Potts),
Anthony Anderson (Matthew Vault),
Cheryl Hawker (Mindy Platt),
Robert Clendenin (Benjamin Winter),
Gina Philips (Sandy Hingle),
Margeurite MacIntyre (Debra Schoefield),
Christine Tucci (Nancy Raleigh Sicklen),
Jenny Gago (Dr Pontes), Albert Hall (Judge Seymore Walsh),
Helen Eigenberg (Assistant District Attorney Kettering),
Harry Danner (Hallen), Joe Hanna (Clerk),
Reagan Browne (Police Officer#1),
Skip O'Brien (Police Officer#2), Libby Bancroft (Technician)

Note: Although credited, Lisa Nicole Carson, Vonda Shepard and Jane Krakowski do not appear.

Paul Potts, one of the 'Oddball Parade', is arrested for the murder of his former employer. John Cage defends with Richard as second chair and Ally as third. However, proving him innocent could be rather difficult and involve some unorthodox tactics. Billy's recent behaviour is finally, terribly explained.

Everything Stops For Ally: Ally claims to have always wanted to do a murder case, which seems to fly directly in the face of both her oft-stated fear of criminals and her reactions in 120 'The Inmates'.

The Boy Next Door: Billy hallucinates Matthew as a stunningly beautiful woman in a small pink dress, and accidentally walks into Nelle's office believing it to be his own. He forgets an important meeting, snogs Nelle, hallucinates tiny imp versions of Georgia and Ally jumping up and down on his desk, and then imagines that his neurologist is actually Georgia. After Billy hits on Matthew, Sandy quite reasonably demands of him, 'Man or woman, what the hell are you doing hitting on him or her?'

Fishisms: Richard reacts to the news of the murder trial like a small child who's been offered a particularly exciting toy: 'I've always wanted to do a murder trial, John. I could open and close, cross-examine; move to suppress the murder weapon,' he says, licking his lips. He gets so enthusiastic that he even tries a 'good cop, bad cop' routine on his own client. When John explains to the court that their client has a compulsion that makes him repeat words, Richard helpfully points out that it has so far 'never made him kill'. When asked for his opinion he lip-smacks, 'He did it,' but is prepared to defend him anyway. John points out that 'this is a murder here . . . not some game' but his words fail to dent his partner's enthusiasm for the case. The hearing succeeds where he failed, however, turning Richard off the idea of defending in more murder trials: 'This is why we don't do murder cases, we suck at them.'

Sub Zero: Nelle is vile here, attacking Sandy for trying to protect Billy, and then (under the pretence of concern for his health) arranging for him an appointment with a neurologist which she *knows* will conflict with a meeting he has scheduled. She then chairs the meeting in Billy's absence and steals his biggest client from him. She's clearly planning something big, telling Ling that 'this place . . . needs a few changes' and that she needs power so that she can make them.

Georgia On My Mind: Amusingly the Georgia imp screams, 'Divorce me, divorce me!'

Grrr!: 'They may have cleared the mental one,' she says, denigrating what John, Richard and Ally have spent the whole episode achieving. 'You're doing something despicable, I can tell,' she says to Nelle approvingly.

The Case: Schoefield (the employer of the 'Oddballs') has been murdered; his widow claims that she heard a 'clapping' noise at the crime scene, implicating Paul Potts. After running through a number of alternative possibilities, Ally concludes that Nancy Raleigh Sicklen, a woman she believes to have been the dead man's lover, had him murdered, and sets out to prove it via a complex 'sting' operation. She's wrong on at least one count: Nancy was Debra's lover not Schoefield's, and they conspired together to kill him and frame Paul Potts. Richard and John then capture them by pretending to be the FBI. (Yes, really.)

Fantasy: During Debra's evidence Ally imagines herself being murdered in a shower, in B & W in a blatant homage to *Psycho* (Alfred Hitchcock, 1960).

Fetishes: At the first suggestion that Debra and Nancy might be lovers Richard visibly cheers and chirps, 'Lesbians!' 'Quick,' replies John, 'dial 911.'

Fashion Victims: Richard and John in baseball caps and matching shades. Sooo not them. But then that's the point.

Judge Not: Seymore Walsh who doesn't want a mockery made of his court. When Ally points out that no one is doing that he insists, 'Miss McBeal, when justice is affected by you, Mr Cage and Mr Fish . . . trust me when I tell you a mockery has occurred.'

Kisses: A mentally unstable Billy kisses Nelle, believing her to be Sandy. Oh, any excuse . . .

Sounds Unusual: Billy's 'hand in fist' signature noise makes a welcome reappearance.

The Verdict: This is funny, clever and touching with both an interesting, complex plotline and loads of character stuff. The ending caps the episode, provides an explanation for Billy's behaviour, and renders any audience desperate to see the next instalment. Flawless.

316
The Boy Next Door

#3M16
27 March 2000

Written by David E. Kelley
Directed by Jack Bender

Cast: Kimberley Davies (Angela Prune),
Jay Karnes (Simon Prune), Steven Culp (Anthony Dixon),
Kate Asner (Dr Peters),
Dyan Cannon (Judge 'Whipper' Cone),
Gina Philips (Sandy Hingle),
Roy Brocksmith (Judge Raymond Norway),
Clyde Kusatsu (Billy's Doctor),
Harrison Page (Mark Newman)

Billy informs the office that he has a brain tumour; but that his doctor tells him he is in no immediate danger. As his behaviour grows ever more erratic and his hallucinations more and more extreme, he determines to carry on fighting his current case.

The Boy Next Door: Billy initially tries to joke his way through his medical problems: 'I have a brain tumour in my ass,' he claims, and tells Ally, 'I wanted to tell you personally because you probably helped bring it on.' He tries to push Sandy away from him in order to save her from being hurt by his illness. He tells her that while he likes her, if he has to go into potentially life-threatening surgery it won't be her hand he wants to hold. Billy's doctors initially believe his brain tumour to be benign but are appalled at both its size and the speed with which it's growing. In court later that day, with Ally as second chair, Billy is fighting a case in which a man wants to annul his marriage because his wife didn't tell him she'd had cosmetic surgery. As neither of them believes in pre-marital sex, he only discovered on their wedding night that she'd had silicon breast implants. Billy, like Ally, is appalled by the cynical nature of this bid and the man's attempts to rid himself of his wife for such a reason. As part of his case Billy defends, at length, the very concept of marriage itself. He argues that it's meant to be an institutionalised form of a love so strong it can survive anything. During his closing he begins to babble, telling the judge that he has been married to Ally for twelve years and that they have children. He claims that 'in the end love is the only thing that counts' and that 'it is *so* everything'. He says of Ally that he's 'loved her since I was eight years old . . . and I'll love her for all my days'. He looks directly at her and says, 'All of my heart, for ever.' And then he dies.

Fishisms: When he has to go and tell the hospitalised John that Billy has died, Richard openly weeps; and all John can do is watch. 'When things aren't good I go into surf mode,' he says earlier, meaning that he wants to grab the remote control for life and fast-forward to the happy ending, unaware, of course, that this episode doesn't have one. The fear and concern he shows for Billy when he finds out he's ill, and the rawness of his emotions following Billy's death, show just how much of his shallowness and 'money ethic' is simple bravado.

Sub Zero: Nelle dumps John whilst he is trapped hanging out of the lift. 'I don't mean to be cruel,' she says, but she doesn't seem to mean it. 'He doesn't like me,' she says of John. 'He finds it repugnant that I wouldn't date a janitor.' When she does something that could be seen as unlikeable she embraces 'being a total bitch' because 'there's more power in it'. She rolls her eyes during Ally's oration at Billy's funeral indicating just how emotionally cold she really is.

Grrr!: Ling is annoyed by the fact that John is stuck in the lift, as it means she'll have to use the stairs. During a meeting she expresses the hope that Billy won't 'milk' his brain tumour problem to gain an unfair advantage at work. After Billy's death she expresses the genuine sadness and regret that Nelle seems to find impossible.

Fantasy: What is clever about so much of this episode is the way it takes a lot of the series comic iconography, such as dance routines, fantasies of public nudity and ridiculous hallucinations and uses them to prevent a sinister and quite upsetting look at Billy's mental health.

Song: Billy's doctor sings Bill Withers' 'Lean On Me', or rather Billy imagines him doing so. 'Neighborhood' which has, in a very real sense, become Billy's theme is used to devastating effect as he dies on the courtroom floor. 'You Belong To Me', (King/Stewart/Price) the Johnny Mathis' song to which Billy and Ally danced so often, is used hauntingly. Ally, as part of her funeral oration, speaks lyrics from the Blood, Sweat and Tears' song, 'And When I Die'. Mighty Sam McCain's 'New Man in Town', the song Billy so recently adopted to emphasise his shift in character, is sung by a gospel choir as he's laid to rest, and as a warning for those in heaven to sit up and notice Billy's arrival.

The Case: Prune vs Prune, Billy is first chair. It's a stupid annulment-of-a-marriage case between two blandly hard-line Christians. When, on his wedding night the husband discovered that his wife had undergone cosmetic surgery, including breast and cheek implants, and a tummy-tuck, he resolves to ask for an annulment. He claims that she is not the woman that he thought she was and that it is sufficient grounds for the marriage to be dissolved. It is to Billy's eternal credit that he dies belittling the unworthiness of this case.

McBeal & Thomas (Deceased): Billy's ghost comes to visit Ally as she sits alone in her office. 'Are you going to haunt me now, Billy?' she asks. 'You did it when you were alive, you might as well now you're dead.' She notices that the Billy spectre has dark hair and comments, 'I'm glad your hair is back to normal.' Billy's ghost asks her, 'Have you ever known any two people to have what we had?' and goes on to say that their friendship is 'stronger than death'. (See 115 'Once In A Lifetime'.) Billy had heard that as you're about to pass into the next world, the final truth of this one comes to you. As he died in court all Billy could think of was 'love' and 'how it was all that mattered'. It is unclear here whether Billy is a symptom of Ally's grief or a genuine visit from the ghost of the dead boy-next-door.

The Verdict: 'About forty minutes ago, Billy Thomas passed away.' The silence in the office is palpable as Ally tells her colleagues what the audience already knows. The script to this brilliant episode pivots on a moment: changing in one terrible second from a farce with a serious thread into a bitter tragedy. Gil Bellows, Calista Flockhart and Greg Germann's performances are astonishing. Neither of us is ashamed to admit that we cried during both Billy's death scene and the subsequent montage of Billy and Ally's lives together. Compulsive, beautiful and driven by a terrible tragic momentum, this is one of the finest episodes the series has ever produced.

317
I Will Survive

#3M17
17 April 2000

Written by David E. Kelley
Directed by Bernet Kellman

Cast: James LeGros (Mark Albert),
Loretta Devine (Nora Mills),
Amanda Donohoe (Marianne Holt),
Valerie Mahaffey (Dr Sally Muggins),
Phil Lewis (DA Kessler), Gibby Brand (Judge McGough),
Gloria Gaynor (Gloria Gaynor)

Note: Although credited, Lisa Nicole Carson,
Courtney Thorne-Smith and Peter MacNicol do not appear.

Richard hires somebody new, while Ally tries to cope with Billy being gone.

The Boy Next Door: 'Billy is dead. And we loved him, and he is going to be dead for ever,' says Ally, summing up the feelings of the firm and the audience in one neat, anguished sentence.

Introducing: James LeGros as Mark Albert, a crackerjack criminal lawyer whom Richard has hired to take over Billy's portfolio. Richard hopes that Mark will bring more criminal cases to the firm. Mark tells Ally that as a teenager he went by the handle 'Ally', a diminutive of his surname. She's rather irritated by this.

Everything Stops For Ally: Following Billy's death Ally is cracking up. When told that life must go on she very reasonably responds, 'What is wrong with just staying still and crying? Who made up that stupid rule anyway? That life just goes on?'

Fishisms: 'I loved Billy as much as you did,' Richard claims to Ally, but then climbs down to 'OK, I liked him'. When Ally challenges him over his hiring of a new lawyer to replace Billy, Richard points out that they cannot get behind with the work they have to do. They need another lawyer. He later confesses his real motive: 'We're all trying to survive this, Ally. Maybe you can walk past his empty office all day long. I can't.' Later Nelle attacks Richard over his failure to keep his promise to make her a partner (see 201 'The Real World') to which he responds, 'Promises I make are irrelevant, I don't keep 'em.'

Smile Therapy: John is AWOL. According to Richard he went to New Hampshire on account of Billy being dead or Nelle dumping him. Or something.

Sub Zero: Nelle takes advantage of Ally's severe emotional distress by trying to poach Cindy Snell, one of her clients. Nasty.

Grrr!: After Ally collapses in court Ling tells her that she looks awful and sounds bitchy. Ally's behaviour makes Ling wonder if brain tumours are contagious.

The Other Ally: Mark Albert, the new lawyer hired by Richard to replace Billy. He has a theme song, Queen's 'We Will Rock You', which he likes to play before he goes into court. Ally walks into his office to find him laid out in a dentist's chair having his teeth whitened. With habits like this he obviously fits right into Cage & Fish straight away. Or would do if everyone didn't hate him. He thinks that one of the reasons Ally is being so unpleasant to him is because she senses that he could be the sort of man that she'd have a relationship with. 'I think his bulb is a little dim,' says Ling.

Fantasy: A hallucination of Gloria Gaynor visits Ally, hides in her shower and then chases her through the streets. 'I was being chased,' Ally tells Ling. 'Pygmies?' Ling asks. 'Worse,' Ally replies, 'disco.'

Song: 'Here's a little song for all you romantics out there whose first love just died from a brain tumour,' announces the radio DJ in the first scene; inevitably this leads into 'Neighborhood' being performed, as it really only can be, by Vonda Shepard. The appearance of Gloria Gaynor leads into a performance of her disco masterpiece 'I Will Survive'. Another camp classic, 'Never Can Say Goodbye', is performed in the witness box by Loretta Devine, in character as Lorna. The final montage is shown to a beautiful rendition of 'Goodbye My Friend' performed by Vonda Shepard.

The Case: A man who was having sex with his physiotherapist, was beaten to death by his wife using his artificial leg. Ally and Mark defend what was previously Billy's case, contesting that the defendant is not guilty by virtue of temporary insanity.

Guilty?: Despite Ling's scorn, Mark gets their client acquitted of Murder One, Murder Two and manslaughter.

Also Starring: Amanda Donohoe was a regular on the partially David E. Kelley-scripted *LA Law* and has appeared in a number of bad films, such as *The Lair of the White Worm* (Ken Russell, 1988).

McBeal & Thomas (Deceased): Billy's ghost meets Ally in his office. He advises her to give Mark a chance, and promises to make sure it never rains when she's outside. She refuses to believe him. Later she walks home in the rain, getting soaked. The obvious implication being that Billy's ghost is a symptom of Ally's grief, not a real spectre.

The Verdict: 'Back to work, back to work, back to work.' 'I Will Survive' gets exponentially better as it goes along. There's a fantastic Billy/Ally scene, a better Richard/Ally one, both towards the end, and James LeGros makes a convincing debut. What's more it ends with a beautiful montage of Billy/Ally scenes. It was always going to be a comedown after the previous episode, but a stupid case and an irritatingly inept guest performance from Loretta Devine doesn't help.

318
Turning Thirty

#3M18
1 May 2000

**Written by David E. Kelley and Jill Goldsmith
Directed by Jeanot Szwarc**

Cast: James LeGros (Mark Albert),
Cindy Ambuehl (Lorna),
Vasili Bogazianos (DA), Clyde Kusatsu (Dr Myron Okubo),
Jennifer Holliday (Lisa Knowles), Harrison Page (Minister),
Albert Hall (Judge Seymore Walsh),
Geoffrey Wade (Dr Kipperman), Amy Castle (Young Ally)

Ally turns thirty. Another ridiculous murder case finds its way into Cage & Fish's notice. Billy continues his haunting.

Smile Therapy: John gets up to sing a song for Ally's birthday and publicly acknowledges his debt to her. Before Ally he was 'this lawyer savant' and she, slowly and carefully, has made him realise his potential and has made his life worth living. He thanks her for this and describes her as 'my best friend'.

The Other Ally: Mark demonstrates his inability to remember anyone's names, calling John 'Jim' twice in the space of a minute and referring to him as 'the Cookie' rather than 'the Biscuit'.

Sub Zero: Whilst arguing with Elaine, Nelle tells her, 'With concentration I can pretend the little people in the world don't exist. Too bad I'm not focusing now.' In response Elaine calls her a 'cold-hearted, cunning, conniving bitch'. Nelle explains that the reason that she can't get on with secretaries is that 'amounting to nothing makes them hostile'. She then deliberately hurts Elaine by attacking the one thing she has faith in: her singing voice. Ouch!

Office Gossip: Elaine tries to get everybody to 'do a number' for Ally's birthday. So keen is she to get Mark to take part, she lies, informing him that he's been drawn out of the hat as the one person who has to get up and sing a song for Ally. Ally and Elaine duet on 'The Happening', scrapping with each other as to who is singing lead, and eventually collapsing into a violent ruck. Ladies, please! Elaine butts in on the end of John's song for Ally, which is a bit selfish at the very least.

Song: John sings ''Til There Was You' (Meredith Willson), a song from *The Music Man*, Ally's (and David E. Kelley's) favourite musical. The best-known recording of the song is probably Paul McCartney's vocal on The Beatles' album, *With The Beatles*. An alternative cut is included on the 'Baby It's You' CD single.

Fashion Victims: Ally wears a fantastic white-on-black pin-stripe trouser suit. John has never looked better than here, and perversely Nelle has never looked worse: her horrific red jacket and Technicolor nightmare cravat are amazingly awful. Elaine's red dress when singing is smashing.

The Case: Lorna Flood is accused of murdering her elderly husband, Henry, for his money. The prosecution claim that she deliberately smothered him to death with her breasts. Yes, really.

Judge Not: As you all probably know by now we think Seymore Walsh is great. This paragon of dignity really has his hands full in this episode. Dealing with a ridiculous murder case, John *and* Mark try his patience to the limit, but he manages to keep his cool somehow.

McBeal & Thomas (Deceased): Billy's ghost appears in the window of an antique shop. Ally tells him that she'd hoped he'd be more profound when dead, but Billy explains that he just dropped in to wish her a happy birthday. Later he visits Ally in her office and offers to walk her home, but she refuses.

The Verdict: 'You have beautiful lips.' This is a transitional episode. The repercussions of Billy's death are still being felt, but the consolidation of Mark as a character pushes the episode forward, giving us a glimpse of what the fourth season may well be like. The subplot with Ally's collagen implants isn't very funny and takes up far too much of the episode, but James LeGros continues to impress and Dr Okubo's comment on Billy's death has to be heard to be believed.

319

Do You Wanna Dance?

#3M19
8 May 2000

Written by David E. Kelley
Directed by Michael Lange

Cast: Tim Dutton (Attorney Brian Selig),
Jamie Denton (Jimmy Bender),
Thomas McCarthy (Peter Hanks),
Claire Rankin (Susan Hanks),
Albert Hall (Judge Seymore Walsh),
Holland Taylor (Judge Roberta Kittleson),
Mary Chris Wall (Emerson's Mother),
Jonathan Taylor Thomas (Chris Emerson),
Michele Gregory (Clerk),

Jennings Bryan McMillen (Foreman), Ty Upshaw (Detective), Jorge Luis Abero (Waiter)

Note: Although credited, Gil Bellows does not appear. As his character is dead, he's got a reasonable excuse.

Can the electronic substitute the romantic? Will Cage & Fish finally lose a case? How far will Nelle go? Ally is arrested for statutory rape.

Everything Stops For Ally: 'I just had computer sex. It was amazing.' Ally has been e-mailing a man for four months and, as Renee discovers her, she was just, ahem, having 'computer sex' with him. Ally insists that this is the first time they've done such a thing. Ally arranges to meet with her e-pal, who styles himself 'Thunder Thighs', only to discover he's a sixteen-year-old boy. Within minutes of meeting him she finds herself arrested for attempted statutory rape. John defends her, moving for a Probable Cause hearing, where he demonstrates that there's not only no crime but also no motive involved.

Introducing: Brian Selig, an English lawyer with a propensity for courtroom antics on a Cage scale. Ally's rather attracted to him, despite his Michael Portillo hair, and initially believes him to be the man with whom she has been communicating via e-mail over recent months.

Fishisms: Richard demonstrates to Nelle why she can't become a partner. If he and John are partners they get half each; if they cut Nelle in, they'll only get a third. He's gone so far as to produce a pie chart showing this discrepancy. 'I need to be a good leader, not a charitable sap,' he tells her. Although you can't argue with his logic, this is a direct betrayal of what he told her in 201 'The Real World'.

Smile Therapy: After John insults Nelle during a staff meeting, Ally tells him that he can't talk like that. 'Of course I can,' he retorts. 'You heard me, I didn't even stutter.' John later tells Ally that he has never used the word 'bitch' to describe any woman before, but with Nelle it's just so apposite that he can't help it. He later comments that it's a wonder that, whilst dating Nelle, he didn't lose his penis to frostbite. John defends Ally in court, backed by Richard and Renee. 'Three lawyers?' questions the judge. 'These charges are so outlandish it takes three lawyers to convey the necessary outrage,' John responds.

Sub Zero: John calls Nelle 'Frosty, the snow girl'. She refers to John as Senior Pipsqueak and demands she be made a partner. John insists that this will only happen over his dead body, pointing out that his corpse would still be 'a few degrees warmer than yours, you rich bitch elitist ice-queen'. John goes to Nelle's office to get back a file of his she's taken. She insists that she needed the file because she had to meet with the client due to John being stuck in a lift (see 316 'The Boy Next Door'.) It later transpires that she was, in fact, trying to steal his client, having phoned constantly, telling him to let her handle his account, not John. Nelle confides in Ling that she's planning to move to one of the big firms. When Ling counters by asking Nelle if she realises how long it would take her to make partner at a 'big firm', Nelle calmly responds that with her portables, her hair and her willingness to abuse the sexual harassment laws, she'd be partner within a month. We believe her.

The Other Ally: John tells Mark he has the depth of a bottle cap. He later apologises. He knows that this was cold of him, but feels that becoming cold is inevitable when you hang out with a Popsicle.

Grrr!: Nelle tries to get Ling to start a new law firm with her, to which Ling responds, 'I'm rich. I only go to work to wear my outfits.' Ling likes working for John and Richard, she thinks 'they're fun'. She hates the idea of working with real lawyers and spending more time with clients.

Girl Talk: The first big Ally/Renee conversation in ages occurs right at the beginning of this episode. It's nice to have them, and Lisa Nicole Carson, back.

Fetishes: After discovering Ally has had computer sex, Richard develops an unnatural interest in the type of computer, size of computer and software used.

Kisses: 'One kiss?' asks Chris after the trial, prompting Renee and John to loudly insist 'on the cheek'. So Ally, reluctantly, pecks him gently.

The Case: Jimmy Bender suing his best friend Peter Hanks for emotional distress. Hanks was having sex with Bender's ex-wife whilst they were still married

Guilty?: Ally and Mark lose the case. Their client is ordered to pay his ex-friend damages of $10,000, leaving Ally to fret that this is the price they put on friendship. Mark suggests that in fact this is the price they put on marriage. This obviously fails to cheer Ally in the slightest.

Men: Brian Selig, an English lawyer who acts as opposing counsel in Ally and Mark's case. Ally is drawn to him and at the end of the episode takes him to the bar.

Withdrawn: Mark gets really very nasty in court, but there's no real indication why. Brian pulls all sorts of bizarre courtroom tricks, including substituting 'gophering' for 'badgering', claiming it's a recognised legal term in England, and shouting 'Pope Paul' at inappropriate moments. This is apparently something to do with Winston Churchill, but he later admits to Ally that he's making it all up.

Judge Not: A new judge, middle-aged Roberta Kittleson, who's presiding over Ally's statutory rape case. She's clearly quite taken with Chris Emerson herself, which makes her rather unsuitable to judge the case, really.

Also Starring: Jonathan Taylor Thomas was a regular in *Home Improvement*, the Tim Allen sitcom.

Hit The Bar: At the bar John dances with Renee. 'C'mon, Biscuit, it's been too long' she tells him. 'Indeed,' he replies. Richard dances with Elaine. 'I think we have something here,' he notes, looking at John and Renee. 'It's about time,' Elaine says, smiling back.

The Verdict: Another 'sex and teens' episode (see 201 'The Real World') that leaves people in Europe shaking their heads in bewilderment. Aside from that this is a straightforward instalment mostly concerned with getting back to something resembling business as usual (Billy's death isn't mentioned once). James LeGros continues to impress and Nelle's master plan gets advanced a few inches. That aside, there isn't anything here that we've not seen before. That's not to say it's bad, of course; average *Ally* is still a cut above almost everything else on television.

320
Hope And Glory

#3M20
15 May 2000

Written by David E. Kelley
Directed by Mel Damski

Cast: Alicia Wit (Hope), Tim Dutton (Brian Selig),
Albert Hall (Judge Seymore Walsh),
Mary Pat-Green (Julia 'Bulldog' Braddel),
Allen Williams (Milton Meyers)
Special Appearances by James LeGros (Mark Albert),
Macy Gray (herself)

Note: Although credited, Gil Bellows does not appear in this episode due to Billy staying dead.

Nelle's plot to set up her own firm, taking several of Cage & Fish's clients with her, reaches fruition. To do that she persuades Elaine to help her.

When Nelle leaves, the case goes to binding arbitration. Will Julia 'Bulldog' Braddel back up Nelle's claims of abuse, or Cage and Fish's claims that Nelle stole from them?

Sub Zero: This is Nelle's episode, as all her scheming comes to a head and she betrays the firm. Nelle needs Elaine to help her steal the files on the clients who will leave with her when she departs Cage & Fish. Of course, Nelle doesn't even like Elaine, which means she has to jump through hoops to flatter

Elaine's ego. Nelle continues her allusion to John as the Mayor of Munchkinland by quoting *The Wizard of Oz*, cementing her gay-icon status. Nelle offers Elaine over double her current salary to be her paralegal, thereby convincing Elaine that although Nelle may not like her, she does respect Elaine's abilities and potential. She then withdraws the offer, saying that Richard and John vetoed Elaine's promotion – this is, of course, a lie. The next stage is to reveal her desire to leave, and to ask Elaine to come with her. Elaine accepts, and when she seems reluctant to copy computer files for Nelle, she instead gives Nelle the password – thereby allowing Nelle to steal the files as intended. Nelle doesn't actually seem to enjoy scheming and takes little pleasure in deceiving Elaine. Nelle goes to the office to announce her resignation and finds that through Myers the partners already know she's left. 'I bet you'd really like to spank me now, John!' she tells Cage. In arbitration Nelle is partly play-acting, but she does have a strong case when she refers to the spanking, the 'clicker' used on her heels and hair, the fact that the unisex means the men can corner her in the toilets, etc. The fact that John then calls her a 'lying, manipulative, conniving bitch' only helps her case. She asks for a break, seeming upset, and says she's afraid to go to the unisex on her own. When arbitration is over Nelle is left with a fine of $300,000 and no friends, alone and unhappy in her new office.

Everything Stops For Ally: Ally believes she has problems evaluating men one on one, so she takes Brian to the bar in the hope that some of her friends will see them together. She kisses Brian passionately as they dance and walks down the street in a happy daze imagining her own wedding. This is Ally being *happy*, a startling character development. Ally also does a lot to stop the firm falling apart, bringing Elaine back into the fold to testify and forcing John and Richard to shake hands and make up after they have a fight.

Smile Therapy: John says his therapist has told him to go straight into a smile when he meets Nelle, rather than waiting for her 'typically horrendous behaviour'. When Nelle leaves, he has one repetitive response, as he and Richard breathe into paper bags to try to calm down: 'I want to get her.' He also keeps saying 'Balls'.

Fishisms: When one of Richard's prize clients, Milton Myers, tells Richard he's leaving for Nelle Porter's new firm, it's the first Richard has heard of it. His response is hysterical, setting off alarms and running around the office telling everyone Nelle isn't allowed back in. He soon finds out she's stolen the files: 'Talk about dishonest. I hired her to steal from her old firm, she ends up stealing from me.' Richard is transfixed by the wattle hanging off arbiter Julia 'Bulldog' Braddel's tricep, and after arbitration is over he asks her to help him perform a test. Richard lifts Bulldog's arm and slaps the wattle, timing how long the vibrations last. Everyone else seems to feel ill as the tricep wattle shudders in slow motion, but Richard is very impressed.

Office Gossip: Elaine is flattered by Nelle fanning the flames of her huge ego and is tempted by the offer to become a paralegal. It's not like she couldn't do with the money – face bra sales are apparently down. Elaine's acceptance of what Nelle tells her, including the obvious lie about Richard and John vetoing her promotion, and Nelle's equally transparent flattery of Elaine's abilities, shows just how self-absorbed and dumb Elaine can be. However, her analysis of Nelle's 'philosophical differences' with the firm is pretty sharp: 'You mean with the philosophical way they wouldn't make you partner?' However, when Nelle leaves Elaine leaves too, in spite of the disapproval of her colleagues. Elaine doesn't realise Nelle lied until Ally comes to Nelle's new office to tell her. Ally asks what Nelle could need from Elaine to go to all the effort to poach her, and Elaine realises Nelle was only ever after the passwords. Ally tells Elaine that Nelle didn't just copy the files, she deleted the originals and stole them. Elaine returns to Cage & Fish and her old job, testifying as to what Nelle did: 'I was totally duped, and I can't believe I fell for it.' She tells Nelle she isn't a nice person and that she admires honesty. However, when Hope tries to flatter Elaine again, Elaine wavers once more – her ego being stronger than her common sense. This time common sense wins out. She thanks Ally for letting her come back to her old job.

Grrr!: Ling is suspicious of the fact that she hasn't seen much of Nelle lately, especially when Nelle turns down the chance to go to lunch. She seems offended that Nelle didn't tell her what was going on.

All We Need Is Hope: Introducing Alicia Witt as Nelle's flame-haired friend – and Richard's old flame – the sharp-tongued, lethally attractive Hope Merson. It's Hope who advises Nelle on how to screw her firm and on the need to take Elaine so as to steal the required client files. Hope once slept with Fish, but says that isn't an issue: 'I have no problem being dastardly with men I've slept with. I'm dastardly during.' She offers Nelle advice on how to handle her departure from the firm: 'Above all, don't forget to enjoy yourself – this is nasty fun.' During a break in arbitration, she talks to Richard about the time they had sex: 'I can't tell you how many nights I lie in bed, thinking about that night. Regretting it.' She goes on to say that once arbitration is over she hopes Richard will give her 'a little something to regret again'. Hope kisses Richard and lets him go down on her 'inny' navel. Hope tells Ally she loves her hair.

Men: Brian the English lawyer reappears, undeterred by Ally's jailbait experience in the previous episode. He says all women turn out to be monsters sooner or later, so he only dates obvious monsters so as to make an 'informed decision' should he decide to get married. When he casually suggests he might like to have sex that evening, Ally coughs and sprays mineral water over him – Brian admits he deserved it. Brian knows a rumour about Hope but he doesn't reveal what it is.

Fashion Victims: Brian wears a horrid pink shirt with a clashing yellow tie. Urgh!

Kisses: Ally and Brian kiss passionately on the dance floor. Hope kisses Richard, telling him she wants him.

Toilet Humour: In the unisex, Mark asks Ally if she and Brian are serious. When pressed, Mark tells Ally that if she wasn't serious with Brian he would have asked her out for dinner. Ally says that she's serious enough with Brian for dinner with Mark to be inappropriate. Mark feels stupid for asking; even more so when three consecutive cubicles open, Richard, John and Brian all emerging from the stalls. Later, during a break in arbitration, John and Richard have a confrontation over John's aggressive behaviour towards Nelle and how it is about to lose them their case. Richard tries to tell John to go home and they start pushing one another. Finally they wrestle on the floor and Hope has to come along to break them up. When they've gone Bulldog emerges from a cubicle, having heard the whole sorry thing.

Fantasy: Ally looks into the window of a bridal shop and sees herself wearing the dress rather than the mannequin.

Song: Macy Gray performs her runaway hit 'I Try' in the bar. Donna Summer's 'This Time I Know It's For Real' plays as Ally walks happily down the street, imagining herself in a wedding dress. Vangelis' theme from 'Chariots of Fire' plays when Richard watches Bulldog's tricep wattle shake.

. . . And Dance: Brian and Ally slow dance at the bar.

Judge Not: It never really amounts to a full-blown case, but Mark goes to Judge Walsh to try to get an injunction against Nelle when she takes the files. Hope argues strongly in Nelle's favour, mentioning Richard's broken promise of partnership, the spanking incident (see 302 'Buried Pleasures'), and the retaliatory action by John since the end of their relationship. Hope argues for binding arbitration, as there's a lot of dirty laundry involved. Walsh agrees to pick an arbiter – the man-hating Julia 'Bulldog' Braddel. Bulldog ends up settling for Nelle to pay damages of $300,000.

The Verdict: 'Tell all your little friends to stay hidden; I'm a *bad* witch.' Funny, exciting and packed with plot twists, 'Hope And Glory' gives us the climax to the conflict between Nelle and John and, as their dissatisfactions and resentments come out, no one is safe in the crossfire. A shame to see poor Mark being sidelined so soon into his run on the show, but Brian makes for an interesting and dryly humorous boyfriend for Ally, while Alicia Witt makes a fairly stunning and bizarre debut as Hope. With Ally in a bright new relationship and conflict in the firm, all seems set for a spectacular season finale.

321
Ally McBeal: The Musical, Almost

#3M21
22 May 2000

Written by David E. Kelley
Directed by Bill D'Ella

Cast: Special Guest Star: James LeGros (Mark Albert).
Special Appearances by: Randy Newman (himself),
James Naughton (George McBeal),
Jill Clayburgh (Jeannie McBeal), Alicia Witt (Hope),
Tim Dutton (Brian), Amy Castle (Young Ally),
Dakota Fanning (5-year-old Ally),
Michael Rothhaar (Stanley Kupcheck), Joshua Finkel (Waiter)

John's got the blues because he's thirty-six, Nelle's got the blues because she's all alone, Ally and Brian are dueting, while Ally's parents have their own songs to sing. When everything's a production number, can we expect a happy ending before the fat lady sings?

Titles: Something special here: the female cast sing 'Searching My Soul', intercutting their performance with various song and dance related clips from the series so far. This is the first episode not to have a title credit for Gil Bellows, who does not appear in the episode.

Fantasy: This whole episode is a musical, so much of the action has a fantasy element to it. Probably best not to worry about how many of the routines are 'real' or not; that way lies madness.

Song: Most of the songs come from the Randy Newman canon: Nelle, John, Renee and Vonda sing 'The Blues'; 'Relax, Enjoy Yourself' is performed by the waiter, Brian, and Ally's parents (with the rest of the restaurant providing backing); Vonda sings 'Falling in Love'; John turns Newman's 'Davy the Fat Boy' into 'Jonny the Fat Boy'; Fish's theme song turns out to be 'Can't Keep A Good Man Down', with Elaine, John and Brian providing backing; Randy Newman and Vonda sing 'I Want You To Hurt Like I Do'; Elaine, Renee and Georgia perform 'Take Me Back' (although Georgia's mike is turned down); Vonda performs 'Forever'; Newman, Hope and Renee sing 'There's A Party At My House'; while finally we have Ally's father's song for her, 'Real Emotional Girl', another Newman composition. Aside from the Randy Newman material, we also get the female cast members singing the theme song, Hope's racy performance of Madonna's 'Hanky Panky', and a quick blast of Gloria Gaynor's classic floor-filler 'I Will Survive'. There's also a song from *The Music Man*, David E. Kelley (and Ally's) favourite musical: Ally and Brian sing 'Lida Rose', with flashbacks to Young Ally singing the same song with her father.

. . . And Dance: Way too many to mention, but of note are Elaine's dance routine to 'Can't Keep A Good Man Down', Hope's dance for John during 'Hanky Panky', and any scene where Brian and Ally dance close together.

Everything Stops For Ally: It's always a challenge introducing a partner to your family, and for Ally doubly so. Her father's response to Brian is openly hostile, leading to a disastrous dinner where Ally giggles nervously as her father randomly insults the English. This leads to a major falling-out with her parents, and her desire to sleep with her disapproved-of boyfriend just to get back at her dad. She is disgusted when Brian has too many scruples to go along with this: 'Brian, you are a man, you are supposed to take it any way you can get it.' Ally and her father used to sing 'Lida Rose' together, side by side at the piano. The thirty-year-old Ally instead sings it with Brian. (Unbeknown to Ally, her father walks in on the duet and remembers her as a child.) Ally's mother tries to reconcile father and daughter, while Ally is insistent that she's an adult and doesn't need to tolerate her parents' disapproval. Ally's mother feels that only through the father–daughter bond can she connect to her own daughter. She argues with her father about Billy's funeral and how he didn't attend. On the other hand, Ally's relationship with Brian is going unbelievably well; she has a stable boyfriend at last. 'It's been a long time since I felt this,' she tells Brian. She finally achieves some kind of reconciliation with her father, as he tells her about the pain he felt at Billy's death. Ally encourages her father to sing the song he says he wrote for her. The song is called 'Real Emotional Girl', and he sings it as the episode ends.

Smile Therapy: It's John's birthday again, and he's now thirty-six. He doesn't feel he's achieved anything with his life, that what he's achieved as a person isn't real: 'Except for Richard Fish, all my friends work for me.' 'I am a little curmudgeon toad,' he says, 'it's what I was put on this earth to be.' His view on Nelle is simple: 'I hate her.' He tells Richard how he hates being humiliated, how when he was five or six he was so fat he was used as a 'Guess the Weight' item at a charity gala, and how ever since he has not allowed himself to be ridiculed in that way. He offers to pay Richard not to sing, and says Fish can't hit a note (ironic, considering Greg Germann is a far better singer than Peter MacNicol). John goes to Nelle's office where she tells him he couldn't love her because he couldn't like her. 'You know I loved you,' he retorts and Nelle replies that John could never love her as much as he loved 'her' (presumably referring to Ally). John finally reconciles his differences with Nelle and allows her to rejoin the firm. He feels they should be completely honest with each other – and so tells Nelle when she has vomit on her nose. John considers Hope's version of 'Hanky Panky', where she publicly encourages him to spank her with a hairbrush, unacceptable.

Fishisms: Richard is surprised by John's vehemence towards Nelle: 'I never even thought you had the capacity to hate.' He's arranged a meeting with Nelle and wants John to talk to her, to try to get through his anger. When Nelle wants to rejoin the firm, Richard leaves it to John to decide.

Sub Zero: Nelle is regretting her departure, pining for her old firm. She really used to like it there and she only left to punish 'the dweeb': John Cage. As she tells Hope about her unhappiness, she starts talking about her childhood. She walks in on John talking about his humiliation and says he cares about what others think, whereas she primarily cared about what *he* thought: 'You so fundamentally disapproved of who I am. What I am. It's a lot more painful than being stuck in an elevator.' She understands John's desire not to see her: 'You didn't want me in your life. I get that. I got it even before you did.' Nelle is clearly wounded by John's disapproval and their fighting, and when he visits her she tells him not to 'come in here trying to compare pain'. At the bar, while throwing back shots to give her courage, Nelle tells John and Richard how sorry she is and how she wants to rejoin the firm. 'The practice of law is only as good as the people you work with,' she says. 'I want to work with you.' Nelle keeps drinking, and although she does get back into the firm, she also spends much of John's birthday bash face-down unconscious or throwing up in the ladies'.

All We Need Is Hope: Hope sums up what Nelle has just done succinctly: 'Honey, you screwed your friends.' Richard encourages Hope to 'perform' for John. Not too difficult – Hope likes performing. Her version of 'Hanky Panky' is a riot if, as John says, 'unacceptable'.

Grrr!: Ling prompts Nelle to cry while apologising to John and Richard, but Nelle refuses to fake anything. Ling wants to get back together with Richard.

Georgia On My Mind: If this is Georgia's last episode as rumoured, then it's a very low-key exit, with Georgia singing the refrain to Elaine and Renee's lead vocals – and even then with the mike turned down.

Men: Brian refuses to have sex with Ally the day after the disastrous dinner date with her parents: 'I'm not about to go to bed with you simply because you're angry at your father.' *The Music Man* is one of Brian's favourites. He tells Ally his father disappointed him too – by not being perfect.

The Verdict: 'Wow. I have a boyfriend.' A fantastic way to end the season, full of regrets and reconciliations, and stressing the importance of moving forward and forgiving rather than carrying anger around with you. Nelle and John, so violently at each other's throats for the last few episodes, painfully work through their problems with each other and decide to get on with their lives. More importantly, Nelle realises that her ice queen persona is just that, and that she really does want to be part of the Cage & Fish team. Most importantly Ally herself is beginning to get on with her life, finding a new love and working through the problems with her parents that have blighted her life for so long. All this, and songs and dance routines in buckets. We can't wait for the next season – but at least this one ended on a definite high note.

Miscellany

The *Ally McBeal* completist might consider tracking down the following:

Several episodes are commercially available on video on both sides of the Atlantic. In the UK FOX have released a couple of individual tapes, comprising miscellaneous episodes, and a boxed set of Season One. In the States early episodes have been bundled together, seemingly at random, on a number of tapes and one DVD. Unfortunately, there doesn't seem to be any plan to release the full run in broadcast order any time soon.

A clip-show, *The Life and Trials of Ally McBeal*, was shown in the US on the same night as the first broadcast of 'Just Friends'. In the UK Channel Four produced their own documentary, *McBeal Appeal*. Fronted by Davina McCall and featuring contributions from British TV professionals as well as members of the show's cast, it's well worth seeking out for those interested in a British slant on the *Ally* phenomenon.

Two CDs of Vonda Shepard's songs from the programme have been released. The first, *Songs From Ally McBeal*, comprises 'Searchin' My Soul', 'Ask The Lonely', 'Walk Away Renee', 'Hooked On A Feeling', 'You Belong To Me', 'The Wildest Times Of The World', 'Someone You Use', 'The End Of The World', 'Tell Him', 'Neighborhood', 'Will You Marry Me?', 'It's In His Kiss (The Shoop Shoop Song)', 'I Only Want To Be With You' and 'Maryland'. The second CD, *Heart and Soul: New Songs From Ally McBeal,* features 'Read Your Mind', '100 Tears Away', 'Someday We'll Be Together', 'To Sir With Love', 'Sweet Inspiration', 'Crying', 'Vincent', 'What Becomes Of The Brokenhearted?', 'World Without Love', 'Confetti', 'Baby, Don't You Break My Heart Slow', 'This Is Crazy Now', 'This Old Heart Of Mine (Is Weak For You)' and 'I Know Him By Heart'. While both CDs are well worth having, it's a shame that broader soundtrack CDs from the series, perhaps including segments from Danny Lux's score, original recordings used in the show such as those by Barry White and Gloria Gaynor, and some of the songs performed by the cast, have been rejected in favour of such a Vonda-centric view of the series' music. One can only hope that '*Ally McBeal*: The Musical, Almost' will lead to a reappraisal of this situation.

Appendix 1: *Ally*

In parallel to the second season of *Ally McBeal* series creator David E. Kelley sanctioned a 'spin-off' series called *Ally*. *Ally* consisted of truncated 22-minute versions of several episodes of *Ally McBeal* transmitted in a half-hour slot. Kelley spoke excitedly about the project to a number of publications, detailing how the shorter versions of these episodes, concentrating on just one plot strand, would allow him to insert scenes cut from the one-hour versions for timing reasons.

Despite some of the strongest first season episodes being chosen to receive the re-editing treatment, the experiment was not a success. These *Ally* episodes seem lacklustre compared to their full-length counterparts, and it seems odd to take something as good as 'One Hundred Tears Away' or 'Boy To The World' and attempt to improve it by making it shorter. We don't propose to review *Ally* episodes individually; the episodes are little more than curios which pale in comparison to the full-length versions reviewed elsewhere in this book. The following transmission information is included for completeness' sake only. Writer/director credits and cast information can be found with the reviews of the full versions of these episodes.

First Season

28 September 1999	ALY–115	Once In A Lifetime
5 October 1999	ALY–106	The Promise
12 October 1999	ALY–105	One Hundred Tears Away
19 October 1999	ALY–108	Drawing The Lines
26 October 1999	ALY–107	The Attitude
2 November 1999	ALY–109	The Dirty Joke
9 November 1999	ALY–112	Cro-Magnon
7 December 1999	ALY–203	Fools Night Out
14 December 1999	ALY–110	Boy To The World
28 December 1999	ALY–113	The Blame Game

Appendix 2: *Ally* on the Web

Like any major cultural phenomenon these days, *Ally McBeal* has a major presence on the internet. A few sites are of particular note.

First stop should be the official FOX site for the show, accessible through www.fox.com. There you'll find a wealth of info and updates behind a very flash presentation. UK residents not wanting to trip over spoilers, however, should make their first port of call Daniel Rees' excellent www.allymcbeal. co.uk, a cleanly laid-out and presented site full of useful information and links. Daniel also runs a mailing list which offers regular updates for UK fans of the show.

Now that you've got a taste for this kind of thing, it's worth heading to one of the big American fan sites. Dana Bonistalli's website, 'Dana's Ally McBeal Page', is an immense resource and the authors of this book wouldn't live without it. Of particular note is the list of songs featured in episodes compiled by the mysterious 'Monkey Girl', while the synopses and reviews written by Dana and Josh Bermont are comprehensive and incisive. While Dana has retired from running the site to start a family, the site itself lives on under the TKTV banner at allymcbeal.tktv.net.

It's worth noting that most of the sites above have comprehensive links sections, as well as pointing the way to useful bulletin boards, mailing lists, newsgroups and places to purchase merchandise. The above is only a small selection of the sites around, but many of the others can be reached via the sites listed here.

Water Cooler Rumours: Season Four

At the time of writing, little has been confirmed about Season Four of *Ally McBeal* apart from the fact that there *will* be a fourth season. However, some scraps of information have been released and we're not averse to a little speculation.

Gil Bellows, who played Billy, left the series as a regular in Season Three, and although he is set for a number of cameo appearances in Season Four he will not be a regular. With her screen husband departing the series, Courtney Thorne-Smith will also be leaving the show, although it is uncertain whether this will be immediate – there is certainly no sign of her being 'written out' at the end of Series Three.

The new male character introduced towards the end of the third series, Mark Albert (James LeGros), will be a regular fixture, while there are rumours of a new regular female character. This could perhaps be Alicia Witt's character Hope, who made such an impression in the last two episodes of Season Three. With Lucy Liu's career in the ascendant, Witt could be a natural to fill a Ling-type role in the show, should Liu become unavailable. Certainly, their characters have a similar temperament and sharp wit, and one could be exchanged for the other in scripts at very short notice if necessary. Latest rumours suggest Robert Downey Jr will be appearing in several episodes, possibly as a love interest for Ally.

As for the long-awaited return of Dr Greg Butters, played by Jesse L. Martin, nothing has been announced at the time of writing. However, with the twists and turns in Ally's life story so far, we know by now that David E. Kelley always has plenty of surprises ready. With major changes in the cast forcing new dynamics into the show, Season Four should be very interesting to see.

Credits

Substantial thanks go to our research team – James Ambuehl, Holly Johnson and Daniel Rees – without whom we wouldn't have had anything to write about.

Many *Ally* fans have provided useful insights into how they view the show. Thanks for these water-cooler conversations to Sarah J. Archibald, Caroline Bedding, Meena Naidu, Jennifer Naylor, Shola Oni and Kathryn Pozzi.

We'd also like to thank our predecessors and contemporaries here at Virgin's episode guide range, many of whom gave useful advice and all of whom provided inspiration: Paul Cornell, Paul Condon, Martin Day, Keith Topping and Jim Sangster stand out from a distinguished list. Thanks also to Mark Wright and Covan Scott – great minds may think alike, but synchronicity still sucks!

Finally, this book would not have been possible without the patience of all the friends, family and colleagues who tolerated your *Ally*-fixated authors as they toiled away, absorbed in one TV series through the months this book took to write. You can all come out now – we're capable of talking about other things again.

Also available:

FRIENDS LIKE US

The Unofficial Guide to *Friends*
Revised and Updated

Jim Sangster and David Bailey
ISBN 0 7535 0439 1

'So no-one told you life was gonna be this way . . .'

From its humble beginnings in 1994, *Friends* has turned into a worldwide TV phenomenon. Everyone can identify with at least one of the six characters (just don't rely on Joey for subtle tips on flirting). *Friends* manages to tap into the lives of an entire generation as it covers love, sex, TV, junk food, dead-end jobs and every other facet of modern life, with humour and compassion.

This revised and updated edition takes a light-hearted look at every episode from all six series. Complete with 'Phoebisms', 'Slow Joey', and 'Freaky Monica' categories, this unofficial guide highlights all those classic scenes and celebrity guest appearances, as well as explaining obscure cultural references and keeping track of the forever fluctuating Ross and Rachel relationship.

Essential for all *Friends* fans.

GOODNIGHT, SEATTLE
The Unauthorised Guide to the World of *Frasier*

David Bailey and Warren Martyn
ISBN 0 7535 0286 0

'I'm Frasier Crane, and I'm listening.'

Meet the extended, eccentric family of radio psychiatrist Frasier Crane:

- His father Martin, who owns the world's ugliest chair and lives with it in Frasier's chic apartment
- Martin's disturbing terrier, Eddie
- Martin's live-in carer, the daffy Daphne, who is much admired by . . .
- Niles, Frasier's prissy younger brother
- Roz, Frasier's man-hungry producer

Together they are *Frasier*, Paramount's award-winning comedy series.

Goodnight, Seattle puts *Frasier* through some intensive therapy, laying the series on the couch and listening to its innermost secrets. From Niles's unrequited romantic clinch with Daphne on the dance floor to Martin's telescopic flirtation with the woman in the skyscraper next door, every aspect of the show is covered in this detailed and loving guide to the world's smartest sitcom.

SLAYER
The Revised and Updated
Unofficial Guide to *Buffy the Vampire Slayer*

Keith Topping
ISBN 0 7535 0553 3

'There are things I will not tolerate. Students loitering
on campus after school. Horrible murders with hearts
being removed. And also smoking.'

Slayer is the only complete and up-to-date guide to the weird
yet undeniably cool world of *Buffy the Vampire Slayer*.

Slayer analyses every episode in all four TV series and also
focuses on the original feature film, the novels and the many
fan websites.

The highlights of each episode are presented in categories
such as **Dudes & Babes**, **Authority sucks!**, **Bitch!**, **Denial,
Thy Name is Joyce** and **A Little Learning is a Dangerous
Thing**.

Vampires, violence, non-conformism and teenage angst.
Whether you're a seasoned Slayerette or a novice, *Slayer* is
your indispensable guide to Sunnydale and its Hellmouth.

HOLLYWOOD VAMPIRE
The Unofficial Guide to *Angel*

Keith Topping
ISBN 0 7535 0531 2

'Los Angeles. You see it at night and it shines . . .
people are drawn to it. People and other things. They
come for all sorts of reasons. My reason? No surprise
there. It started with a girl.'

And so begins Angel's new existence. He has his soul back,
but the price is his relationship with Buffy. He must atone for
his past by fighting for humanity and against evil in the dark,
seedy underside of the superficially glamorous city of L.A.

Hollywood Vampire focuses on *Angel* Season One, explor-
ing the world of Angel, Cordelia, Wesley and Kate. This
episode-by-episode guide encompasses the highlights in categories such as: **Dreaming (As *Buffy* Often Proves) Is Free**;
The Charisma Show; **Dudes and Babes** and **Sex and Drugs
and Rock and Roll**. It also draws attention to logical flaws
and points out popular culture references.

The *Buffy* connection is covered in detail too, as the author
discusses the shared history of *Angel* and *Buffy* and charts the
instances where characters flit between the two.

A unique and essential fan bible.

CUNNING
The *Blackadder* Programme Guide

Chris Howarth and Steve Lyons
ISBN 0 7535 0447 2

'The path of my life is strewn with cowpats from the
devil's own satanic herd.'

Succinct as ever, Blackadder sums up the story of his life.
Caught up in a world where everyone else seems either stupid
or inept, he is at a loss to understand why problems and bizarre
situations should follow him around like a bad smell (much
like Baldrick, in fact).

With only his wit to save him, and often with the burden of
some not-very-cunning plans, Blackadder tries to improve his
lot in life, but barely manages to muddle through at all. The
best of Blackadder's cutting comments, evil machinations,
double entendres and opinions are examined in this detailed
companion to this cult British comedy.

Cunning . . . is a unique guide that covers the entire history
of *Blackadder*, considering each episode from the untrans-
mitted pilot to the new Millennium Special. *Cunning* . . . also
takes a look at TV comedy shows that have been inspired by
Blackadder and tells you everything there is to know about the
much-loved programme.

THE BOND FILES
The Unofficial Guide to the World's Greatest Secret Agent

Andy Lane and Paul Simpson
ISBN0 7535 0490 1

'What are you – some kind of Doomsday machine?'

Torn from the secret files of intelligence agencies around the world – the hidden facts about James Bond that even the world's greatest secret agent has forgotten.

- Which Bond films did Stanley Kubrick and Francis Ford Coppola help out on?
- How many times has 009 been killed?
- When did Bond meet Playboy millionaire Hugh Hefner?
- How many times has the British Secret Service battled dinosaurs?
- For what film was director John Frankenheimer under consideration to play Bond?

With *The World is Not Enough*, James Bond has entered the new millennium in style. There's never been a more pressing need for a book that chronicles his every appearance, from the sublime to the ridiculous, from the best known to the most obscure. This revised, updated version of *The Bond Files* is the only book on James Bond anyone could ever need.

'. . . simply crammed with mouthwatering facts and trivia.' *Film Review*

RED DWARF PROGRAMME GUIDE

Chris Howarth and Steve Lyons
ISBN 07535 0402 2

- How many tons of reconstituted sausage pâté are stored on *Red Dwarf*?
- How did Lister get rid of Rimmer's bridge club chums?
- Who was the first actress to play Kristine Kochanski?

All the answers – along with much, much more non-essential information – can be found in this valuable, yet inexpensive and smeg-free, bestselling guide to the greatest SF comedy series in this universe (and most other universes).

Now fully updated to include the mega-popular eighth season, this book is on the Producer's recommended reading list and is often to be found in the *Red Dwarf* production offices for handy reference.

DELTA QUADRANT
The Unofficial Guide to *Voyager*

David McIntee
ISBN 0 7535 0436 7

'You are erratic, conflicted, disorganised. Every
decision is debated, every action questioned, every
individual entitled to their own opinion. You lack
harmony, cohesion, greatness. It will be your undoing.'
Seven of Nine

Delta Quadrant is the only episode guide to *Voyager* currently
in existence. Every episode is recounted and dissected with
absolute precision. Every significant piece of data is logged,
and those more tricky scientific references are analysed in the
ingeniously-named section: **'Ye Canna Change The Laws
O'Physics'**.

For those of us who aren't primarily SF fans and who
simply enjoy a good storyline, *Delta Quadrant* draws attention
to some of the blindingly brilliant characterisation and dialogue, without being afraid to point out bloopers and puzzles,
lack of continuity and where things could have been done
better.

'Am I the only one so intent on getting home?
Is it just me? Am I leading the crew on a forlorn mission
with no hope of success?'

This is the essential guide to the trials of Captain Janeway and
the rest of the *Voyager* team as they try to bridge 70,000 light
years, and find a way home from the Delta Quadrant.